RAT QUEENS™

VOLUME TWO: THE FAR REACHING TENTACLES of N'RYGOTH

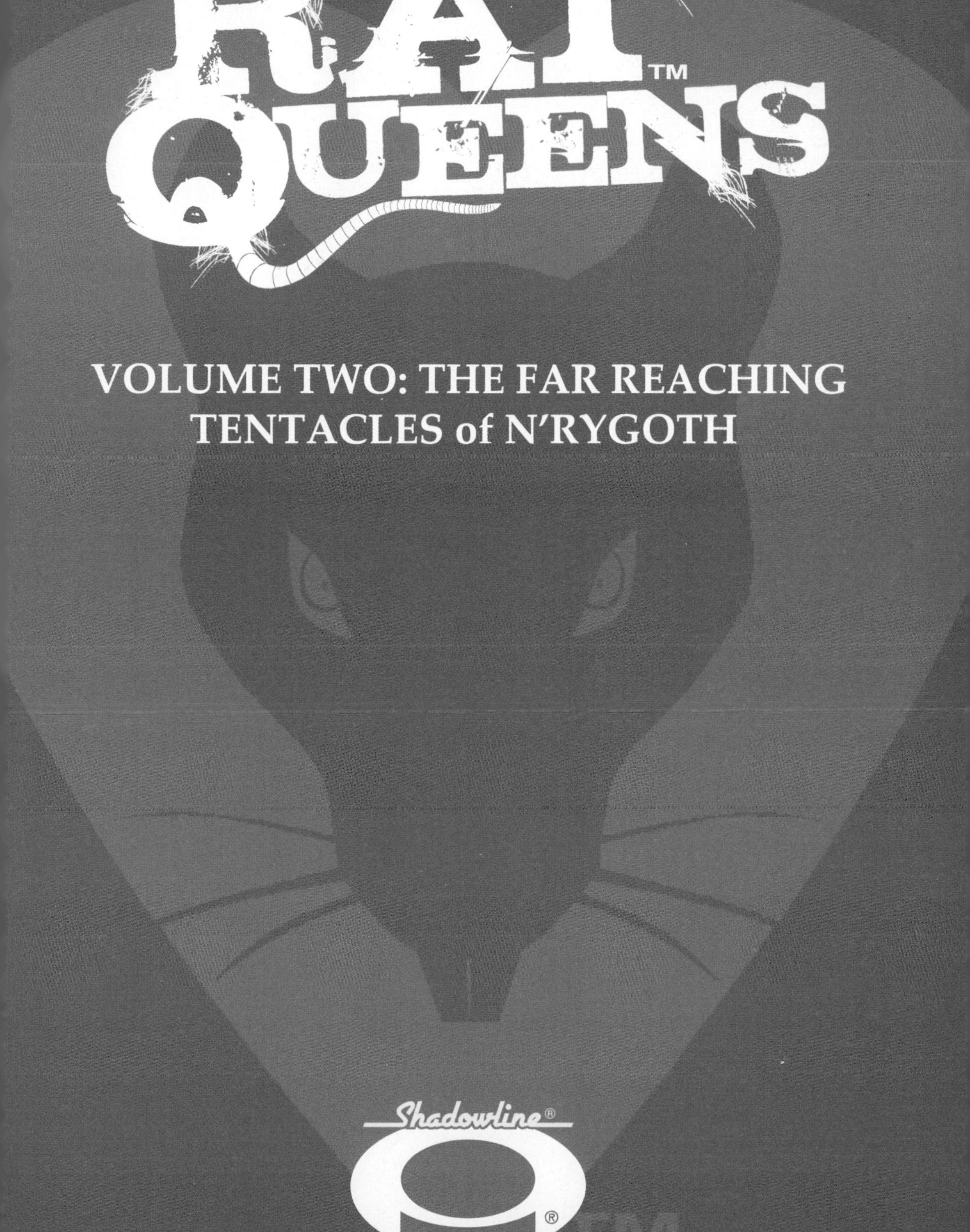

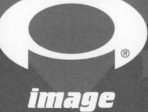

Shadowline®

image

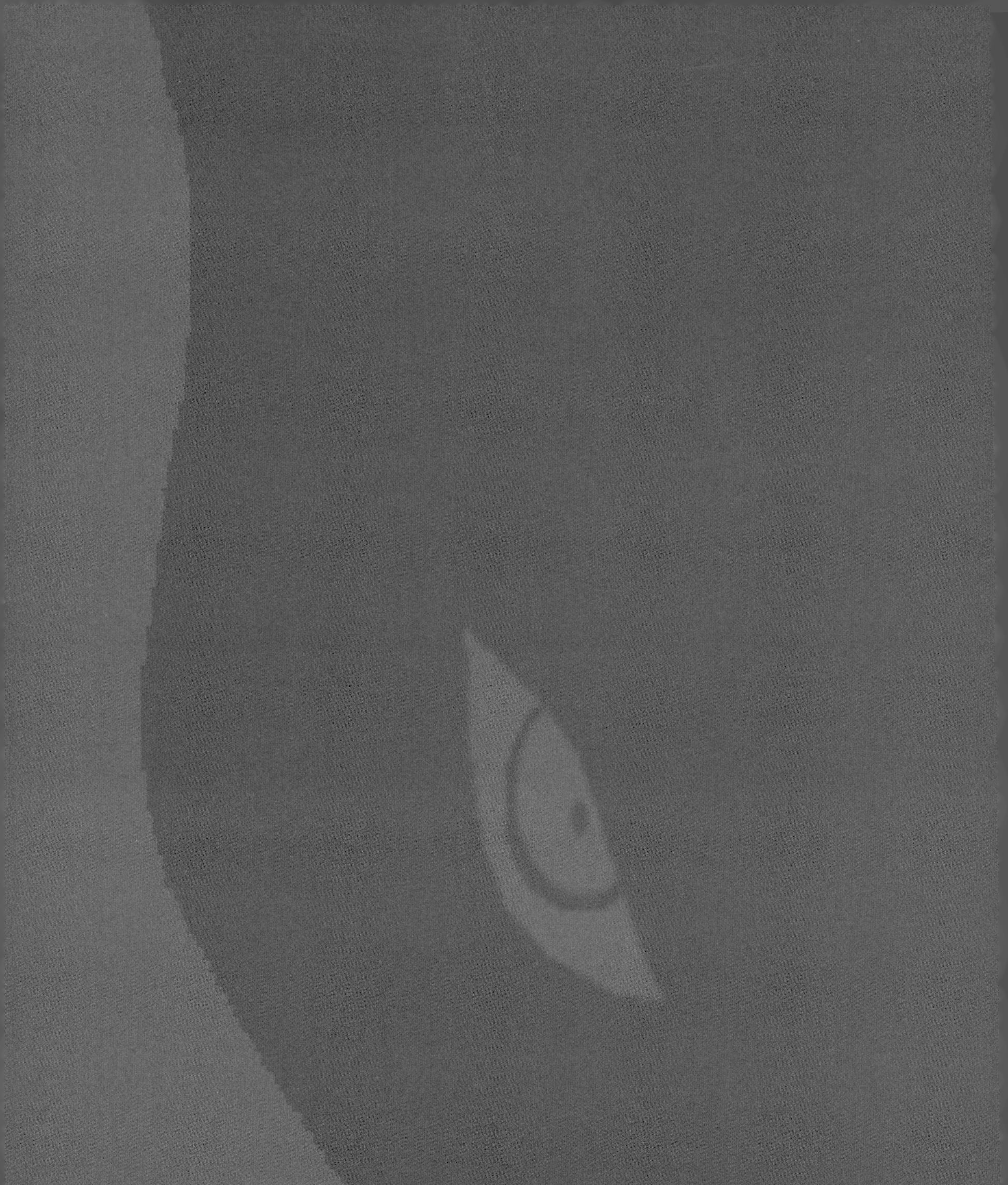

FIRST PRINTING: MAY, 2015

ISBN: 978-1-63215-040-0

RAT QUEENS Volume Two: The Far Reaching Tentacles of N'Rygoth. Published by Image Comics, Inc. Office of publication: 2001 Center St. Sixth Floor, Berkeley, CA 94704. Copyright © 2015 KURTIS J. WIEBE and JOHN UPCHURCH. Originally published in single magazine form as RAT QUEENS #6-10. All rights reserved. RAT QUEENS™ (including all prominent characters featured herein), its logo and all character likenesses are trademarks of KURTIS J. WIEBE and JOHN UPCHURCH, unless otherwise noted. Image Comics® and its logos are registered trademarks of Image Comics, Inc. Shadowline® and its logos are registered trademarks of Jim Valentino. No part of this publication may be reproduced or transmitted, in any form or by any means (except for short excerpts for review purposes) without the express written permission of Mr. Wiebe or Mr. Upchurch. All names, characters, events and locales in this publication are entirely fictional. Any resemblance to actual persons (living or dead), events or places, without satiric intent, is coincidental. PRINTED IN USA. For information regarding the CPSIA on this printed material call: 203-595-3636 and provide reference # RICH – 615634. International Rights/Foreign Licensing -- foreignlicensing@imagecomics.com

KURTIS J. WIEBE
story
ROC UPCHURCH
STJEPAN SEJIC
art

ROC UPCHURCH
STJEPAN SEJIC
TYLER JENKINS
MICHAEL AVON OEMING
JENNY FRISON
covers

ED BRISSON
letters

for
Shadowline®

LAURA TAVISHATI
edits
MARC LOMBARDI
communications
JIM VALENTINO
publisher/book design

 COMICS PRESENTS *Shadowline* PRODUCTION

IMAGE COMICS, INC.
Robert Kirkman – Chief Operating Officer
Erik Larsen – Chief Financial Officer
Todd McFarlane – President
Marc Silvestri – Chief Executive Officer
Jim Valentino – Vice-President

Eric Stephenson – Publisher
Ron Richards – Director of Business Development
Jennifer de Guzman – Director of Trade Book Sales
Kat Salazar – Director of PR & Marketing
Corey Murphy – Director of Retail Sales
Jeremy Sullivan – Director of Digital Sales
Randy Okamura – Marketing Production Designer
Emilio Bautista – Sales Assistant
Branwyn Bigglestone – Senior Accounts Manager
Emily Miller – Accounts Manager
Jessica Ambriz – Administrative Assistant
David Brothers – Content Manager
Jonathan Chan – Production Manager
Drew Gill – Art Director
Meredith Wallace – Print Manager
Addison Duke – Production Artist
Vincent Kukua – Production Artist
Sasha Head – Production Artist
Tricia Ramos – Production Assistant
IMAGECOMICS.COM

CHAPTER SIX

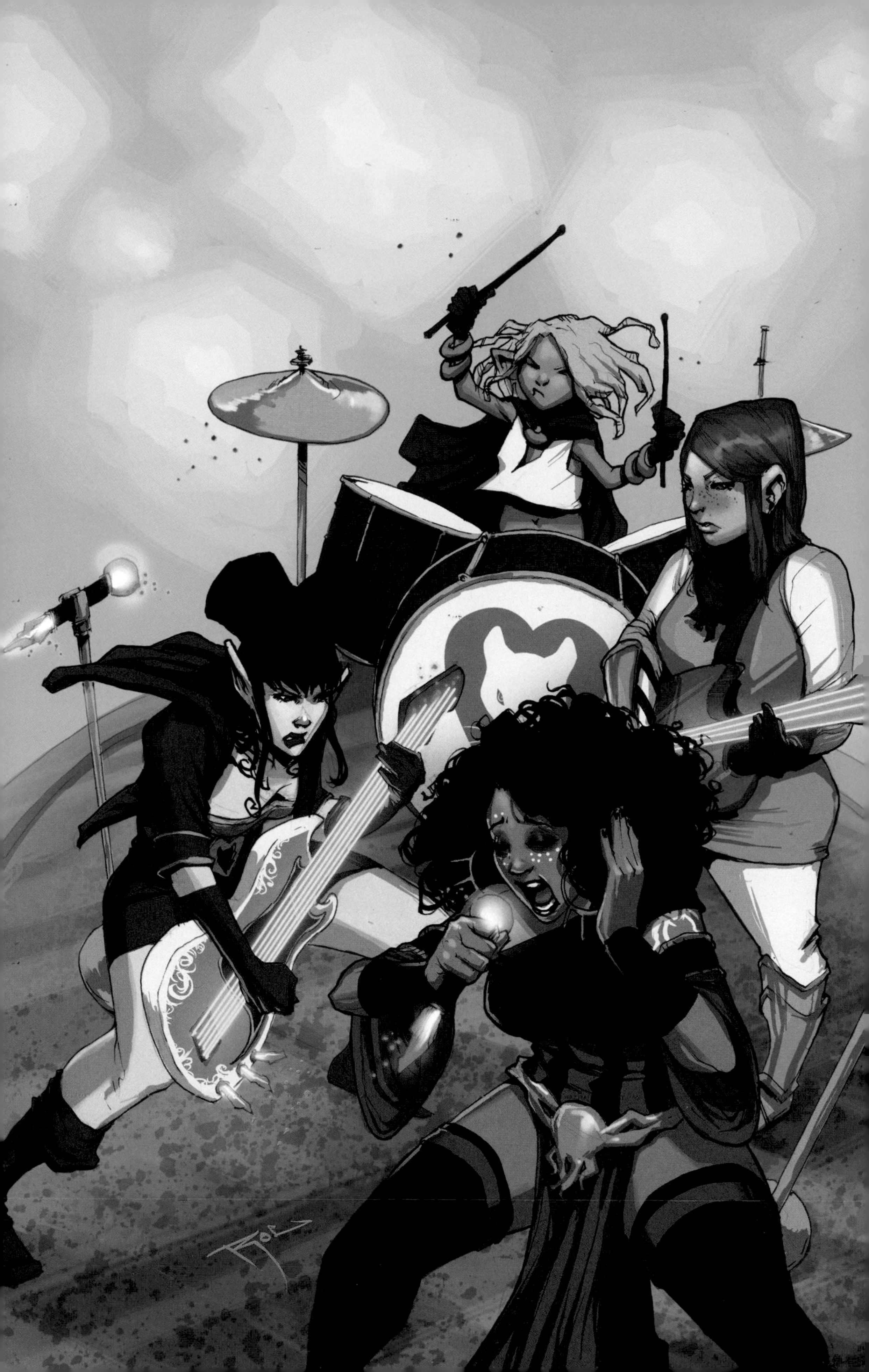

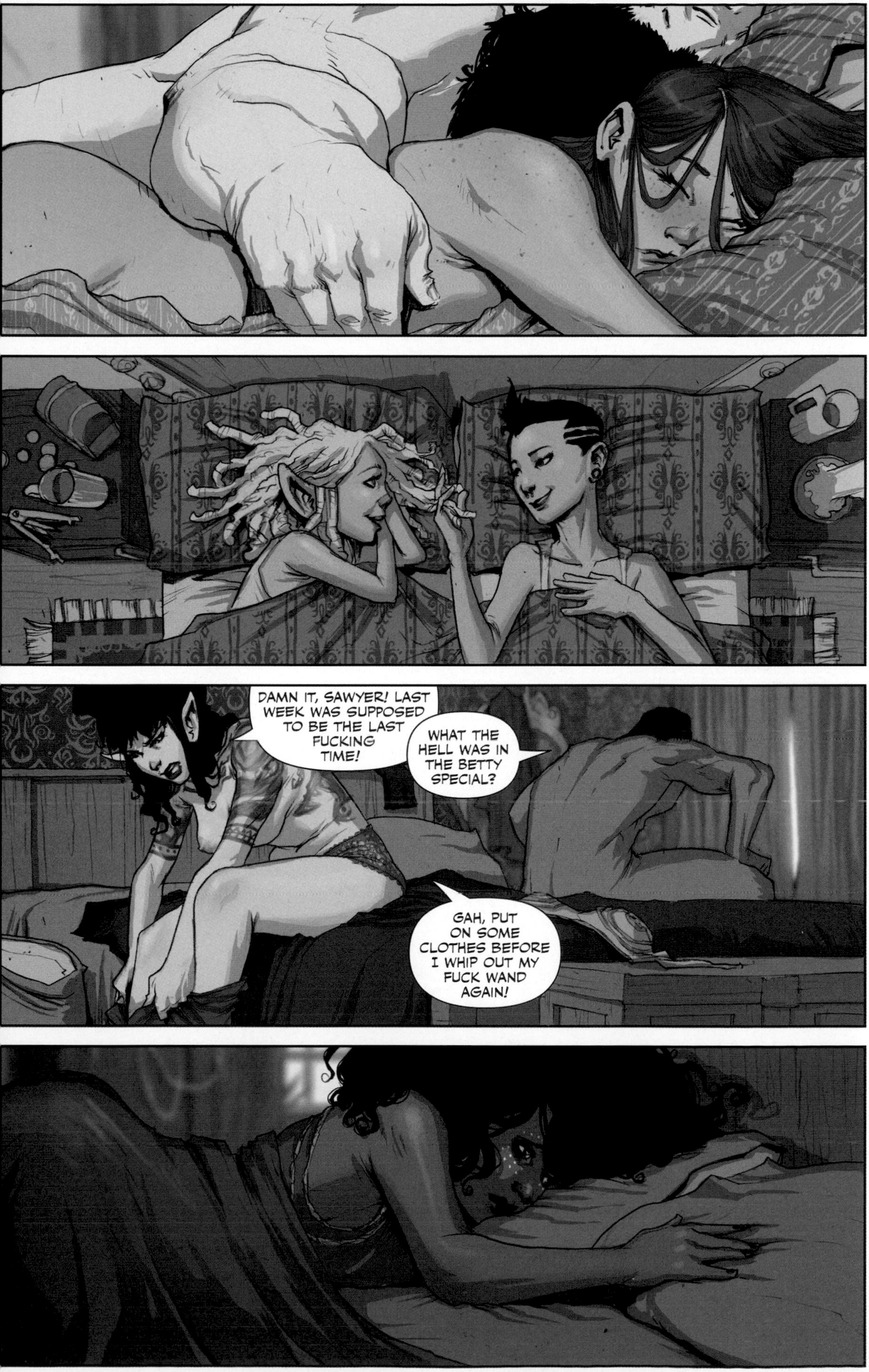
DAMN IT, SAWYER! LAST WEEK WAS SUPPOSED TO BE THE LAST FUCKING TIME!
WHAT THE HELL WAS IN THE BETTY SPECIAL?
GAH, PUT ON SOME CLOTHES BEFORE I WHIP OUT MY FUCK WAND AGAIN!

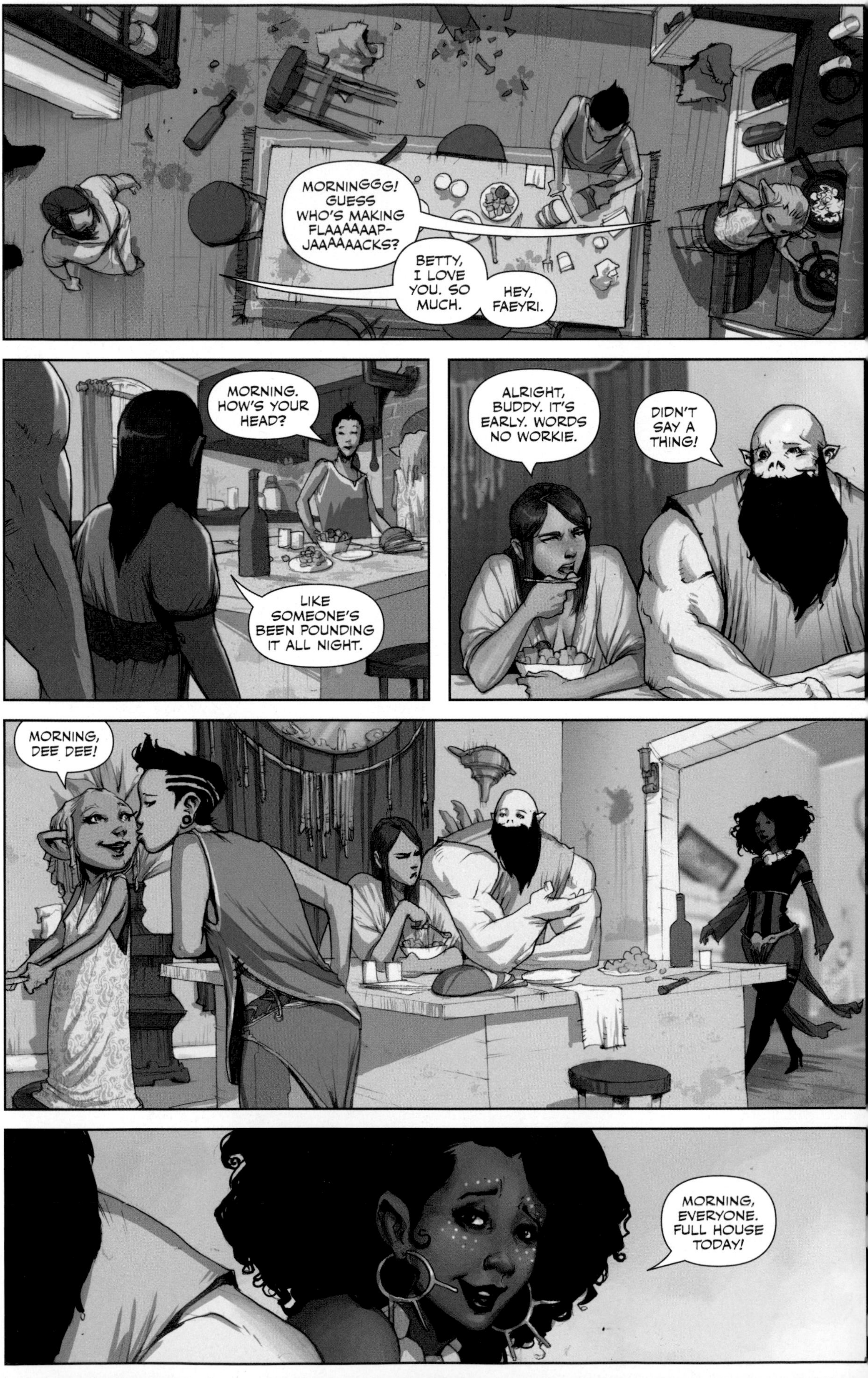
MORNINGGG! GUESS WHO'S MAKING FLAAAAAAP-JAAAAAACKS?
BETTY, I LOVE YOU. SO MUCH.
HEY, FAEYRI.
MORNING. HOW'S YOUR HEAD?
LIKE SOMEONE'S BEEN POUNDING IT ALL NIGHT.
ALRIGHT, BUDDY. IT'S EARLY. WORDS NO WORKIE.
DIDN'T SAY A THING!
MORNING, DEE DEE!
MORNING, EVERYONE. FULL HOUSE TODAY!

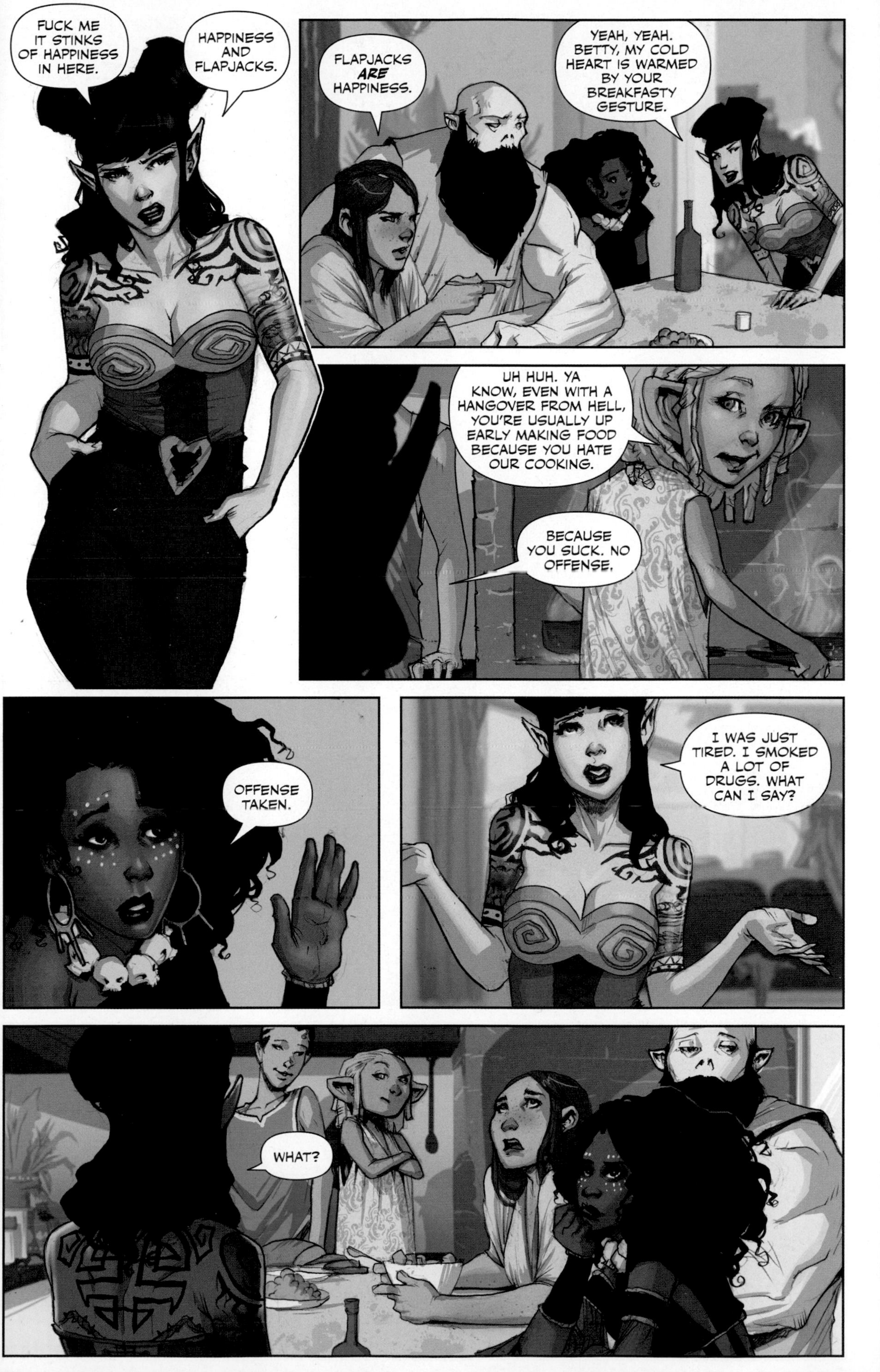
FUCK ME IT STINKS OF HAPPINESS IN HERE.
HAPPINESS AND FLAPJACKS.
FLAPJACKS **ARE** HAPPINESS.
YEAH, YEAH. BETTY, MY COLD HEART IS WARMED BY YOUR BREAKFASTY GESTURE.
UH HUH. YA KNOW, EVEN WITH A HANGOVER FROM HELL, YOU'RE USUALLY UP EARLY MAKING FOOD BECAUSE YOU HATE OUR COOKING.
BECAUSE YOU SUCK. NO OFFENSE.
OFFENSE TAKEN.
I WAS JUST TIRED. I SMOKED A LOT OF DRUGS. WHAT CAN I SAY?
WHAT?

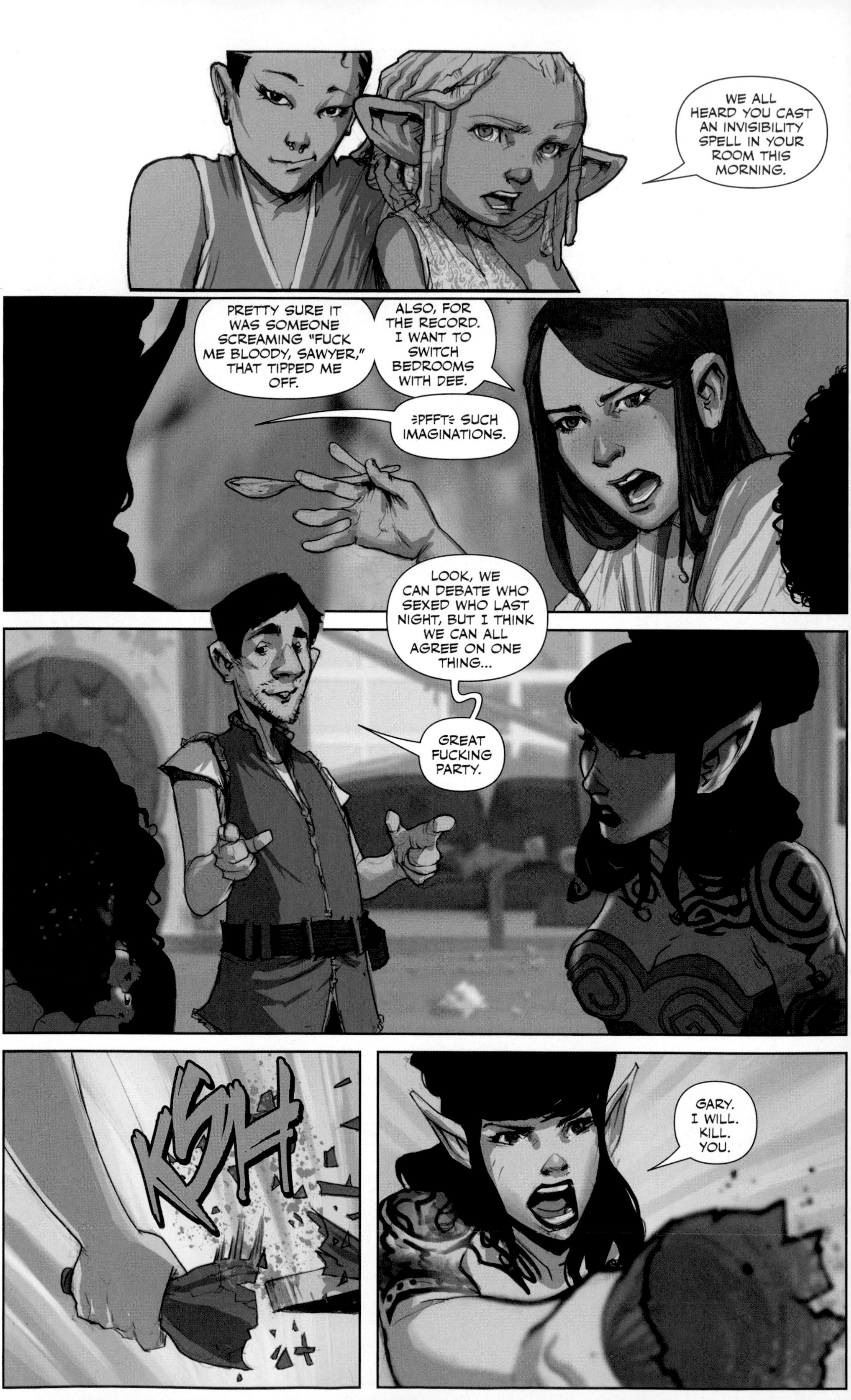
WE ALL HEARD YOU CAST AN INVISIBILITY SPELL IN YOUR ROOM THIS MORNING.
PRETTY SURE IT WAS SOMEONE SCREAMING "FUCK ME BLOODY, SAWYER," THAT TIPPED ME OFF.
ALSO, FOR THE RECORD. I WANT TO SWITCH BEDROOMS WITH DEE.
=PFFT= SUCH IMAGINATIONS.
LOOK, WE CAN DEBATE WHO SEXED WHO LAST NIGHT, BUT I THINK WE CAN ALL AGREE ON ONE THING...
GREAT FUCKING PARTY.
KSH
GARY. I WILL. KILL. YOU.

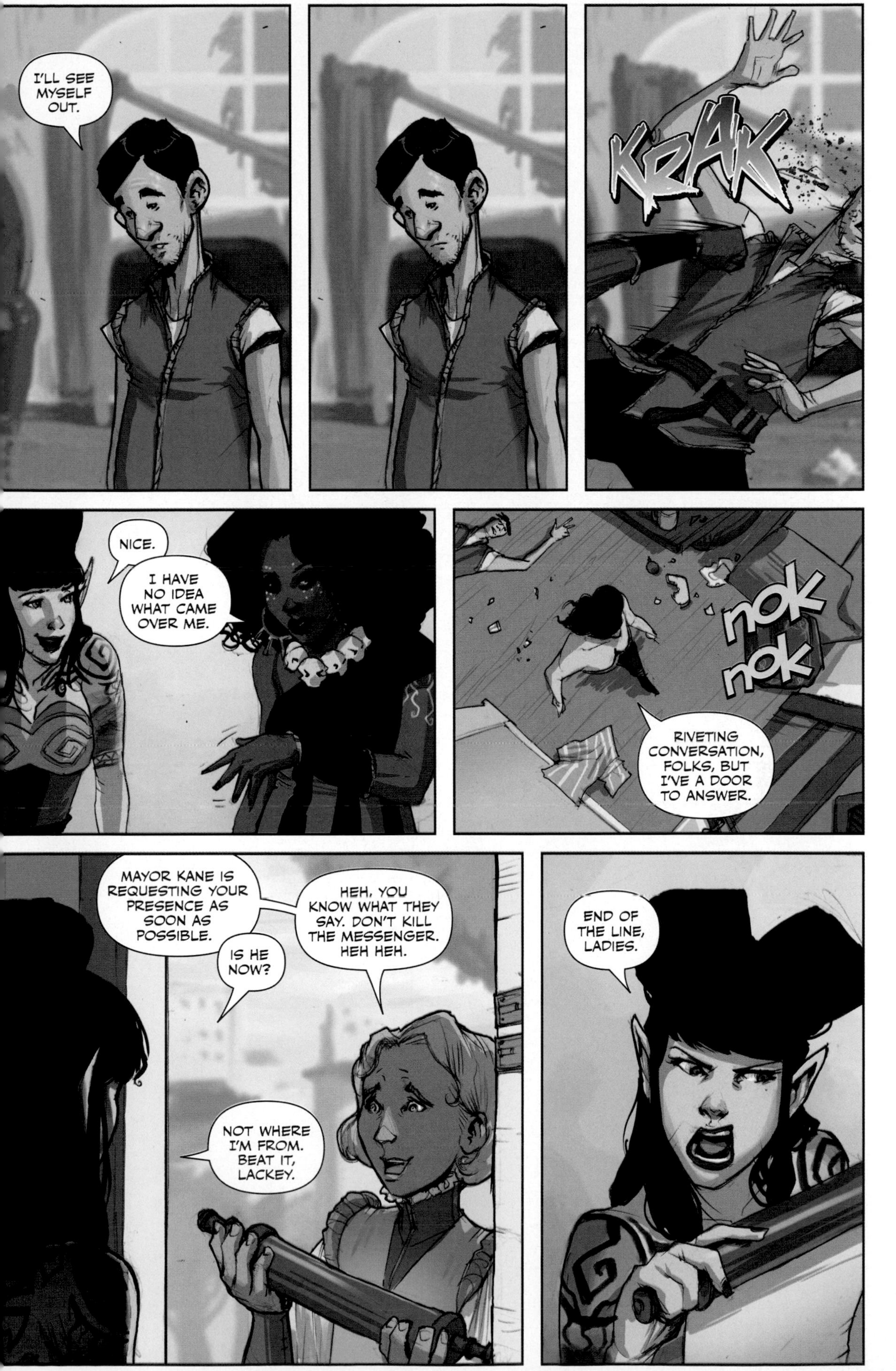
I'LL SEE MYSELF OUT.
KRAK
NICE.
I HAVE NO IDEA WHAT CAME OVER ME.
nok nok
RIVETING CONVERSATION, FOLKS, BUT I'VE A DOOR TO ANSWER.
MAYOR KANE IS REQUESTING YOUR PRESENCE AS SOON AS POSSIBLE.
IS HE NOW?
HEH, YOU KNOW WHAT THEY SAY. DON'T KILL THE MESSENGER. HEH HEH.
NOT WHERE I'M FROM. BEAT IT, LACKEY.
END OF THE LINE, LADIES.

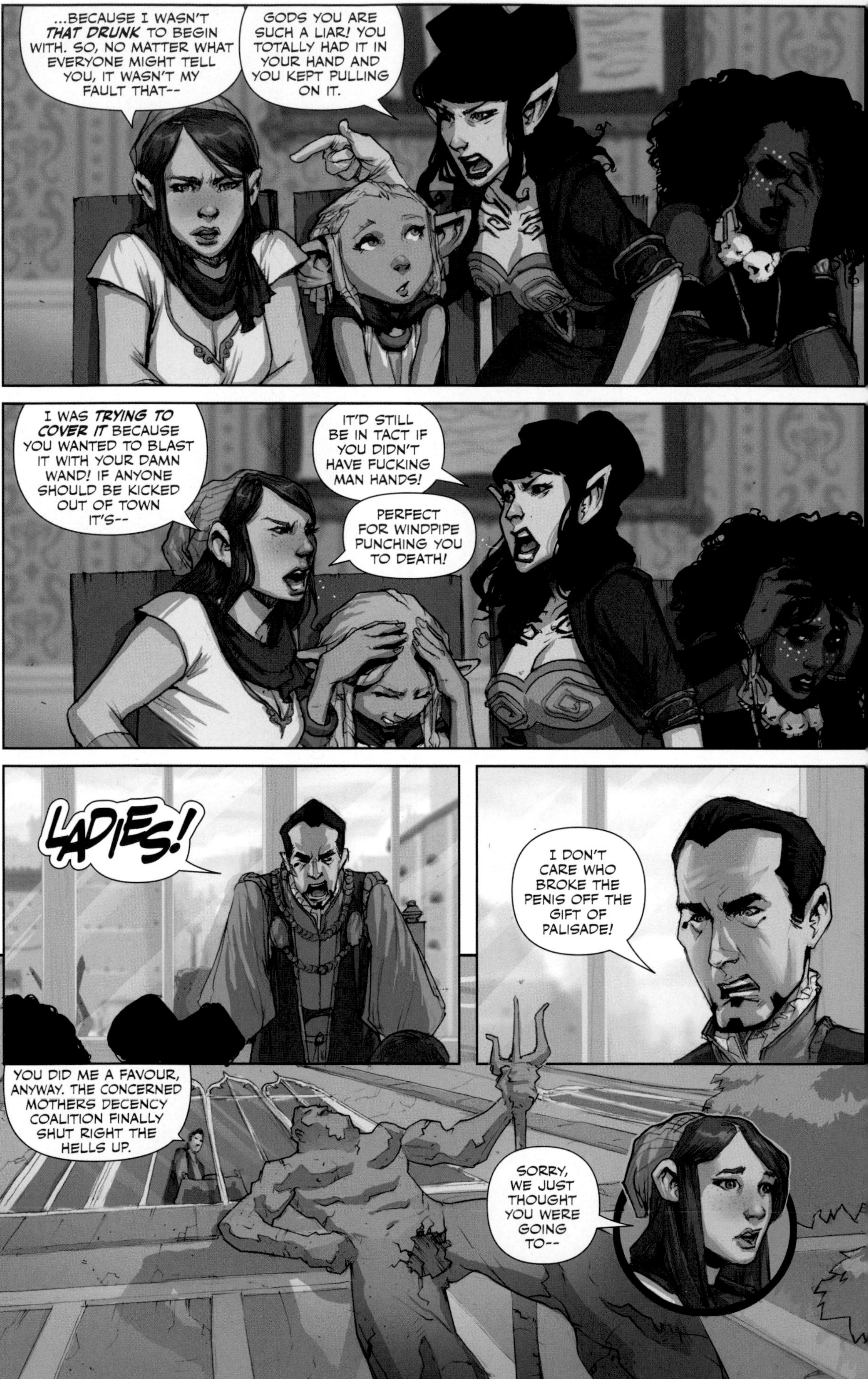
...BECAUSE I WASN'T THAT DRUNK TO BEGIN WITH. SO, NO MATTER WHAT EVERYONE MIGHT TELL YOU, IT WASN'T MY FAULT THAT--
GODS YOU ARE SUCH A LIAR! YOU TOTALLY HAD IT IN YOUR HAND AND YOU KEPT PULLING ON IT.
I WAS TRYING TO COVER IT BECAUSE YOU WANTED TO BLAST IT WITH YOUR DAMN WAND! IF ANYONE SHOULD BE KICKED OUT OF TOWN IT'S--
IT'D STILL BE IN TACT IF YOU DIDN'T HAVE FUCKING MAN HANDS!
PERFECT FOR WINDPIPE PUNCHING YOU TO DEATH!
LADIES!
I DON'T CARE WHO BROKE THE PENIS OFF THE GIFT OF PALISADE!
YOU DID ME A FAVOUR, ANYWAY. THE CONCERNED MOTHERS DECENCY COALITION FINALLY SHUT RIGHT THE HELLS UP.
SORRY, WE JUST THOUGHT YOU WERE GOING TO--

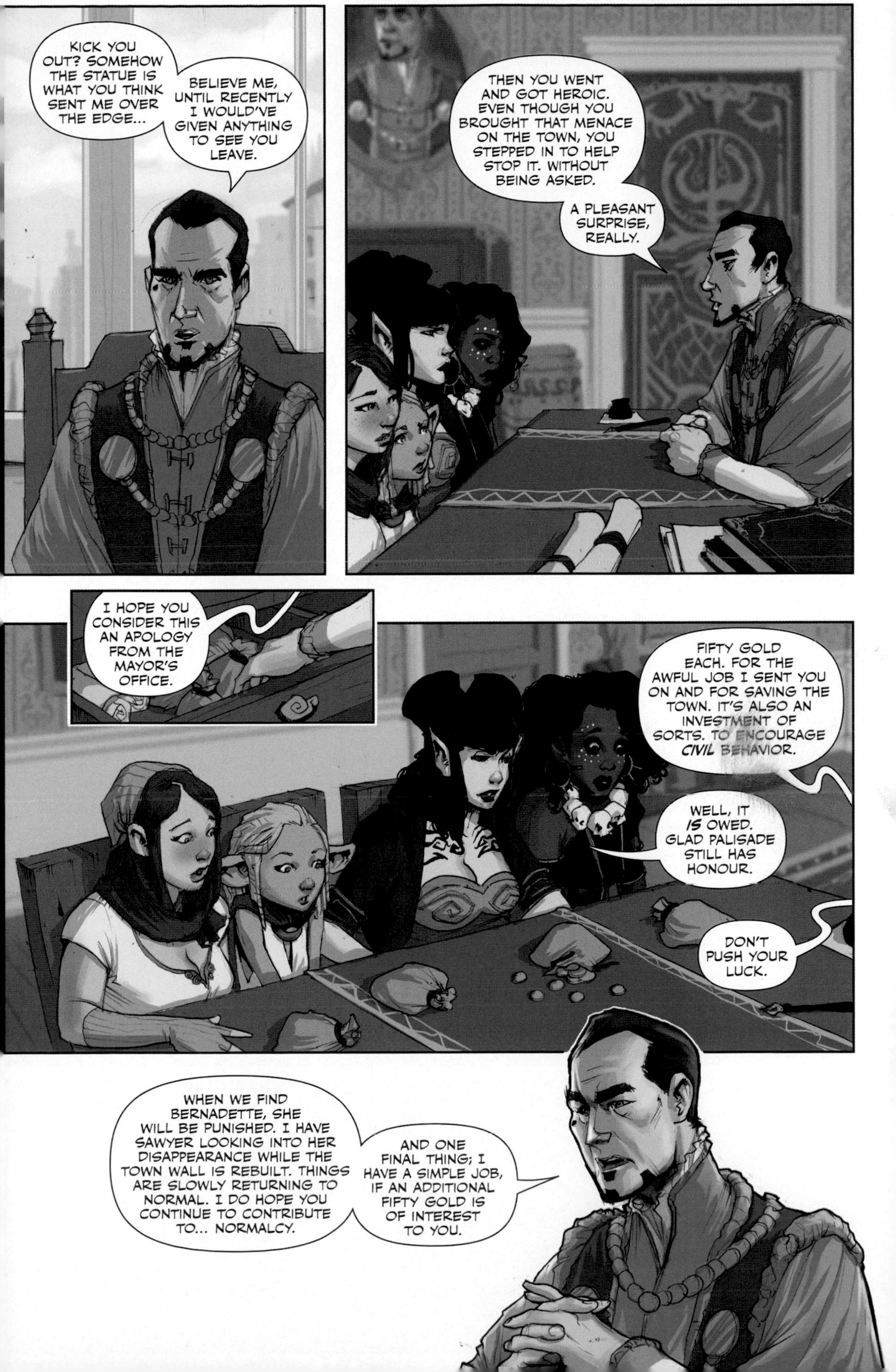
KICK YOU OUT? SOMEHOW THE STATUE IS WHAT YOU THINK SENT ME OVER THE EDGE...
BELIEVE ME, UNTIL RECENTLY I WOULD'VE GIVEN ANYTHING TO SEE YOU LEAVE.
THEN YOU WENT AND GOT HEROIC. EVEN THOUGH YOU BROUGHT THAT MENACE ON THE TOWN, YOU STEPPED IN TO HELP STOP IT. WITHOUT BEING ASKED.
A PLEASANT SURPRISE, REALLY.
I HOPE YOU CONSIDER THIS AN APOLOGY FROM THE MAYOR'S OFFICE.
FIFTY GOLD EACH. FOR THE AWFUL JOB I SENT YOU ON AND FOR SAVING THE TOWN. IT'S ALSO AN INVESTMENT OF SORTS. TO ENCOURAGE CIVIL BEHAVIOR.
WELL, IT IS OWED. GLAD PALISADE STILL HAS HONOUR.
DON'T PUSH YOUR LUCK.
WHEN WE FIND BERNADETTE, SHE WILL BE PUNISHED. I HAVE SAWYER LOOKING INTO HER DISAPPEARANCE WHILE THE TOWN WALL IS REBUILT. THINGS ARE SLOWLY RETURNING TO NORMAL. I DO HOPE YOU CONTINUE TO CONTRIBUTE TO... NORMALCY.
AND ONE FINAL THING; I HAVE A SIMPLE JOB, IF AN ADDITIONAL FIFTY GOLD IS OF INTEREST TO YOU.

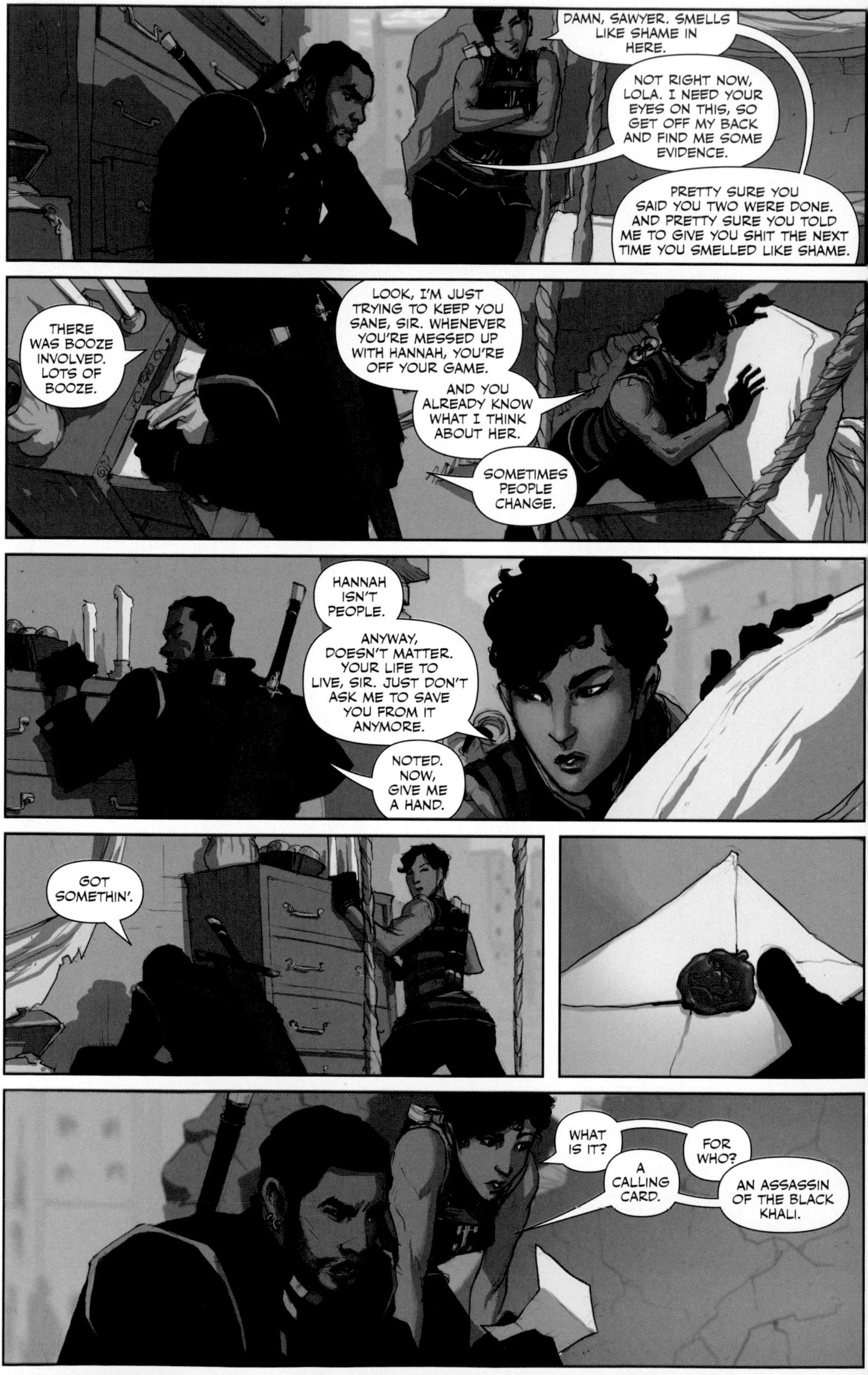
DAMN, SAWYER. SMELLS LIKE SHAME IN HERE.
NOT RIGHT NOW, LOLA. I NEED YOUR EYES ON THIS, SO GET OFF MY BACK AND FIND ME SOME EVIDENCE.
PRETTY SURE YOU SAID YOU TWO WERE DONE. AND PRETTY SURE YOU TOLD ME TO GIVE YOU SHIT THE NEXT TIME YOU SMELLED LIKE SHAME.
THERE WAS BOOZE INVOLVED. LOTS OF BOOZE.
LOOK, I'M JUST TRYING TO KEEP YOU SANE, SIR. WHENEVER YOU'RE MESSED UP WITH HANNAH, YOU'RE OFF YOUR GAME.
AND YOU ALREADY KNOW WHAT I THINK ABOUT HER.
SOMETIMES PEOPLE CHANGE.
HANNAH ISN'T PEOPLE.
ANYWAY, DOESN'T MATTER. YOUR LIFE TO LIVE, SIR. JUST DON'T ASK ME TO SAVE YOU FROM IT ANYMORE.
NOTED. NOW, GIVE ME A HAND.
GOT SOMETHIN'.
WHAT IS IT?
A CALLING CARD.
FOR WHO?
AN ASSASSIN OF THE BLACK KHALI.

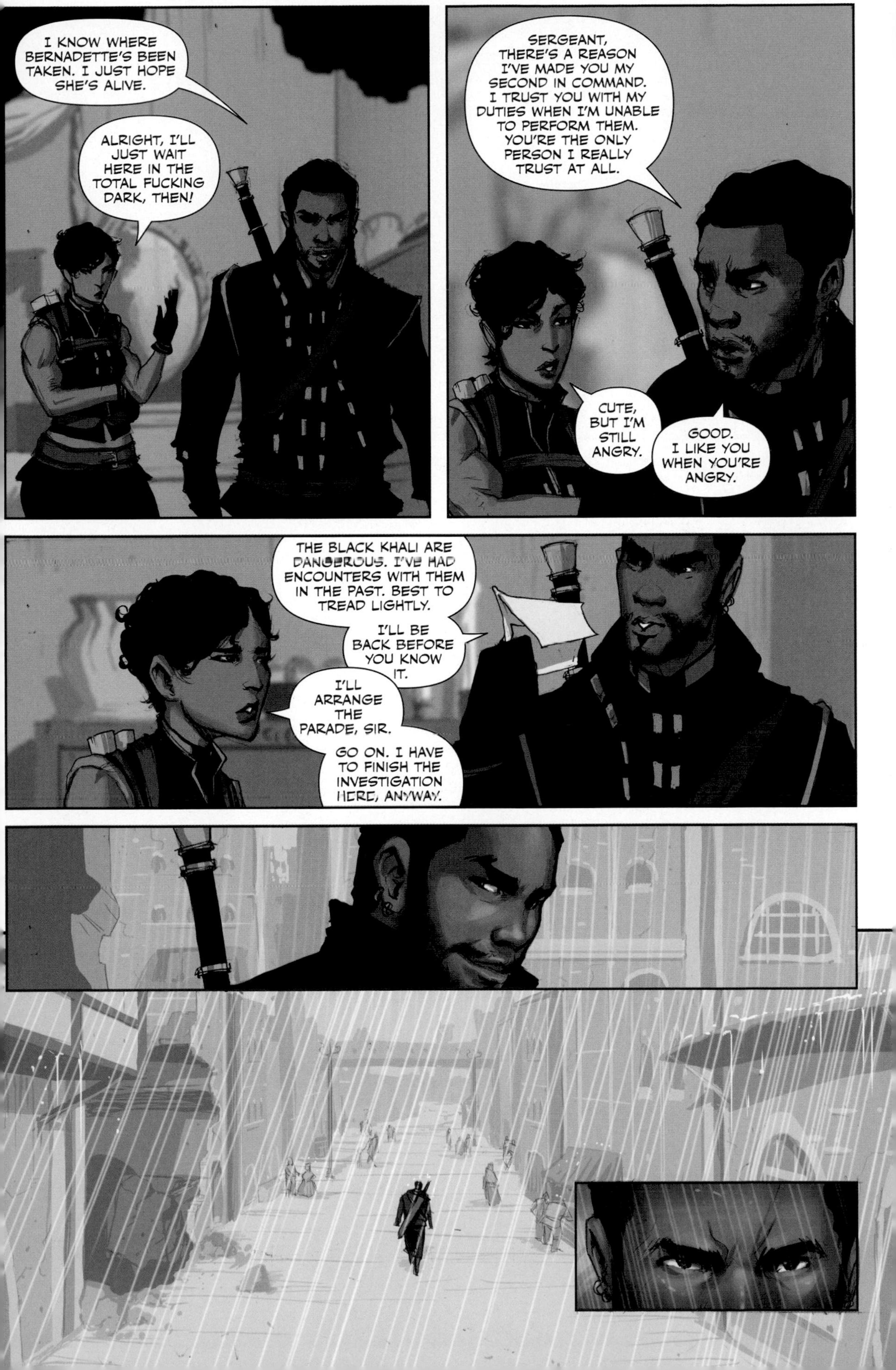
I KNOW WHERE BERNADETTE'S BEEN TAKEN. I JUST HOPE SHE'S ALIVE.
ALRIGHT, I'LL JUST WAIT HERE IN THE TOTAL FUCKING DARK, THEN!
SERGEANT, THERE'S A REASON I'VE MADE YOU MY SECOND IN COMMAND. I TRUST YOU WITH MY DUTIES WHEN I'M UNABLE TO PERFORM THEM. YOU'RE THE ONLY PERSON I REALLY TRUST AT ALL.
CUTE, BUT I'M STILL ANGRY.
GOOD. I LIKE YOU WHEN YOU'RE ANGRY.
THE BLACK KHALI ARE DANGEROUS. I'VE HAD ENCOUNTERS WITH THEM IN THE PAST. BEST TO TREAD LIGHTLY.
I'LL BE BACK BEFORE YOU KNOW IT.
I'LL ARRANGE THE PARADE, SIR.
GO ON. I HAVE TO FINISH THE INVESTIGATION HERE, ANYWAY.

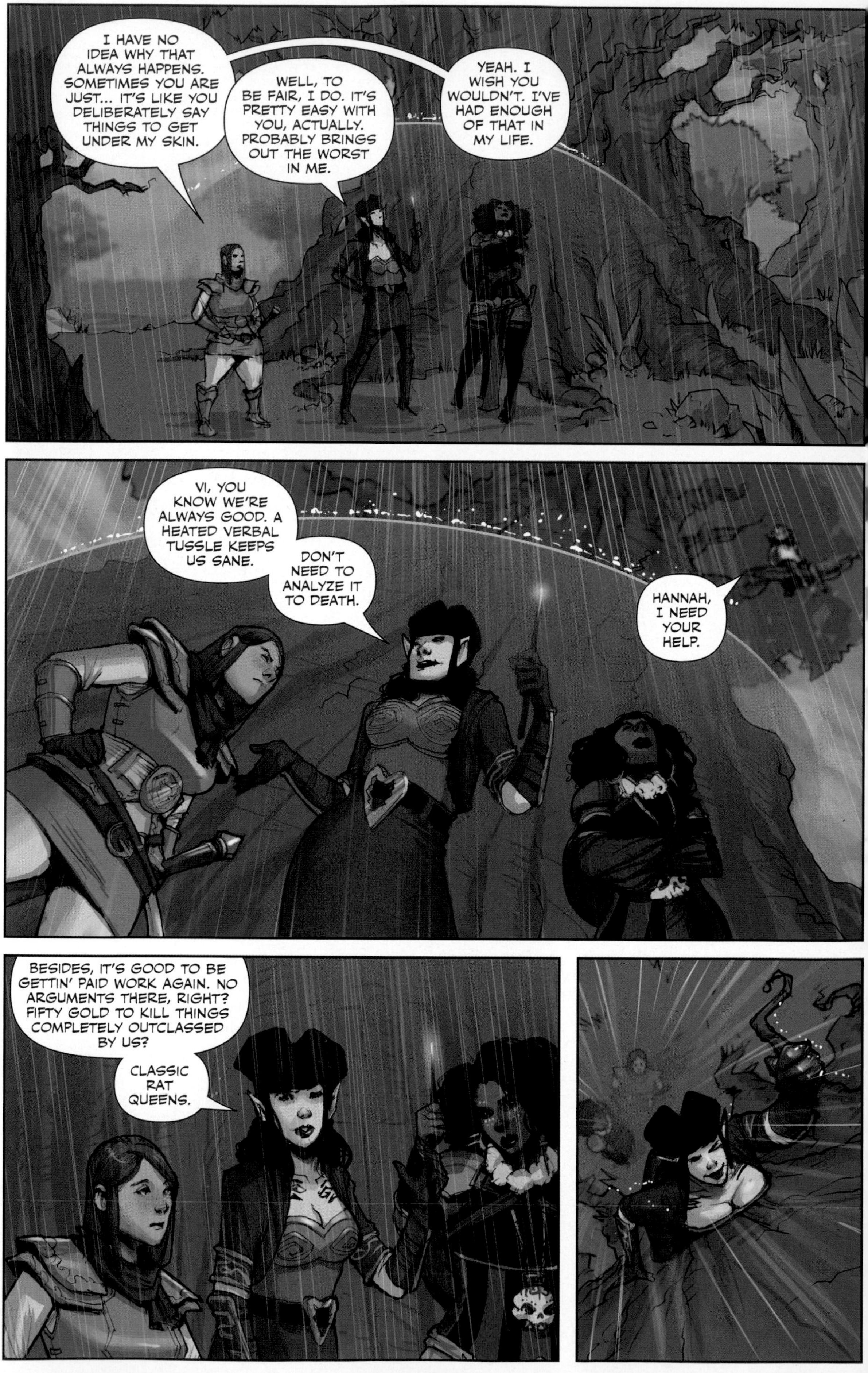
I HAVE NO IDEA WHY THAT ALWAYS HAPPENS. SOMETIMES YOU ARE JUST... IT'S LIKE YOU DELIBERATELY SAY THINGS TO GET UNDER MY SKIN.
WELL, TO BE FAIR, I DO. IT'S PRETTY EASY WITH YOU, ACTUALLY. PROBABLY BRINGS OUT THE WORST IN ME.
YEAH. I WISH YOU WOULDN'T. I'VE HAD ENOUGH OF THAT IN MY LIFE.
VI, YOU KNOW WE'RE ALWAYS GOOD. A HEATED VERBAL TUSSLE KEEPS US SANE.
DON'T NEED TO ANALYZE IT TO DEATH.
HANNAH, I NEED YOUR HELP.
BESIDES, IT'S GOOD TO BE GETTIN' PAID WORK AGAIN. NO ARGUMENTS THERE, RIGHT? FIFTY GOLD TO KILL THINGS COMPLETELY OUTCLASSED BY US?
CLASSIC RAT QUEENS.

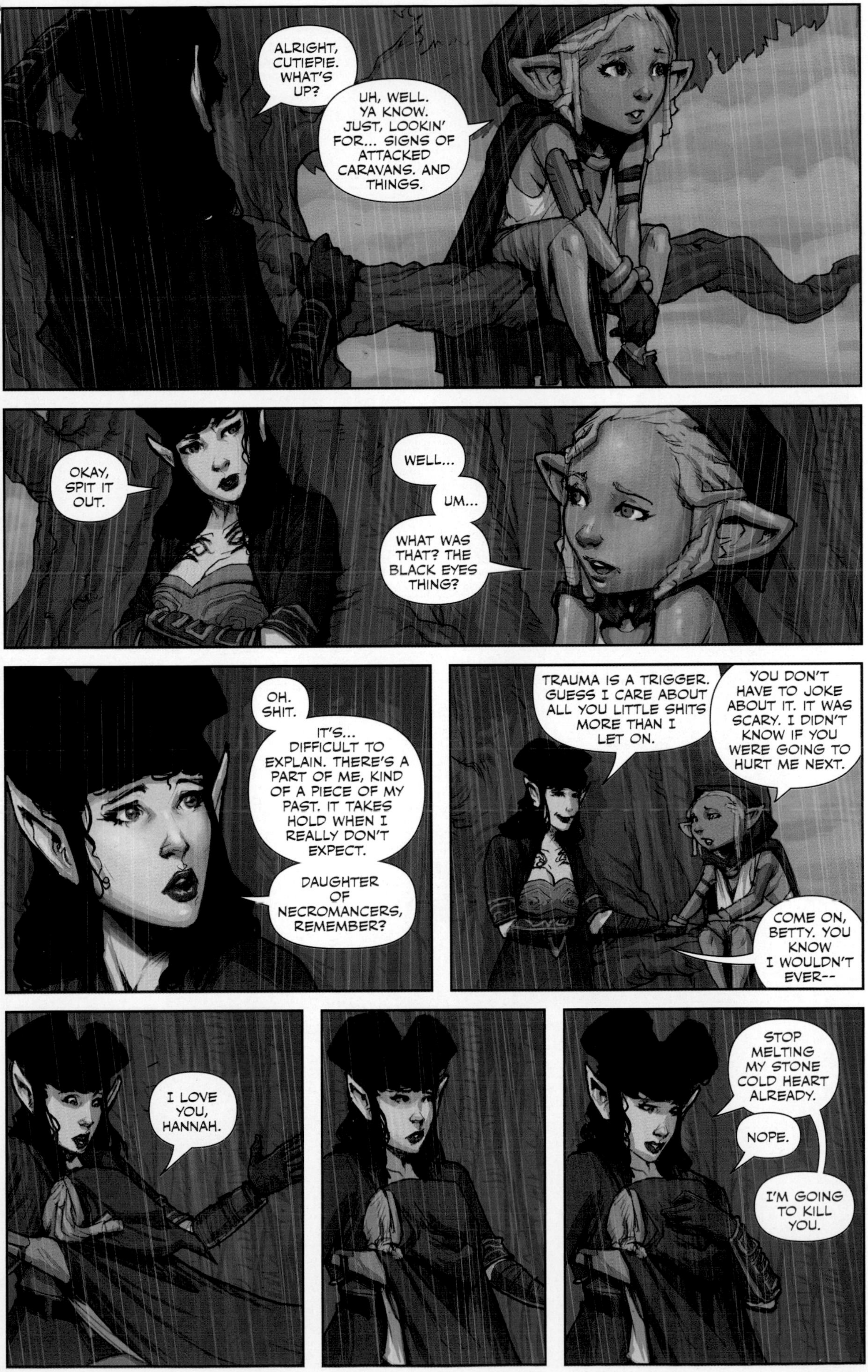
ALRIGHT, CUTIEPIE. WHAT'S UP?
UH, WELL. YA KNOW. JUST, LOOKIN' FOR... SIGNS OF ATTACKED CARAVANS. AND THINGS.
OKAY, SPIT IT OUT.
WELL...
UM...
WHAT WAS THAT? THE BLACK EYES THING?
OH. SHIT.
IT'S... DIFFICULT TO EXPLAIN. THERE'S A PART OF ME, KIND OF A PIECE OF MY PAST. IT TAKES HOLD WHEN I REALLY DON'T EXPECT.
DAUGHTER OF NECROMANCERS, REMEMBER?
TRAUMA IS A TRIGGER. GUESS I CARE ABOUT ALL YOU LITTLE SHITS MORE THAN I LET ON.
YOU DON'T HAVE TO JOKE ABOUT IT. IT WAS SCARY. I DIDN'T KNOW IF YOU WERE GOING TO HURT ME NEXT.
COME ON, BETTY. YOU KNOW I WOULDN'T EVER--
I LOVE YOU, HANNAH.
STOP MELTING MY STONE COLD HEART ALREADY.
NOPE.
I'M GOING TO KILL YOU.

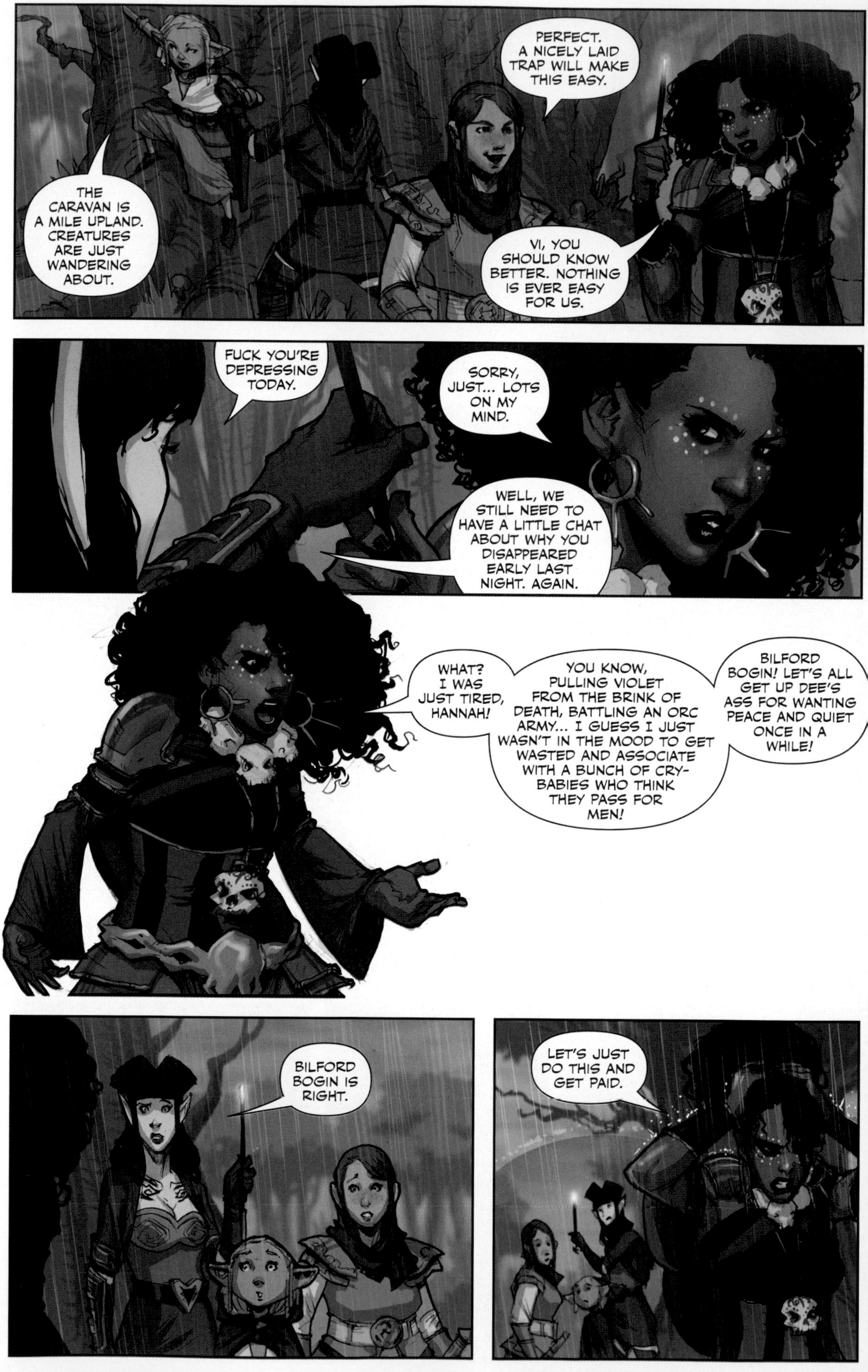
THE CARAVAN IS A MILE UPLAND. CREATURES ARE JUST WANDERING ABOUT.
PERFECT. A NICELY LAID TRAP WILL MAKE THIS EASY.
VI, YOU SHOULD KNOW BETTER. NOTHING IS EVER EASY FOR US.
FUCK YOU'RE DEPRESSING TODAY.
SORRY, JUST... LOTS ON MY MIND.
WELL, WE STILL NEED TO HAVE A LITTLE CHAT ABOUT WHY YOU DISAPPEARED EARLY LAST NIGHT. AGAIN.
WHAT? I WAS JUST TIRED, HANNAH!
YOU KNOW, PULLING VIOLET FROM THE BRINK OF DEATH, BATTLING AN ORC ARMY... I GUESS I JUST WASN'T IN THE MOOD TO GET WASTED AND ASSOCIATE WITH A BUNCH OF CRY-BABIES WHO THINK THEY PASS FOR MEN!
BILFORD BOGIN! LET'S ALL GET UP DEE'S ASS FOR WANTING PEACE AND QUIET ONCE IN A WHILE!
BILFORD BOGIN IS RIGHT.
LET'S JUST DO THIS AND GET PAID.

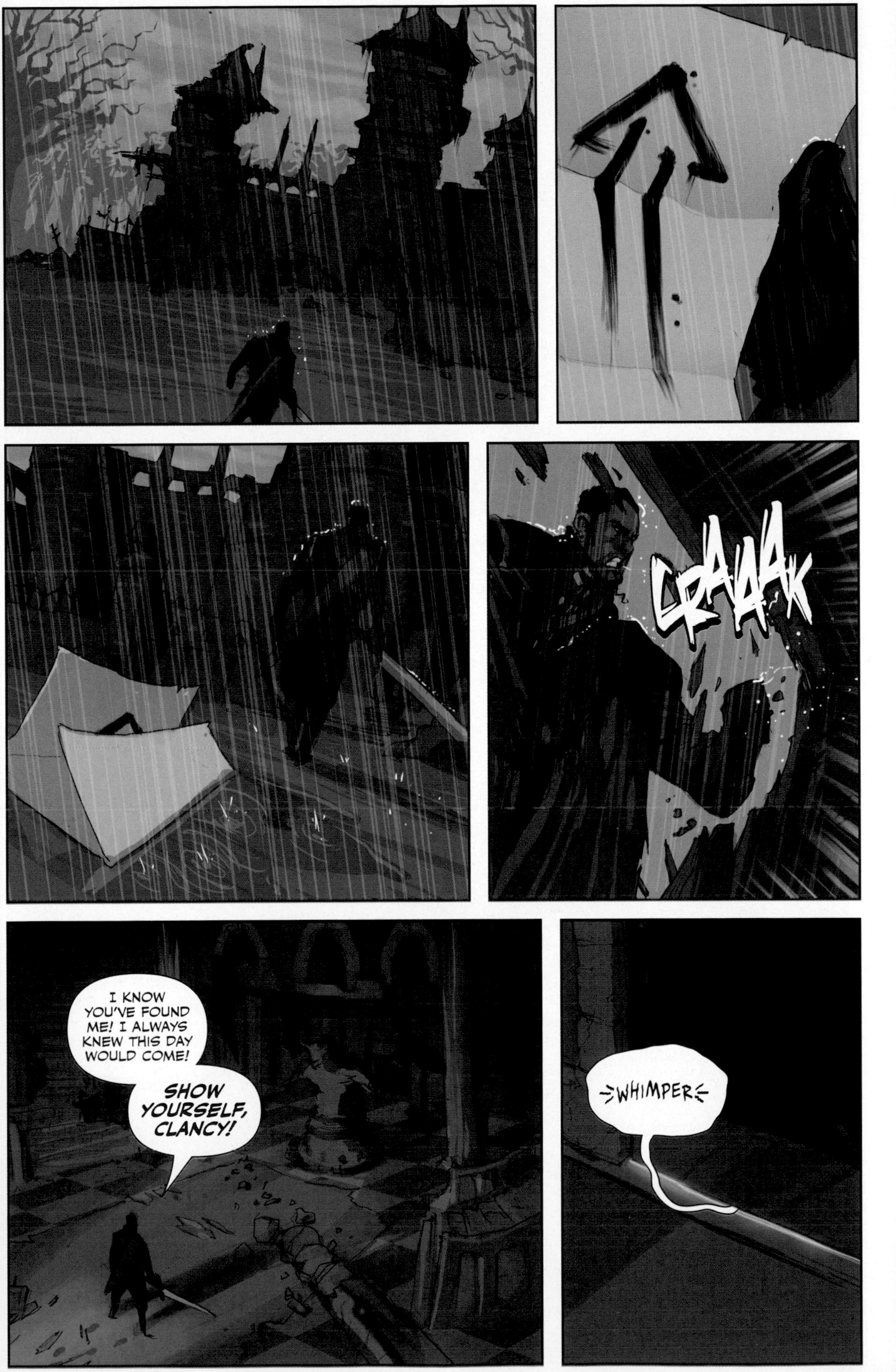
CRAAAK
I KNOW YOU'VE FOUND ME! I ALWAYS KNEW THIS DAY WOULD COME!
SHOW YOURSELF, CLANCY!
WHIMPER

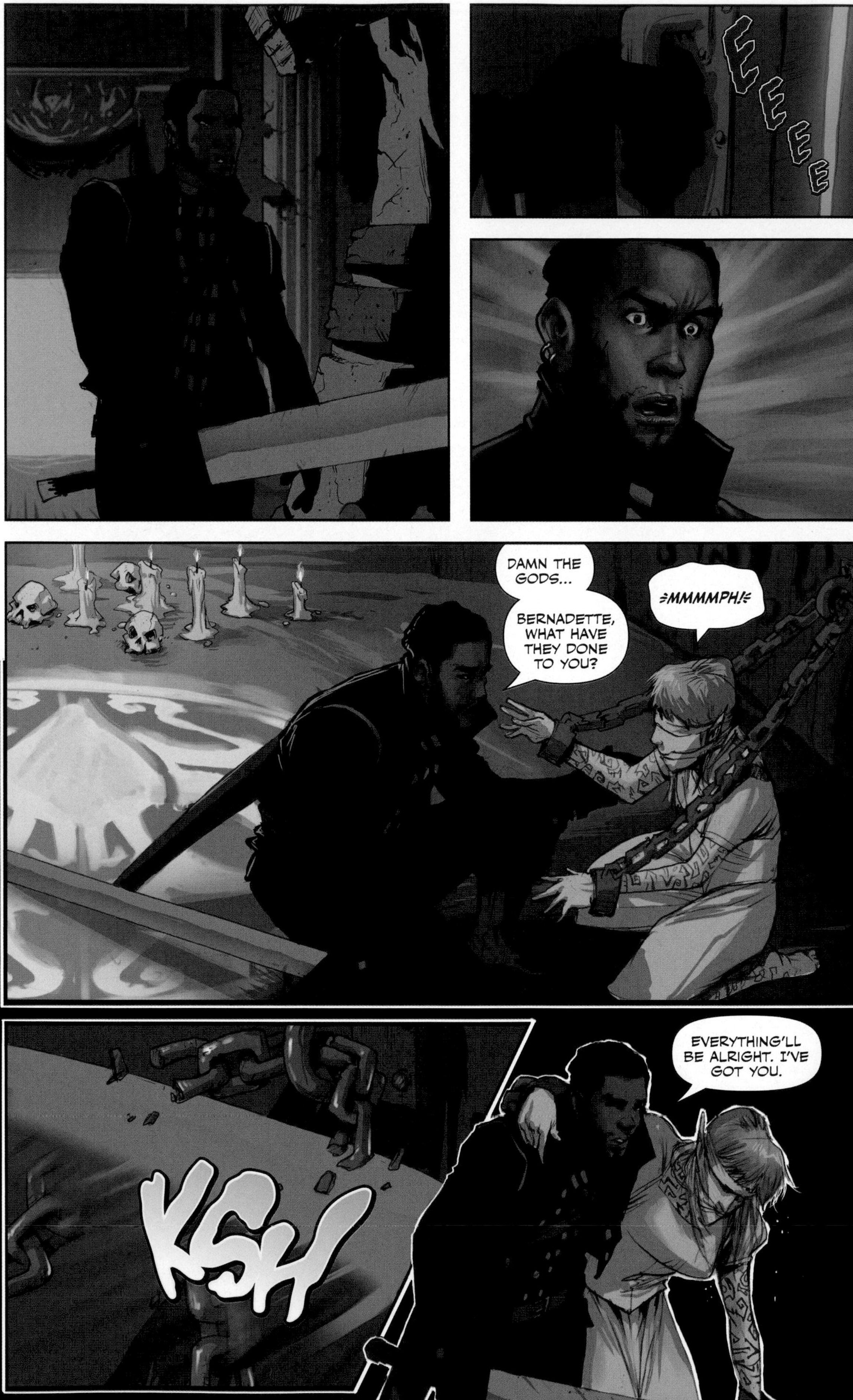
EEEE
DAMN THE GODS...
BERNADETTE, WHAT HAVE THEY DONE TO YOU?
MMMMPH!
EVERYTHING'LL BE ALRIGHT. I'VE GOT YOU.
KSH

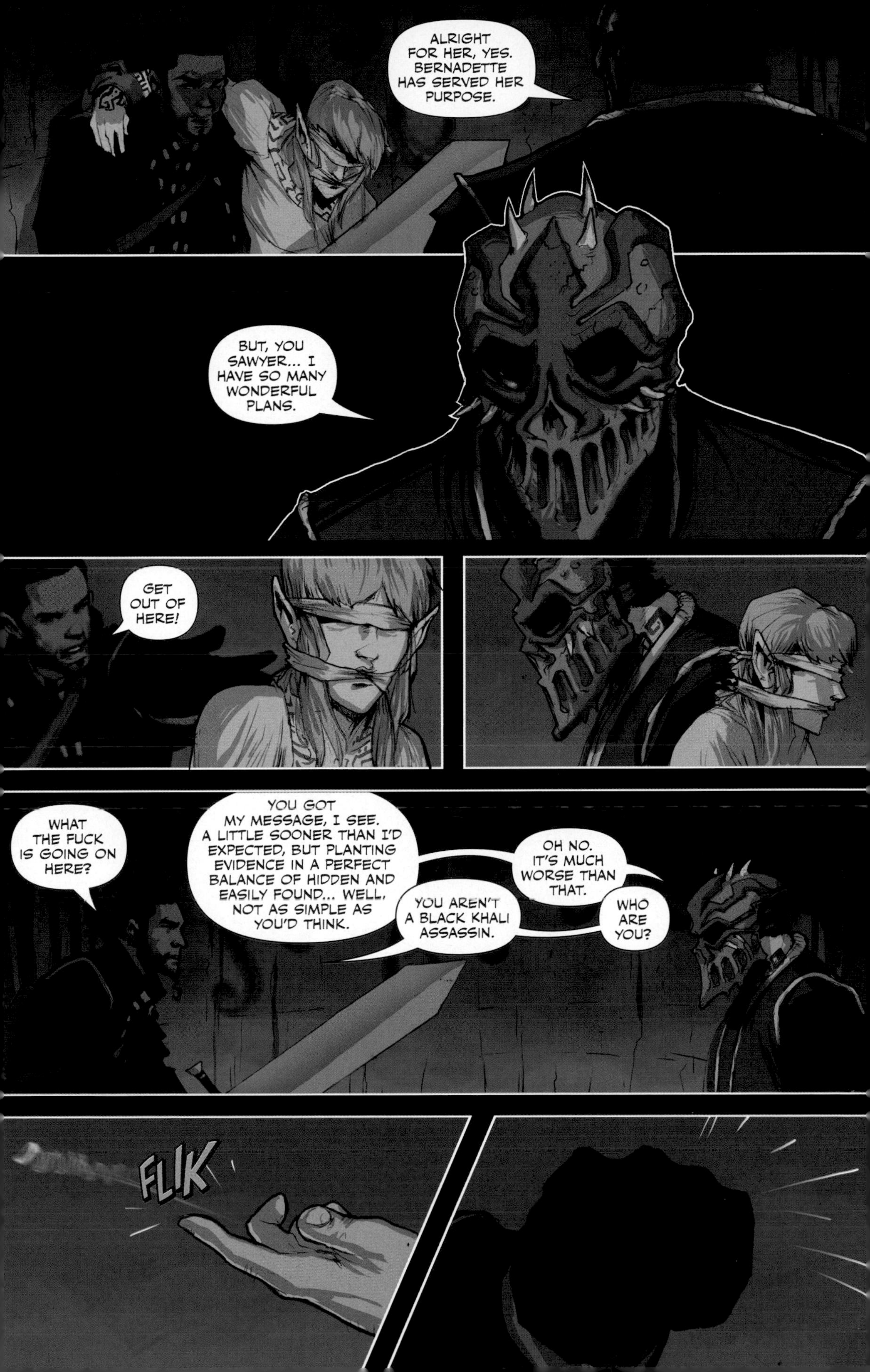
ALRIGHT FOR HER, YES. BERNADETTE HAS SERVED HER PURPOSE.
BUT, YOU SAWYER... I HAVE SO MANY WONDERFUL PLANS.
GET OUT OF HERE!
WHAT THE FUCK IS GOING ON HERE?
YOU GOT MY MESSAGE, I SEE. A LITTLE SOONER THAN I'D EXPECTED, BUT PLANTING EVIDENCE IN A PERFECT BALANCE OF HIDDEN AND EASILY FOUND... WELL, NOT AS SIMPLE AS YOU'D THINK.
YOU AREN'T A BLACK KHALI ASSASSIN.
OH NO. IT'S MUCH WORSE THAN THAT.
WHO ARE YOU?
FLIK

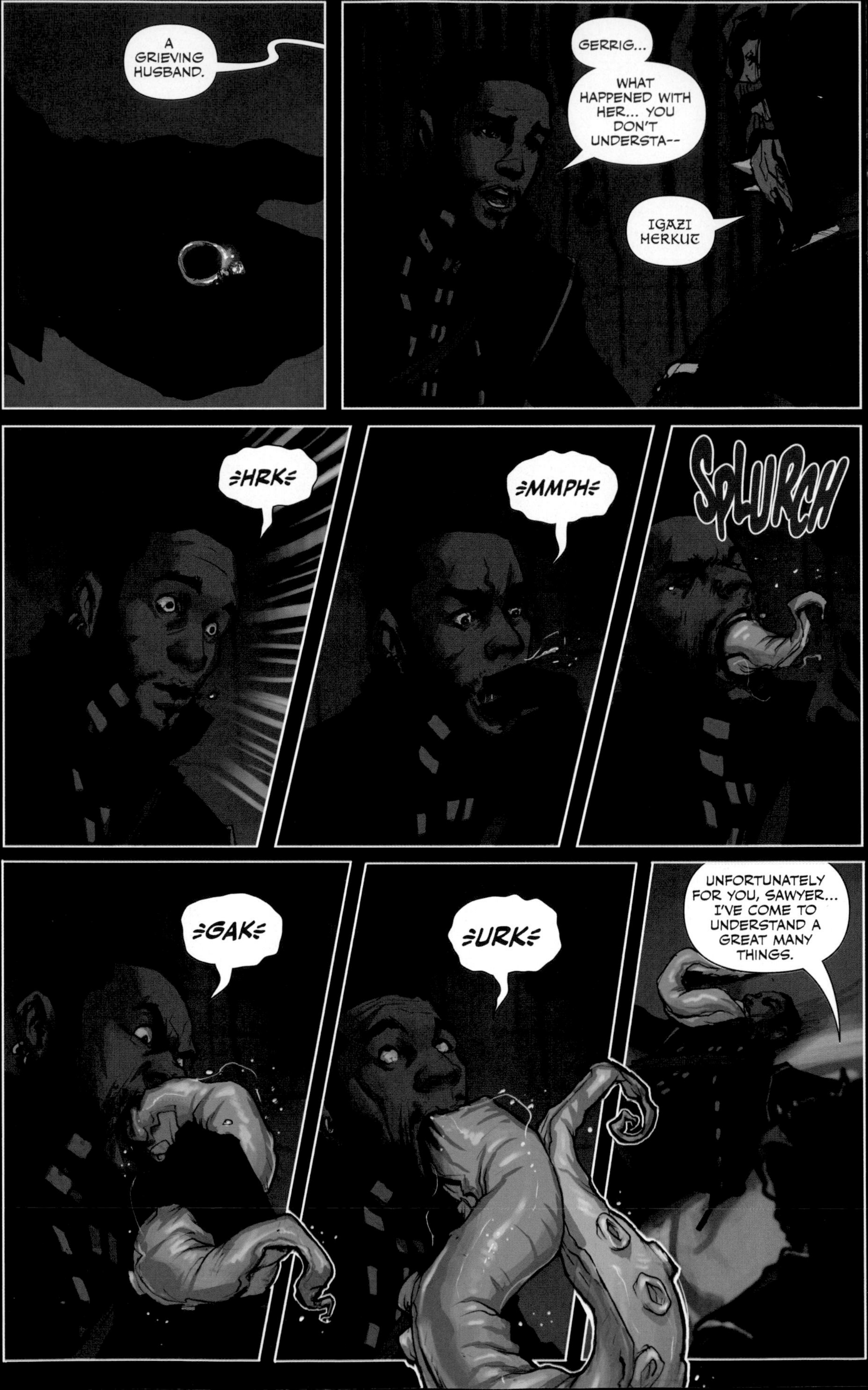
A GRIEVING HUSBAND.
GERRIG...
WHAT HAPPENED WITH HER... YOU DON'T UNDERSTA--
IGAZI MERKUT
HRK
MMPH
SPLURCH
GAK
URK
UNFORTUNATELY FOR YOU, SAWYER... I'VE COME TO UNDERSTAND A GREAT MANY THINGS.

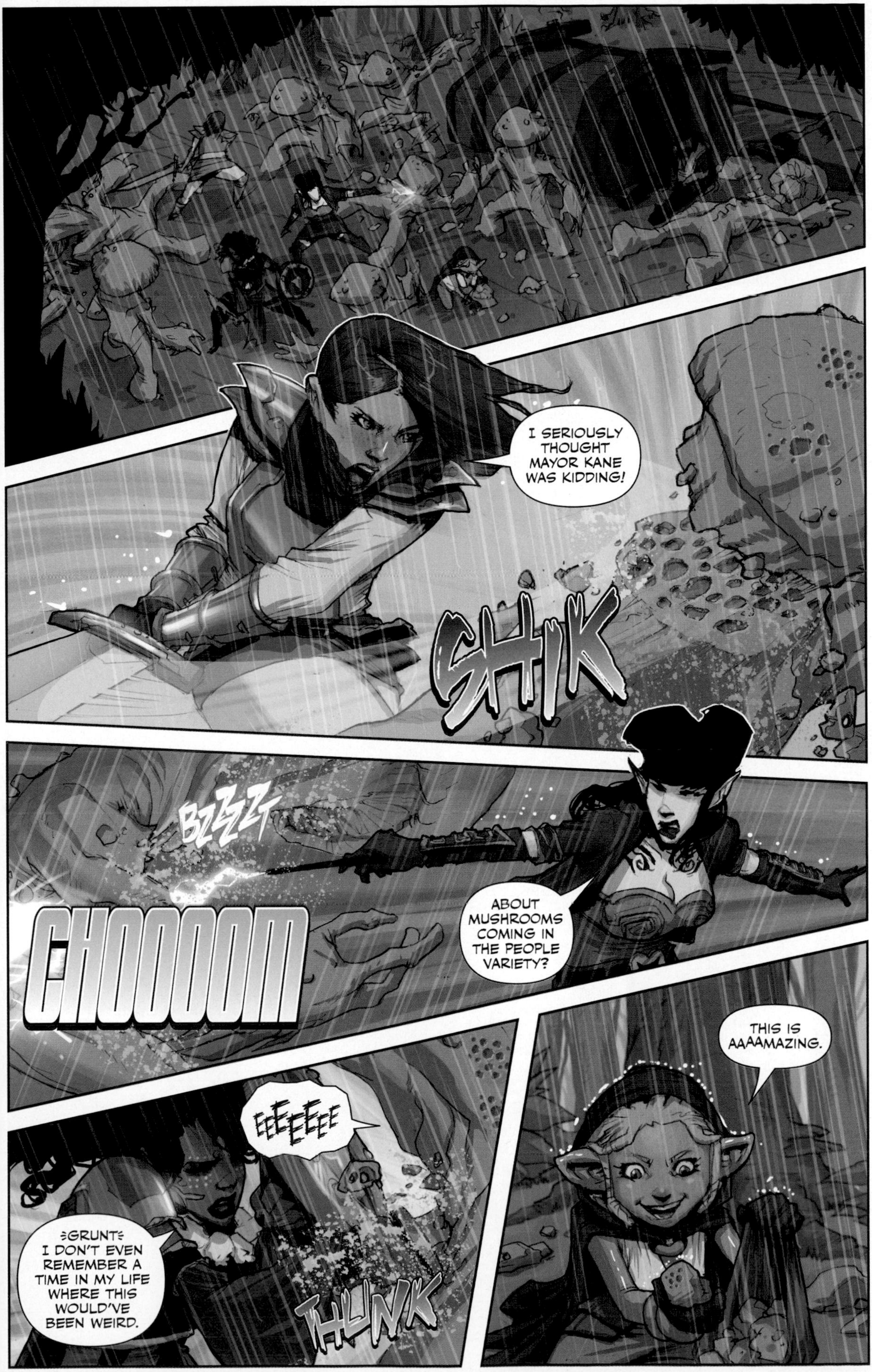

I SERIOUSLY THOUGHT MAYOR KANE WAS KIDDING!
SHIK
BZZZZT
CHOOOOM
ABOUT MUSHROOMS COMING IN THE PEOPLE VARIETY?
EEEEEEE
GRUNT
I DON'T EVEN REMEMBER A TIME IN MY LIFE WHERE THIS WOULD'VE BEEN WEIRD.
THUNK
THIS IS AAAAMAZING.

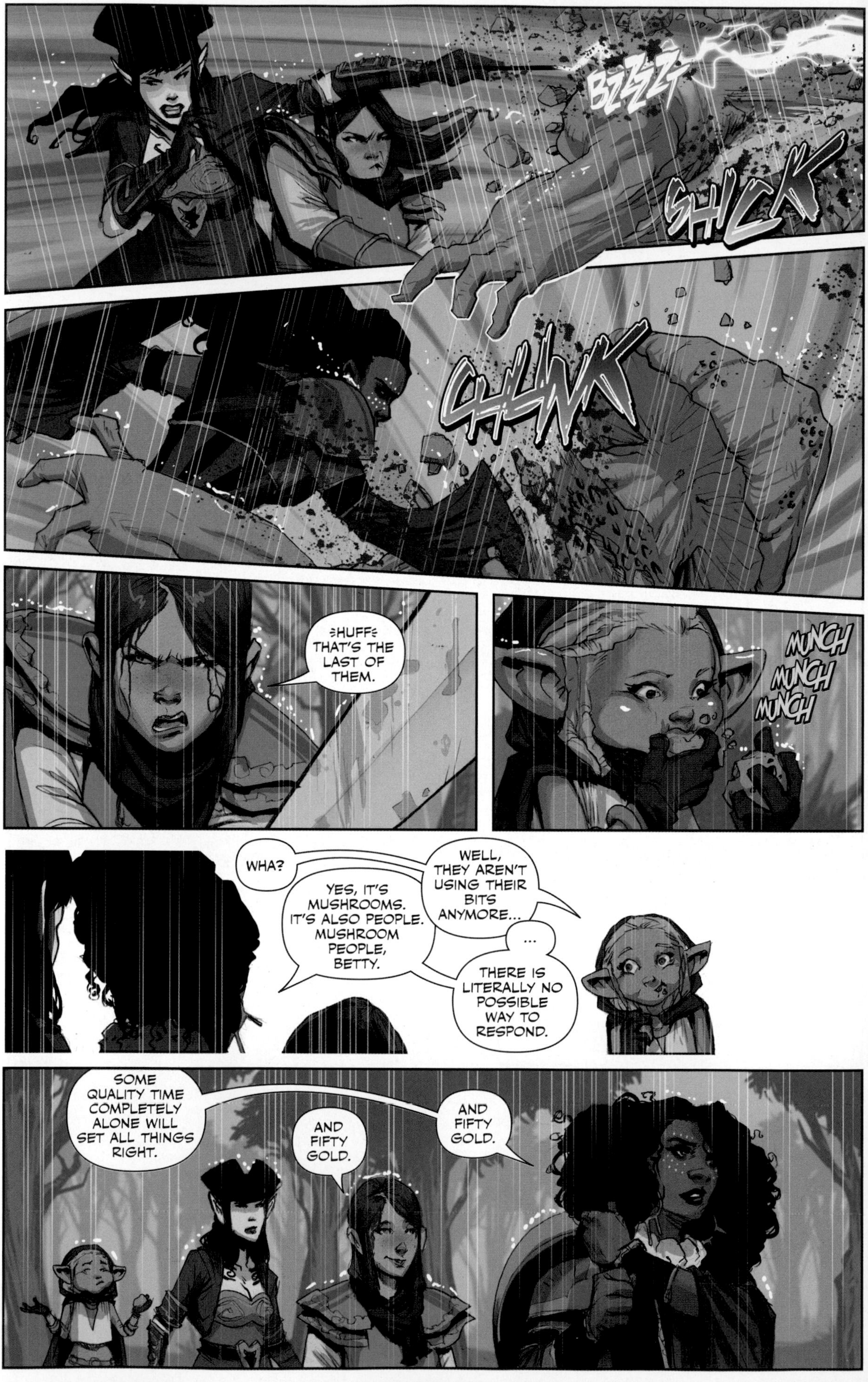
BZZZZT
SHICK
CHLUNK
≶HUFF≶ THAT'S THE LAST OF THEM.
MUNCH MUNCH MUNCH
WHA?
WELL, THEY AREN'T USING THEIR BITS ANYMORE...
YES, IT'S MUSHROOMS. IT'S ALSO PEOPLE. MUSHROOM PEOPLE, BETTY.
...
THERE IS LITERALLY NO POSSIBLE WAY TO RESPOND.
SOME QUALITY TIME COMPLETELY ALONE WILL SET ALL THINGS RIGHT.
AND FIFTY GOLD.
AND FIFTY GOLD.

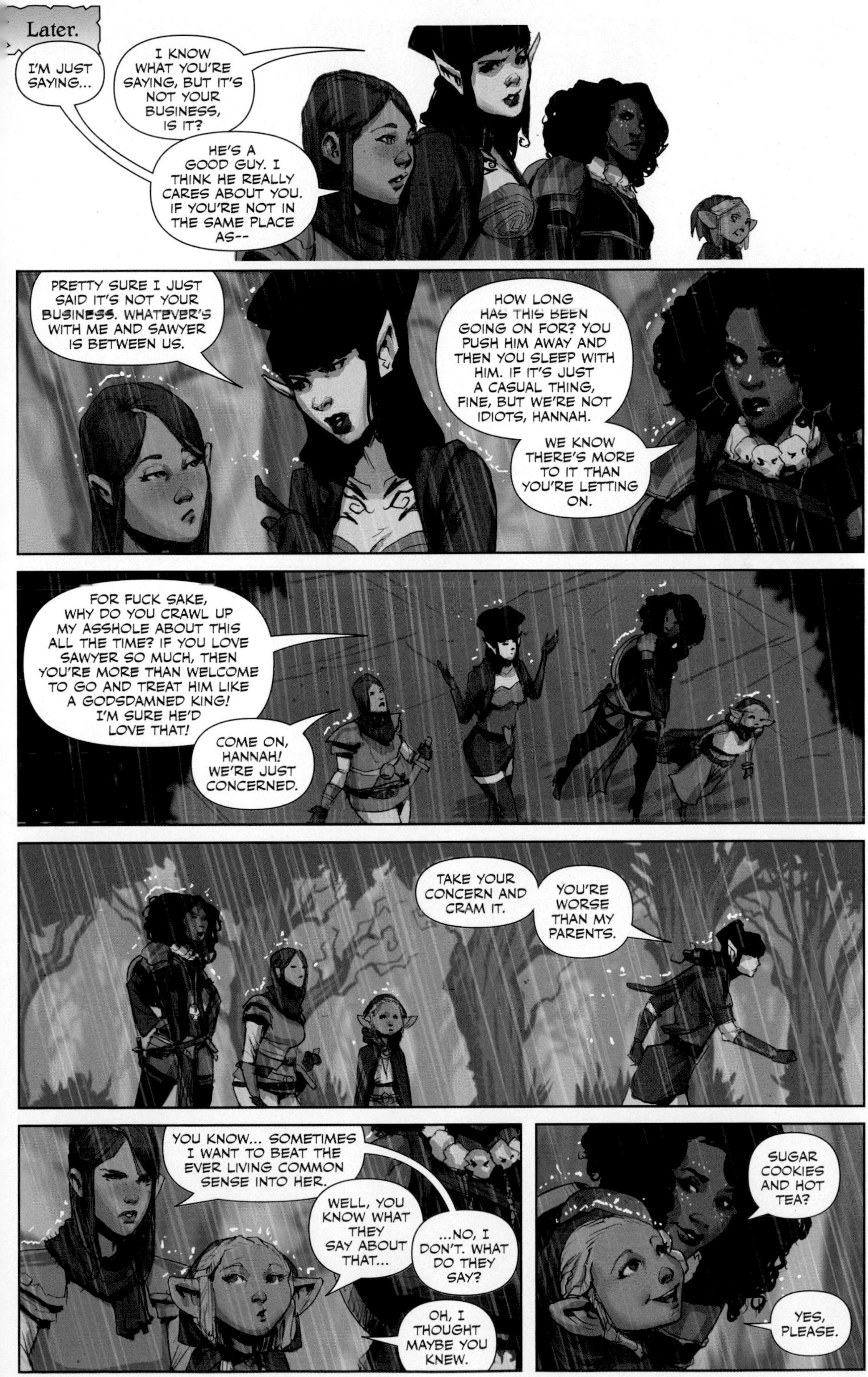
Later.
I'M JUST SAYING...
I KNOW WHAT YOU'RE SAYING, BUT IT'S NOT YOUR BUSINESS, IS IT?
HE'S A GOOD GUY. I THINK HE REALLY CARES ABOUT YOU. IF YOU'RE NOT IN THE SAME PLACE AS--
PRETTY SURE I JUST SAID IT'S NOT YOUR BUSINESS. WHATEVER'S WITH ME AND SAWYER IS BETWEEN US.
HOW LONG HAS THIS BEEN GOING ON FOR? YOU PUSH HIM AWAY AND THEN YOU SLEEP WITH HIM. IF IT'S JUST A CASUAL THING, FINE, BUT WE'RE NOT IDIOTS, HANNAH.
WE KNOW THERE'S MORE TO IT THAN YOU'RE LETTING ON.
FOR FUCK SAKE, WHY DO YOU CRAWL UP MY ASSHOLE ABOUT THIS ALL THE TIME? IF YOU LOVE SAWYER SO MUCH, THEN YOU'RE MORE THAN WELCOME TO GO AND TREAT HIM LIKE A GODSDAMNED KING! I'M SURE HE'D LOVE THAT!
COME ON, HANNAH! WE'RE JUST CONCERNED.
TAKE YOUR CONCERN AND CRAM IT.
YOU'RE WORSE THAN MY PARENTS.
YOU KNOW... SOMETIMES I WANT TO BEAT THE EVER LIVING COMMON SENSE INTO HER.
WELL, YOU KNOW WHAT THEY SAY ABOUT THAT...
...NO, I DON'T. WHAT DO THEY SAY?
OH, I THOUGHT MAYBE YOU KNEW.
SUGAR COOKIES AND HOT TEA?
YES, PLEASE.

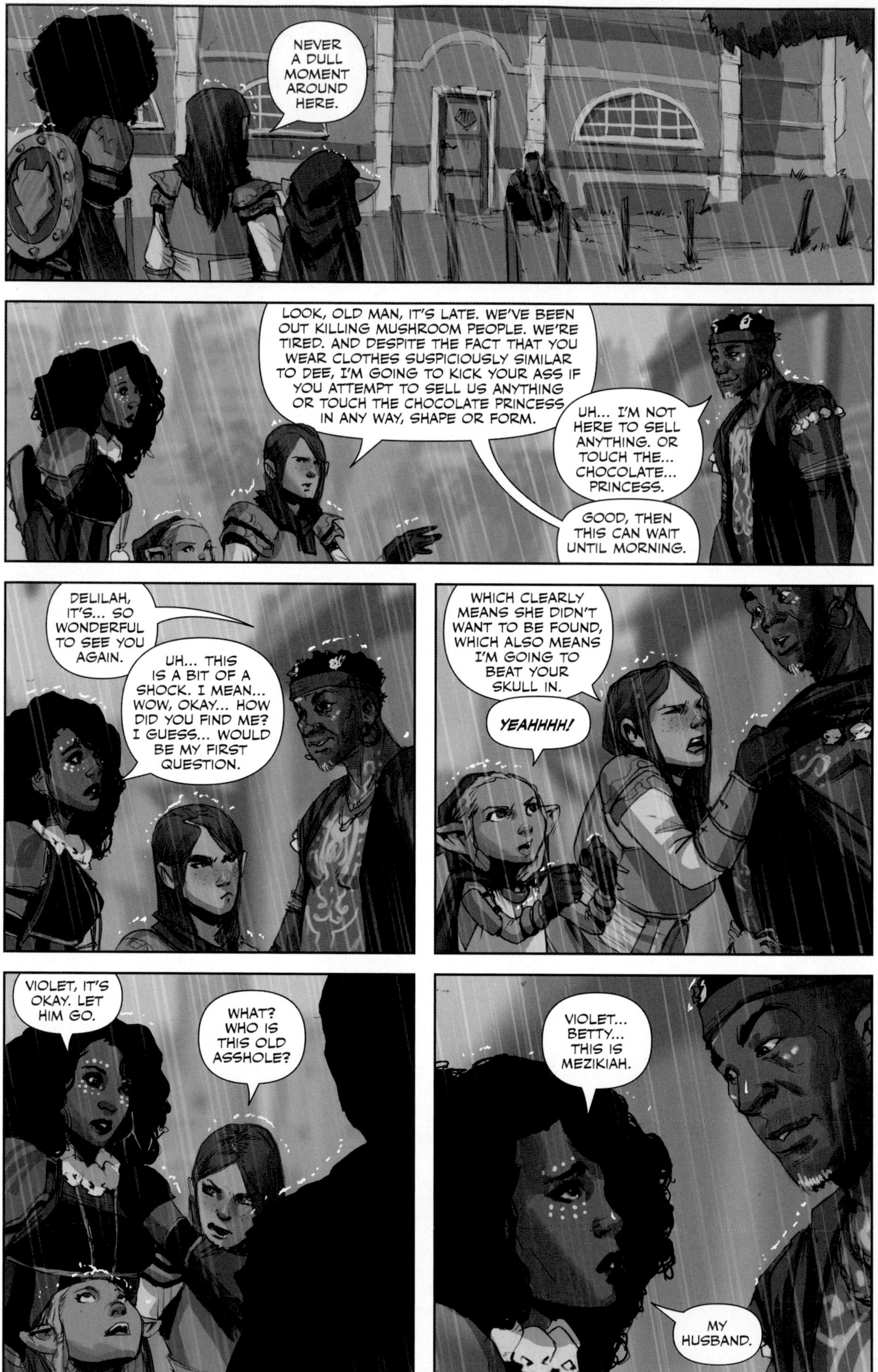
NEVER A DULL MOMENT AROUND HERE.
LOOK, OLD MAN, IT'S LATE. WE'VE BEEN OUT KILLING MUSHROOM PEOPLE. WE'RE TIRED. AND DESPITE THE FACT THAT YOU WEAR CLOTHES SUSPICIOUSLY SIMILAR TO DEE, I'M GOING TO KICK YOUR ASS IF YOU ATTEMPT TO SELL US ANYTHING OR TOUCH THE CHOCOLATE PRINCESS IN ANY WAY, SHAPE OR FORM.
UH... I'M NOT HERE TO SELL ANYTHING. OR TOUCH THE... CHOCOLATE... PRINCESS.
GOOD, THEN THIS CAN WAIT UNTIL MORNING.
DELILAH, IT'S... SO WONDERFUL TO SEE YOU AGAIN.
UH... THIS IS A BIT OF A SHOCK. I MEAN... WOW, OKAY... HOW DID YOU FIND ME? I GUESS... WOULD BE MY FIRST QUESTION.
WHICH CLEARLY MEANS SHE DIDN'T WANT TO BE FOUND, WHICH ALSO MEANS I'M GOING TO BEAT YOUR SKULL IN.
YEAHHHH!
VIOLET, IT'S OKAY. LET HIM GO.
WHAT? WHO IS THIS OLD ASSHOLE?
VIOLET... BETTY... THIS IS MEZIKIAH.
MY HUSBAND.

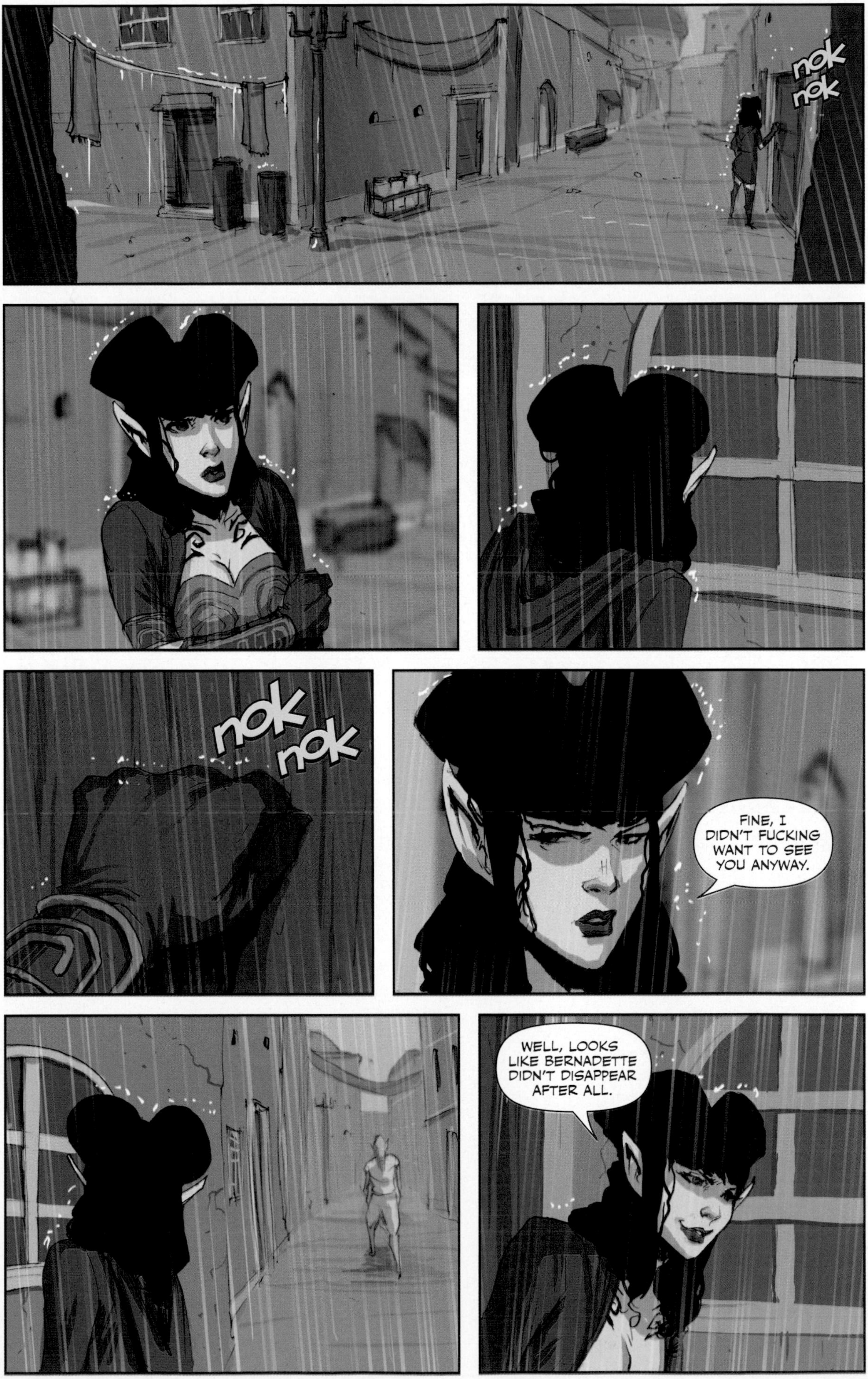
nok nok
nok nok
FINE, I DIDN'T FUCKING WANT TO SEE YOU ANYWAY.
WELL, LOOKS LIKE BERNADETTE DIDN'T DISAPPEAR AFTER ALL.

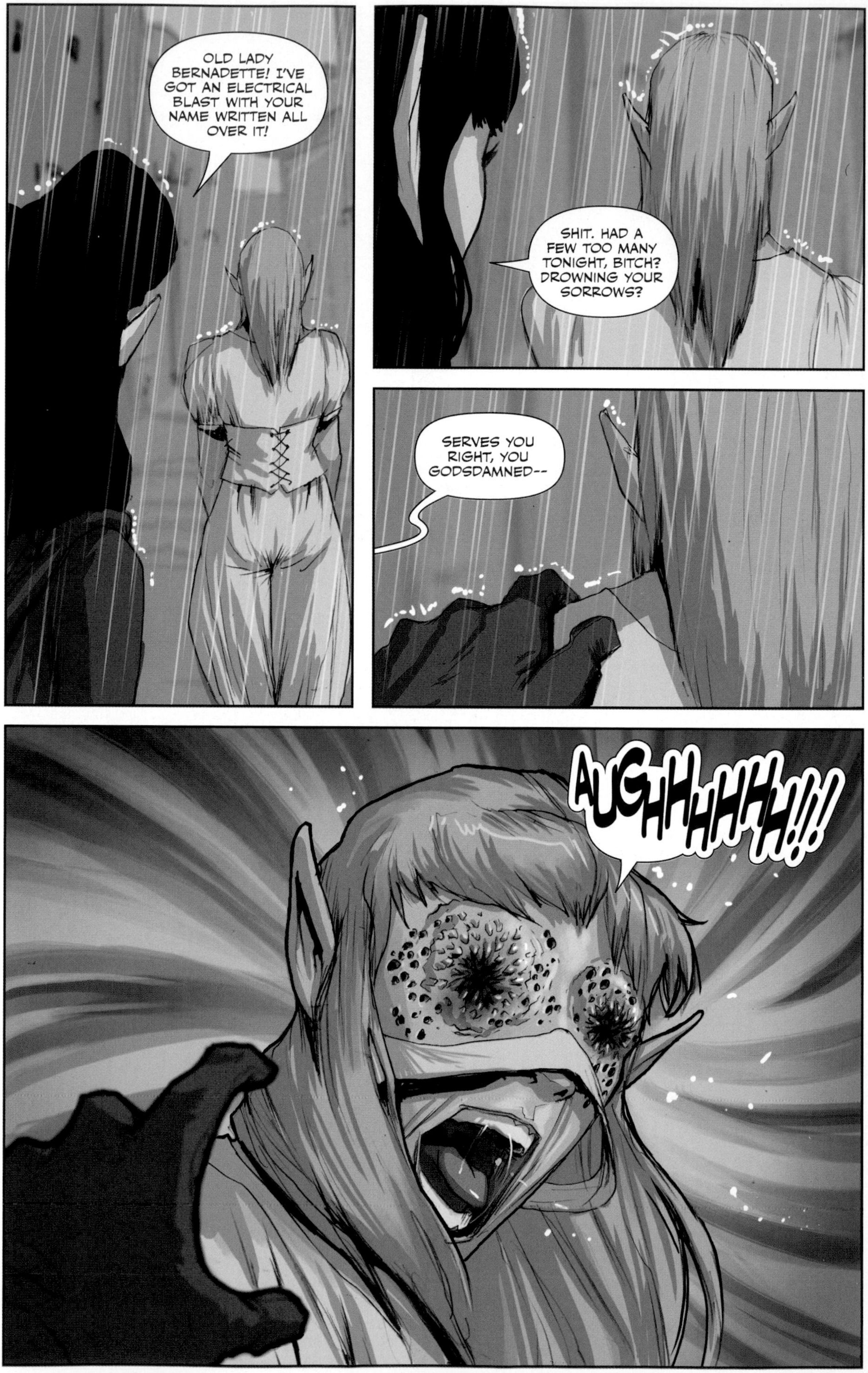
OLD LADY BERNADETTE! I'VE GOT AN ELECTRICAL BLAST WITH YOUR NAME WRITTEN ALL OVER IT!
SHIT. HAD A FEW TOO MANY TONIGHT, BITCH? DROWNING YOUR SORROWS?
SERVES YOU RIGHT, YOU GODSDAMNED--
AUGHHHHHH!!!

CHAPTER SEVEN

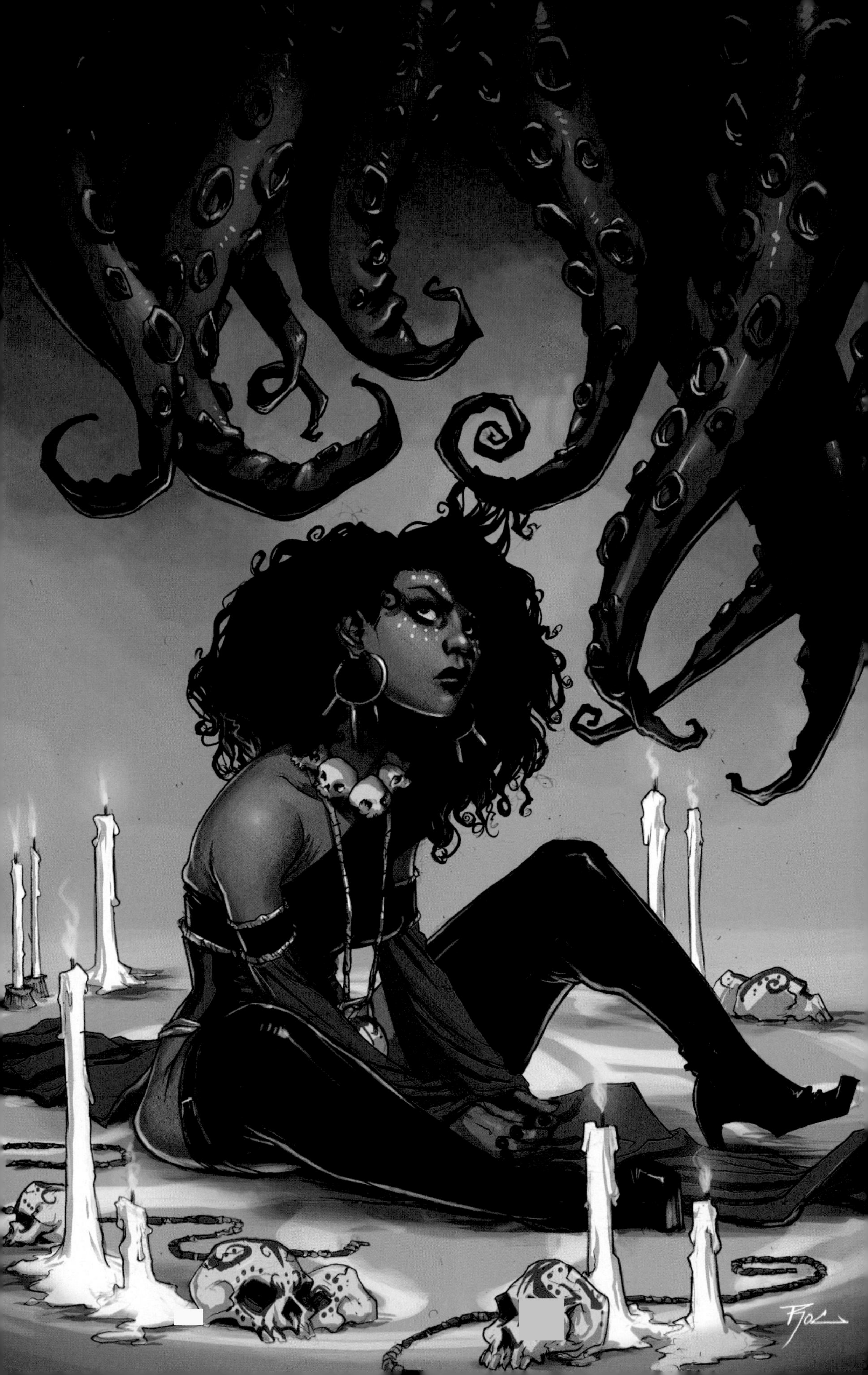

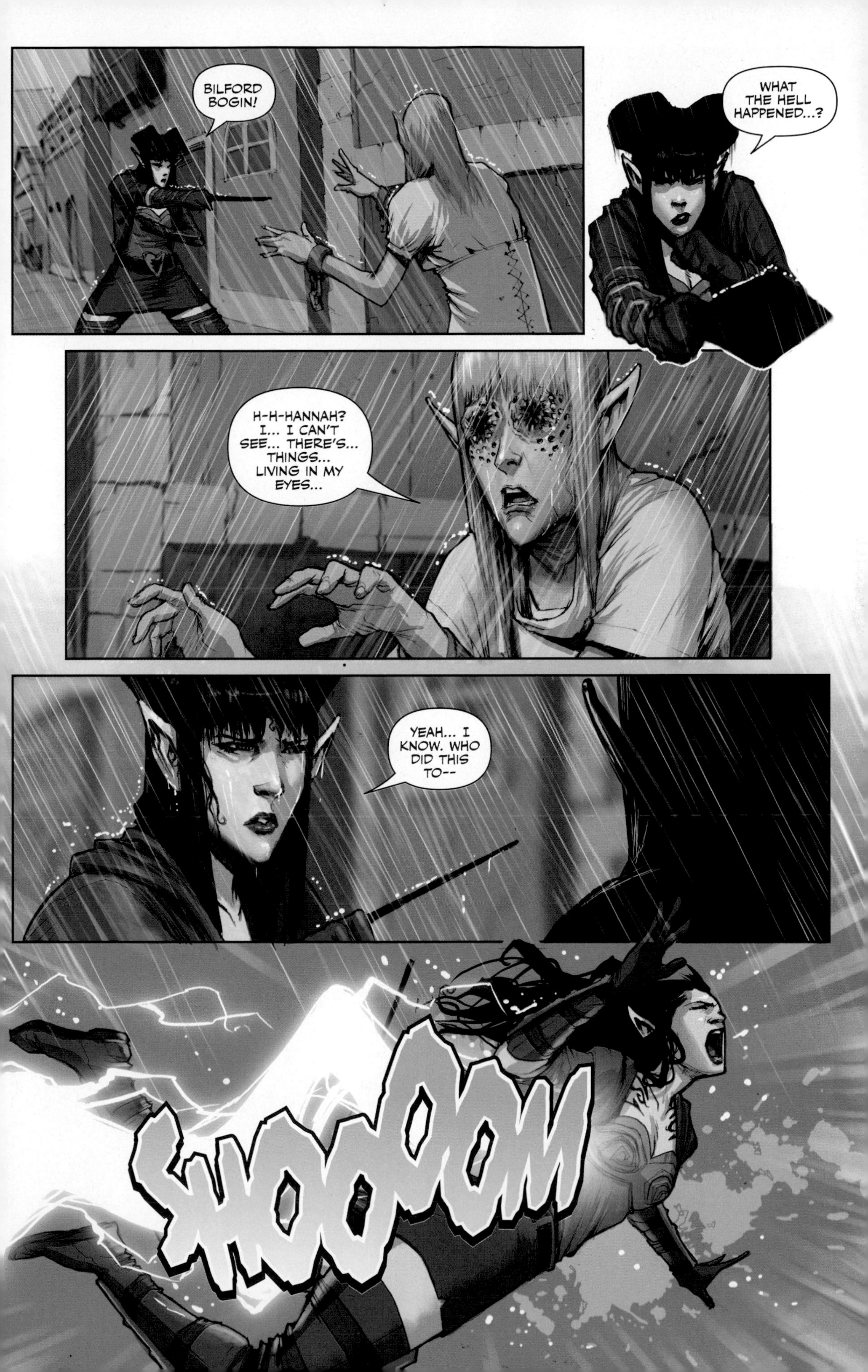
BILFORD BOGIN!
WHAT THE HELL HAPPENED...?
H-H-HANNAH? I... I CAN'T SEE... THERE'S... THINGS... LIVING IN MY EYES...
YEAH... I KNOW. WHO DID THIS TO--
WOOOOM

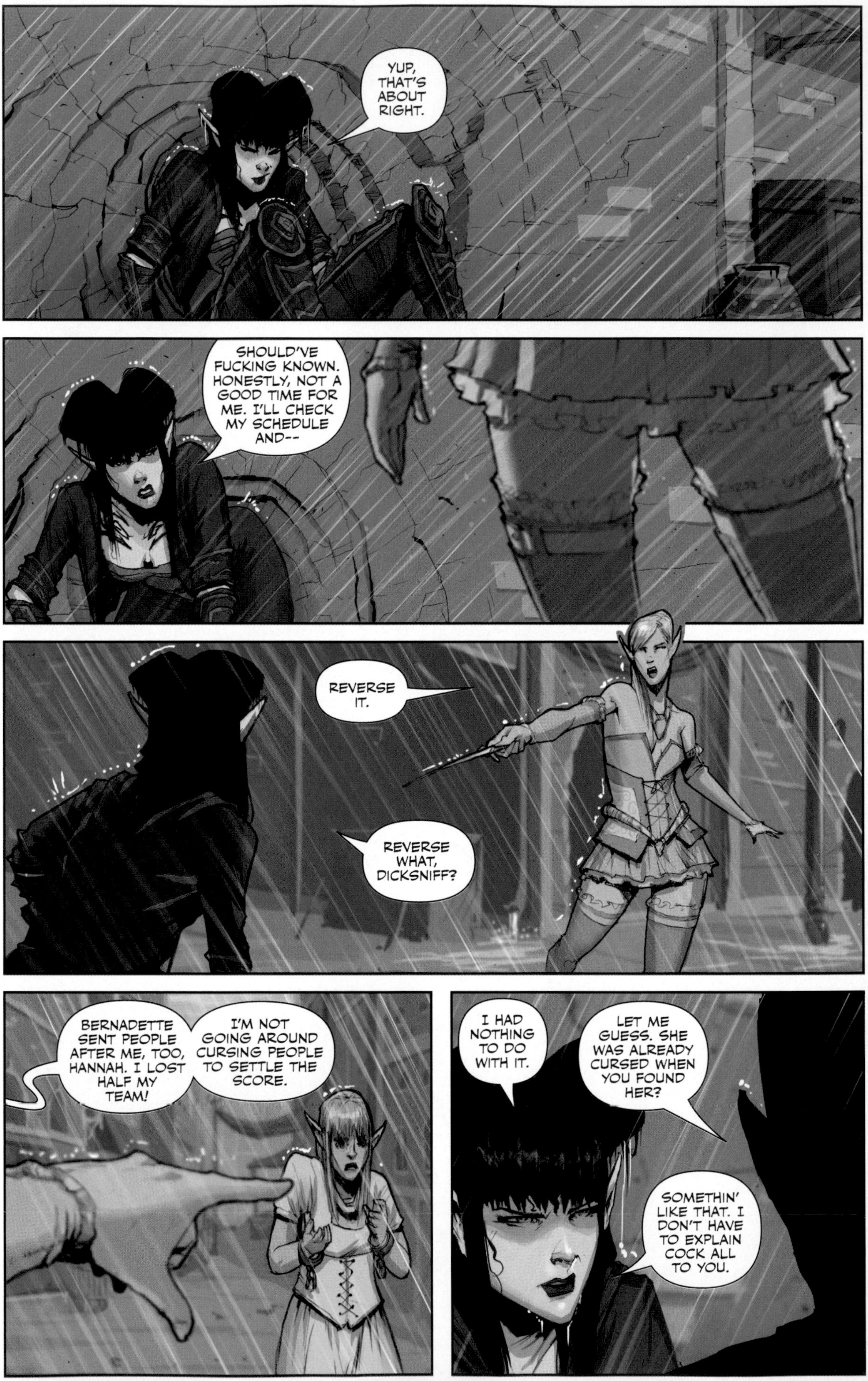
YUP, THAT'S ABOUT RIGHT.
SHOULD'VE FUCKING KNOWN. HONESTLY, NOT A GOOD TIME FOR ME. I'LL CHECK MY SCHEDULE AND--
REVERSE IT.
REVERSE WHAT, DICKSNIFF?
BERNADETTE SENT PEOPLE AFTER ME, TOO, HANNAH. I LOST HALF MY TEAM!
I'M NOT GOING AROUND CURSING PEOPLE TO SETTLE THE SCORE.
I HAD NOTHING TO DO WITH IT.
LET ME GUESS. SHE WAS ALREADY CURSED WHEN YOU FOUND HER?
SOMETHIN' LIKE THAT. I DON'T HAVE TO EXPLAIN COCK ALL TO YOU.

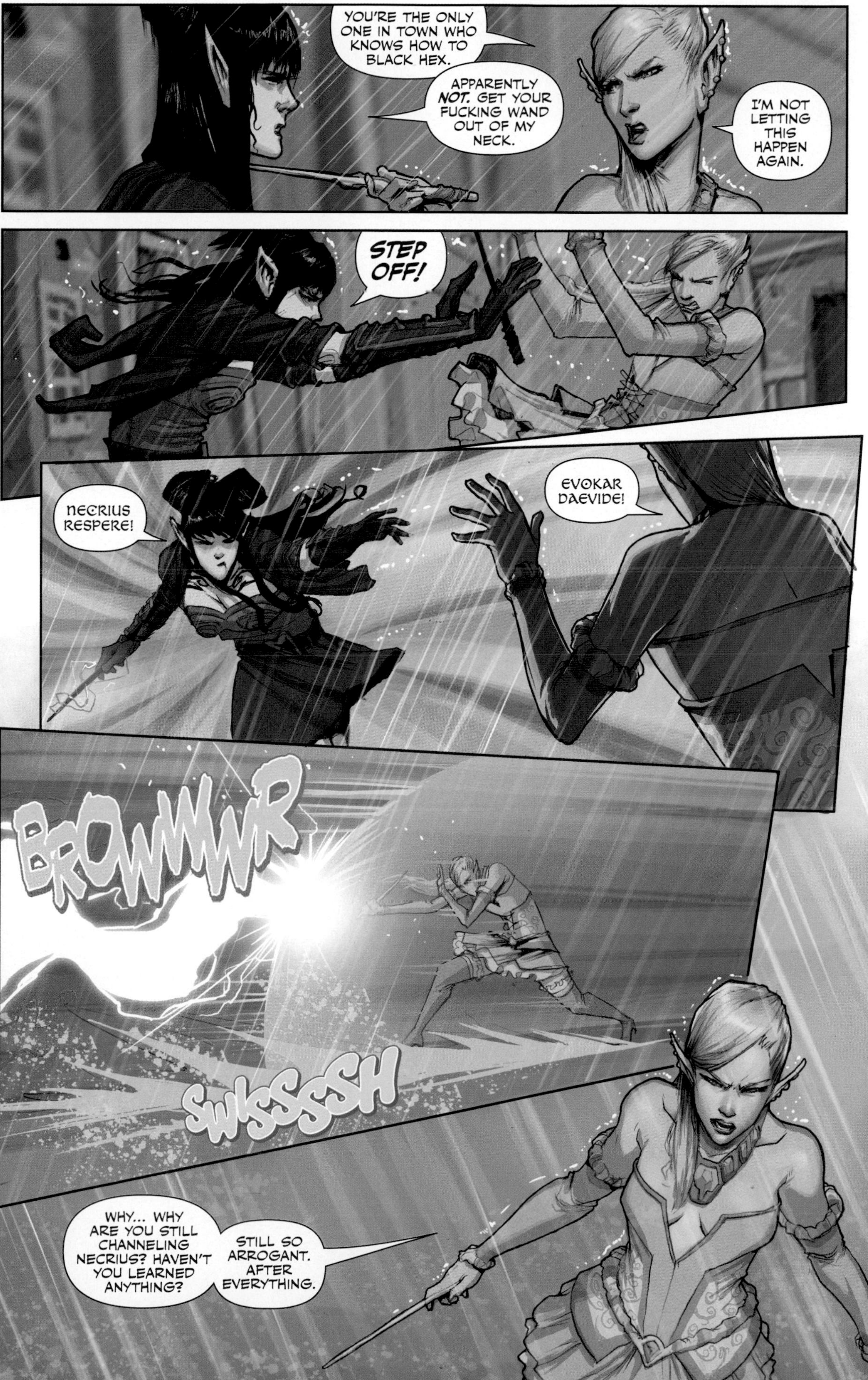
YOU'RE THE ONLY ONE IN TOWN WHO KNOWS HOW TO BLACK HEX.
APPARENTLY *NOT.* GET YOUR FUCKING WAND OUT OF MY NECK.
I'M NOT LETTING THIS HAPPEN AGAIN.
STEP OFF!
NECRIUS RESPERE!
EVOKAR DAEVIDE!
BROWWWR
SWISSSSH
WHY... WHY ARE YOU STILL CHANNELING NECRIUS? HAVEN'T YOU LEARNED ANYTHING?
STILL SO ARROGANT. AFTER EVERYTHING.

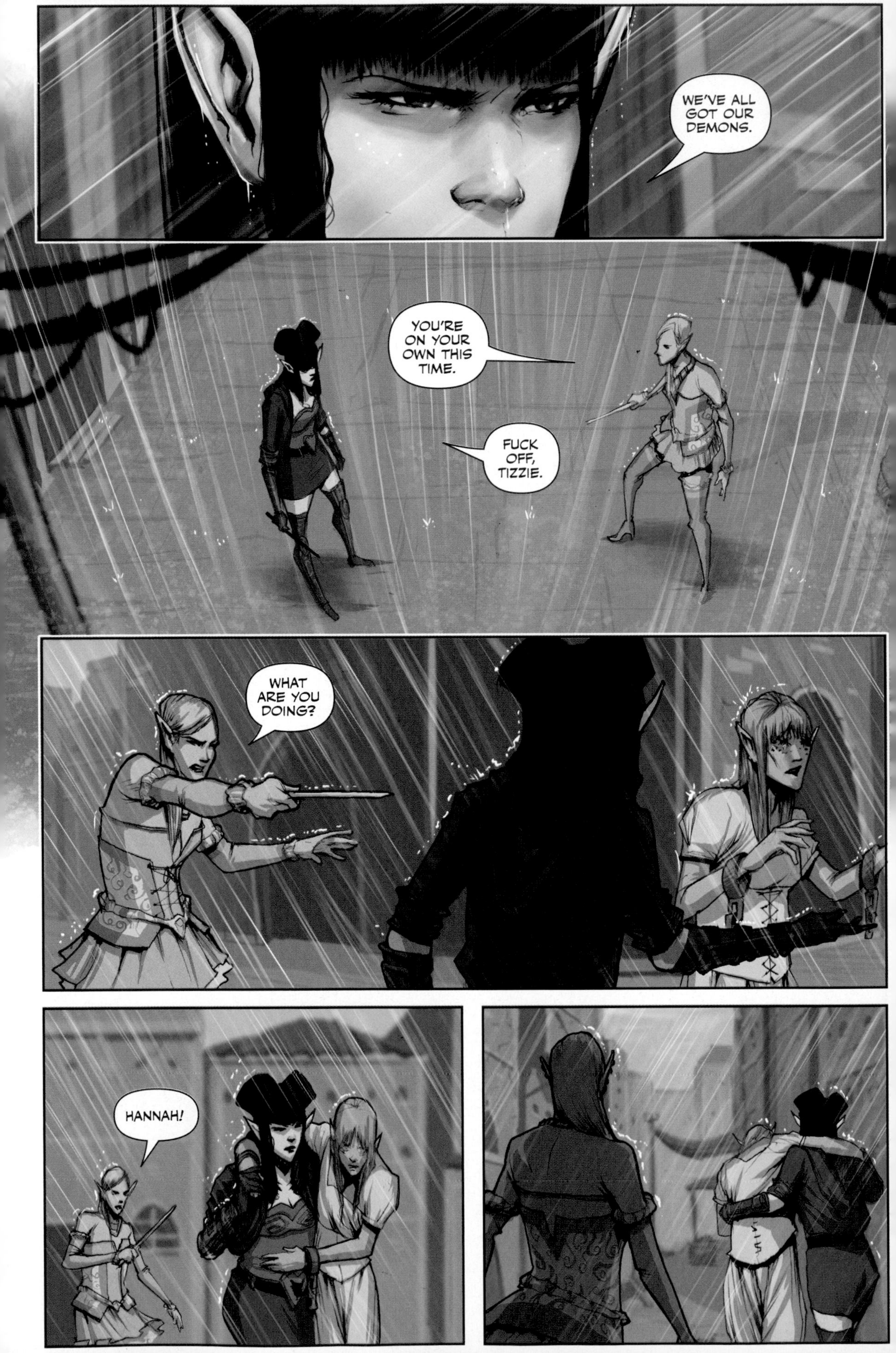
WE'VE ALL GOT OUR DEMONS.
YOU'RE ON YOUR OWN THIS TIME.
FUCK OFF, TIZZIE.
WHAT ARE YOU DOING?
HANNAH!

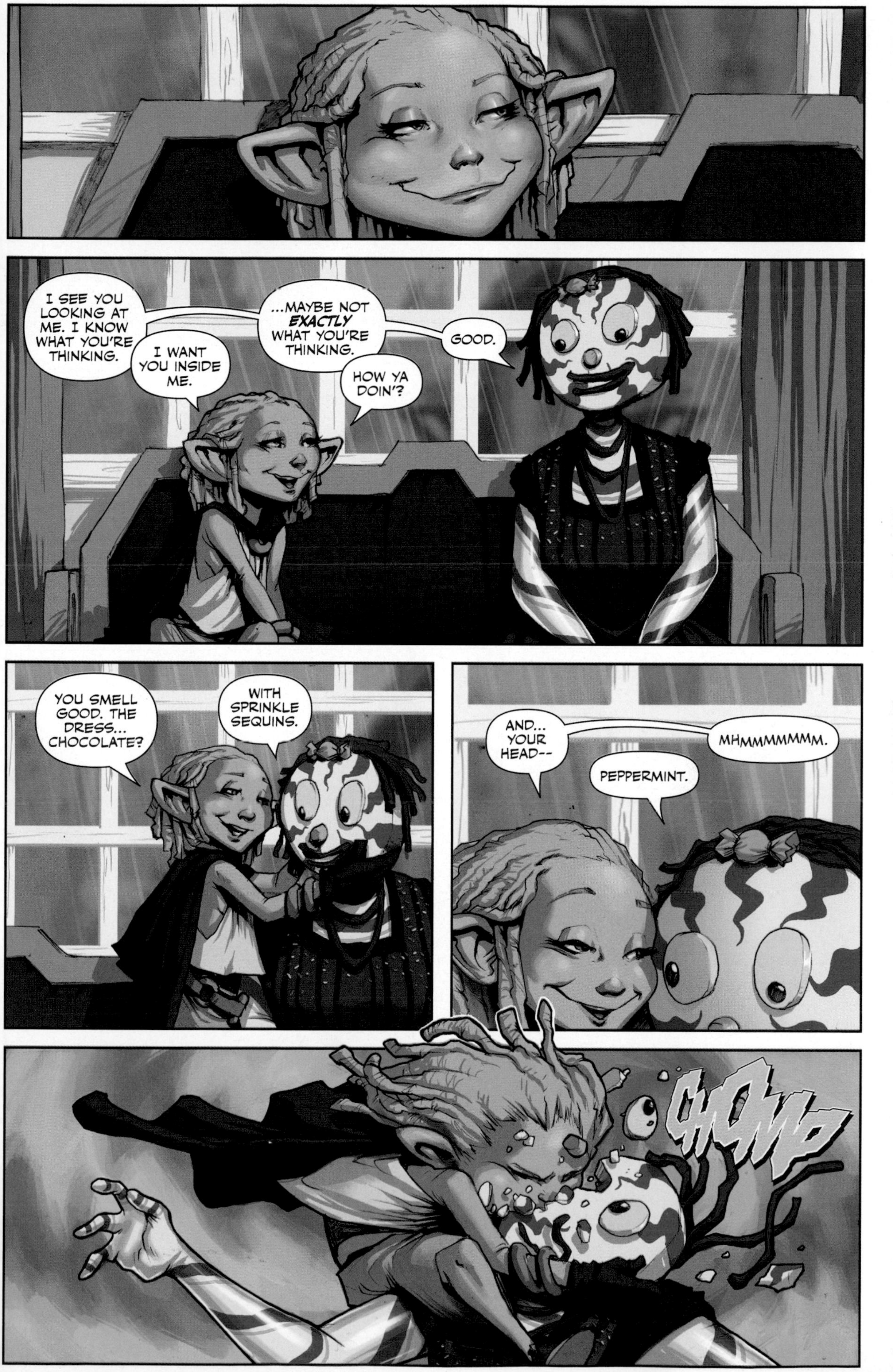
I SEE YOU LOOKING AT ME. I KNOW WHAT YOU'RE THINKING.
I WANT YOU INSIDE ME.
...MAYBE NOT *EXACTLY* WHAT YOU'RE THINKING.
HOW YA DOIN'?
GOOD.
YOU SMELL GOOD. THE DRESS... CHOCOLATE?
WITH SPRINKLE SEQUINS.
AND... YOUR HEAD--
PEPPERMINT.
MHMMMMMMM.
CHOMP

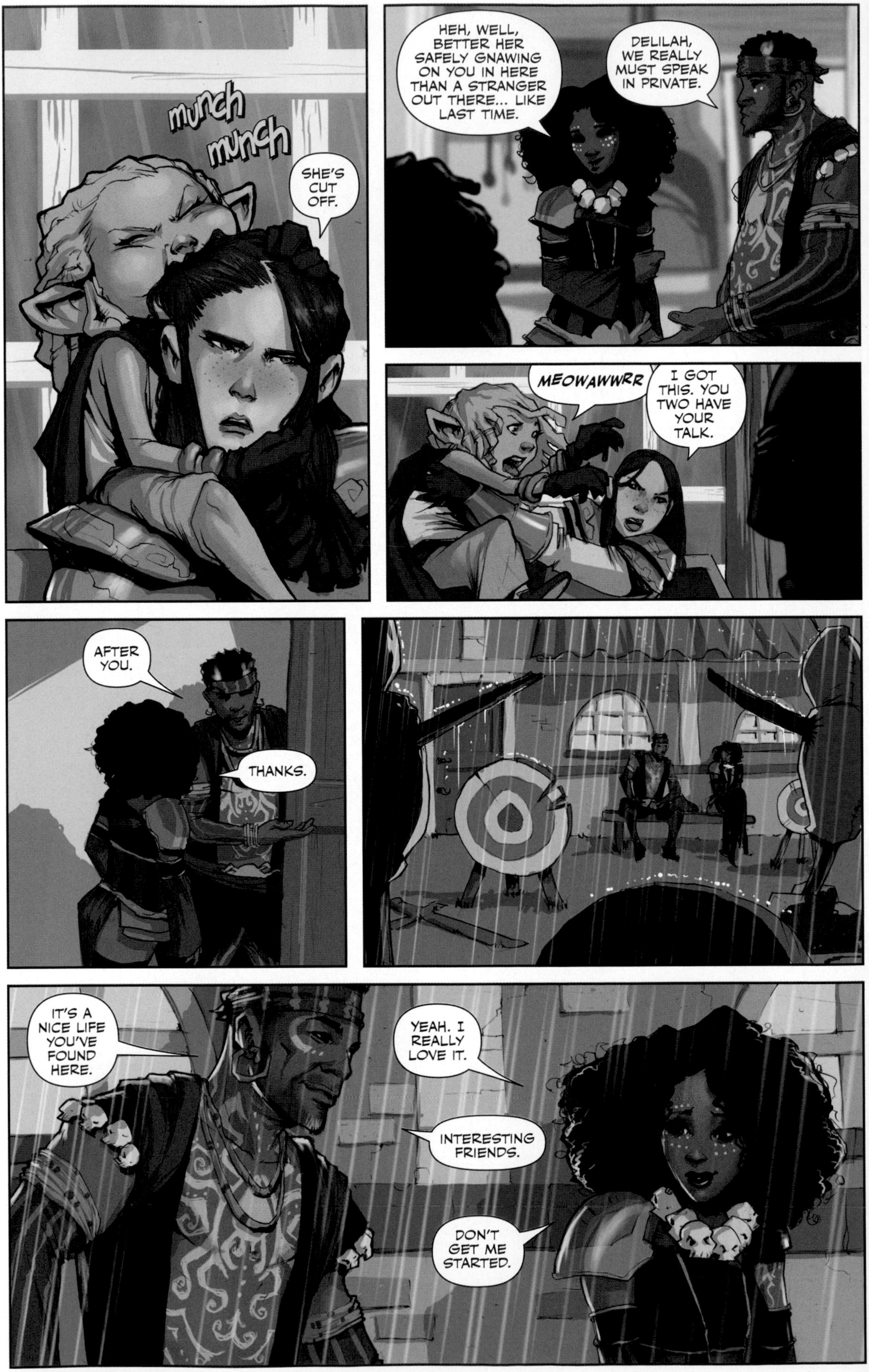
munch munch
SHE'S CUT OFF.
HEH, WELL, BETTER HER SAFELY GNAWING ON YOU IN HERE THAN A STRANGER OUT THERE... LIKE LAST TIME.
DELILAH, WE REALLY MUST SPEAK IN PRIVATE.
MEOWAWWRR
I GOT THIS. YOU TWO HAVE YOUR TALK.
AFTER YOU.
THANKS.
IT'S A NICE LIFE YOU'VE FOUND HERE.
YEAH. I REALLY LOVE IT.
INTERESTING FRIENDS.
DON'T GET ME STARTED.

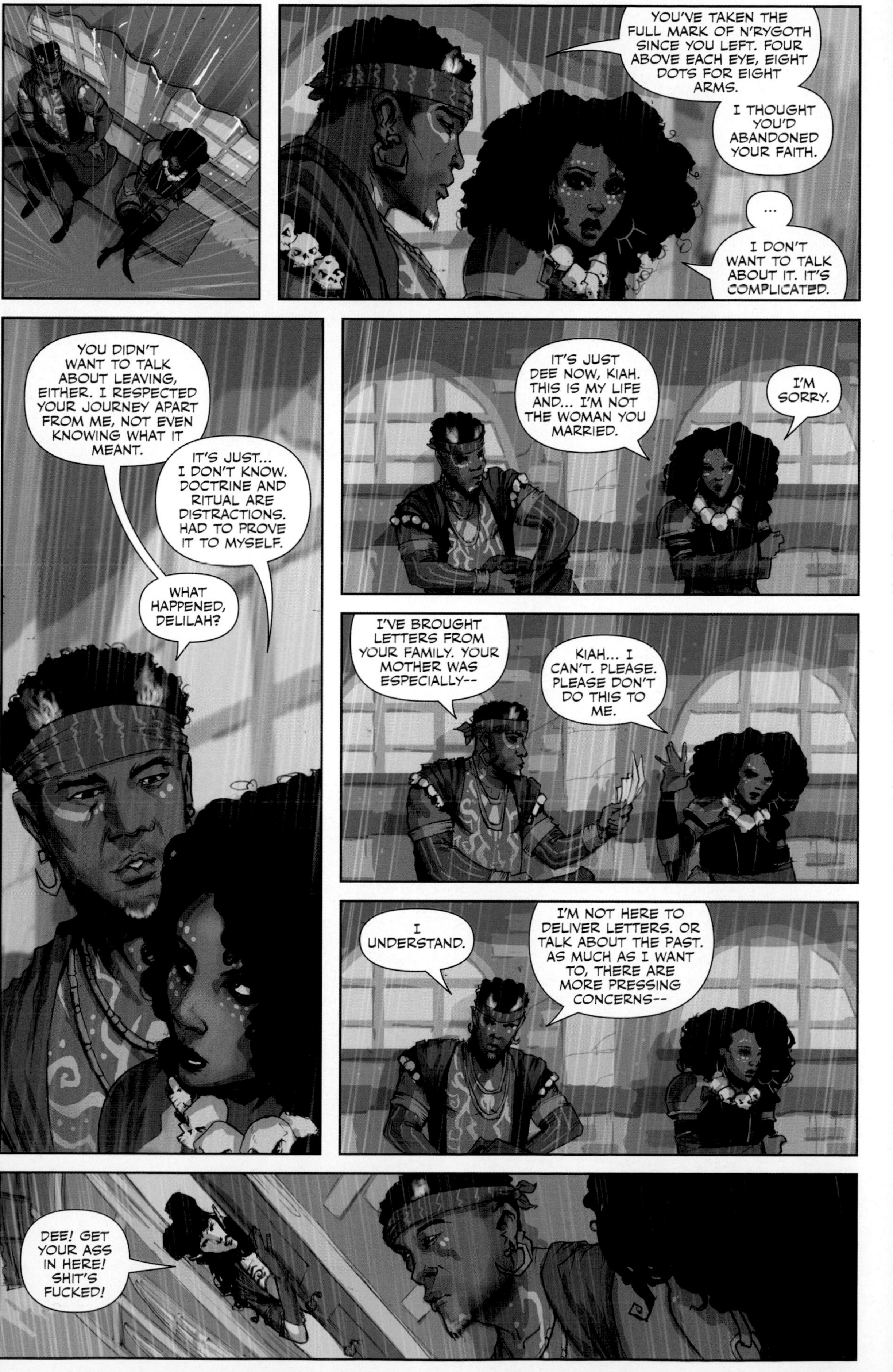
YOU'VE TAKEN THE FULL MARK OF N'RYGOTH SINCE YOU LEFT. FOUR ABOVE EACH EYE, EIGHT DOTS FOR EIGHT ARMS.
I THOUGHT YOU'D ABANDONED YOUR FAITH.
...
I DON'T WANT TO TALK ABOUT IT. IT'S COMPLICATED.
YOU DIDN'T WANT TO TALK ABOUT LEAVING, EITHER. I RESPECTED YOUR JOURNEY APART FROM ME, NOT EVEN KNOWING WHAT IT MEANT.
IT'S JUST... I DON'T KNOW. DOCTRINE AND RITUAL ARE DISTRACTIONS. HAD TO PROVE IT TO MYSELF.
WHAT HAPPENED, DELILAH?
IT'S JUST DEE NOW, KIAH. THIS IS MY LIFE AND... I'M NOT THE WOMAN YOU MARRIED.
I'M SORRY.
I'VE BROUGHT LETTERS FROM YOUR FAMILY. YOUR MOTHER WAS ESPECIALLY--
KIAH... I CAN'T. PLEASE. PLEASE DON'T DO THIS TO ME.
I UNDERSTAND.
I'M NOT HERE TO DELIVER LETTERS. OR TALK ABOUT THE PAST. AS MUCH AS I WANT TO, THERE ARE MORE PRESSING CONCERNS--
DEE! GET YOUR ASS IN HERE! SHIT'S FUCKED!

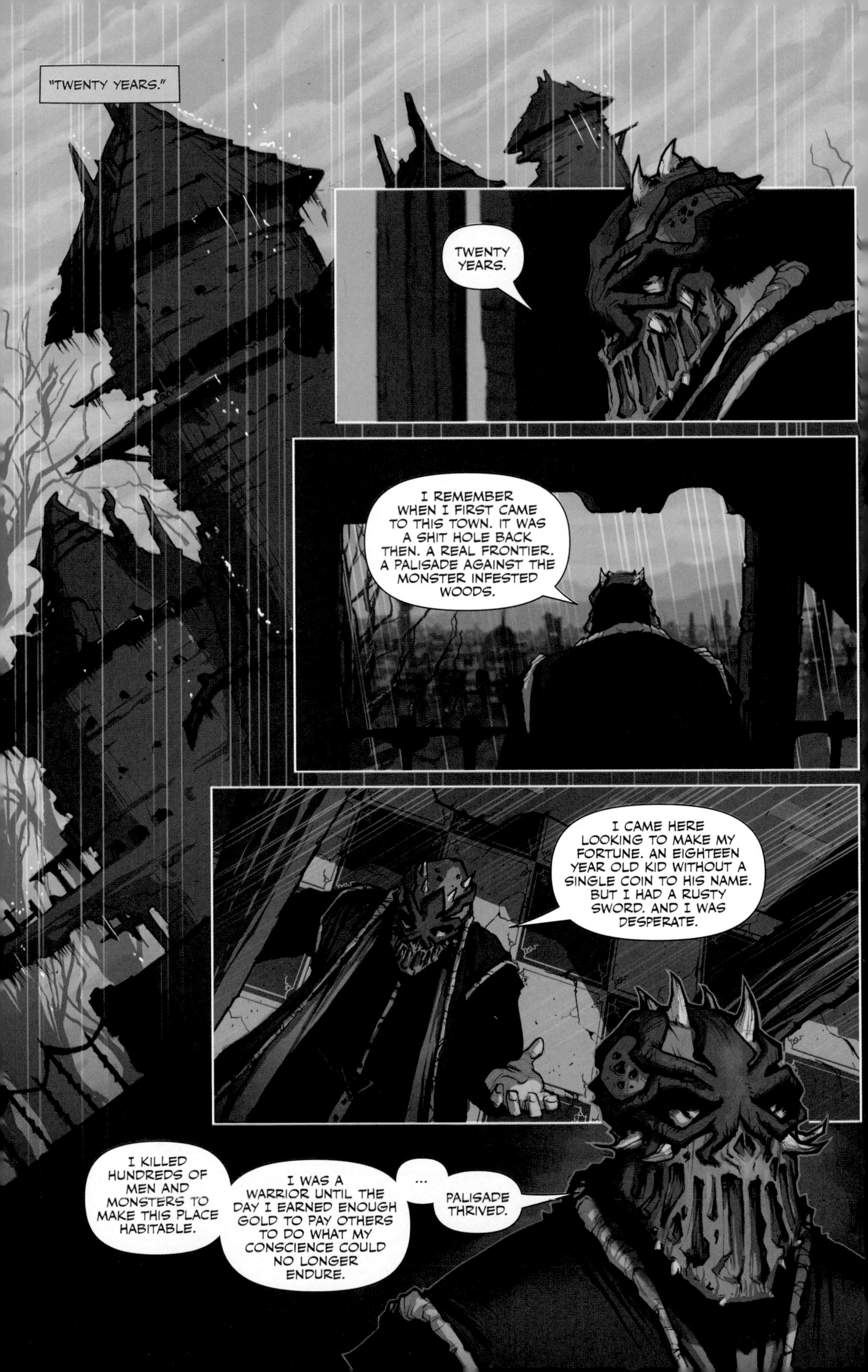
"TWENTY YEARS."
TWENTY YEARS.
I REMEMBER WHEN I FIRST CAME TO THIS TOWN. IT WAS A SHIT HOLE BACK THEN. A REAL FRONTIER. A PALISADE AGAINST THE MONSTER INFESTED WOODS.
I CAME HERE LOOKING TO MAKE MY FORTUNE. AN EIGHTEEN YEAR OLD KID WITHOUT A SINGLE COIN TO HIS NAME. BUT I HAD A RUSTY SWORD. AND I WAS DESPERATE.
I KILLED HUNDREDS OF MEN AND MONSTERS TO MAKE THIS PLACE HABITABLE.
I WAS A WARRIOR UNTIL THE DAY I EARNED ENOUGH GOLD TO PAY OTHERS TO DO WHAT MY CONSCIENCE COULD NO LONGER ENDURE.
...
PALISADE THRIVED.

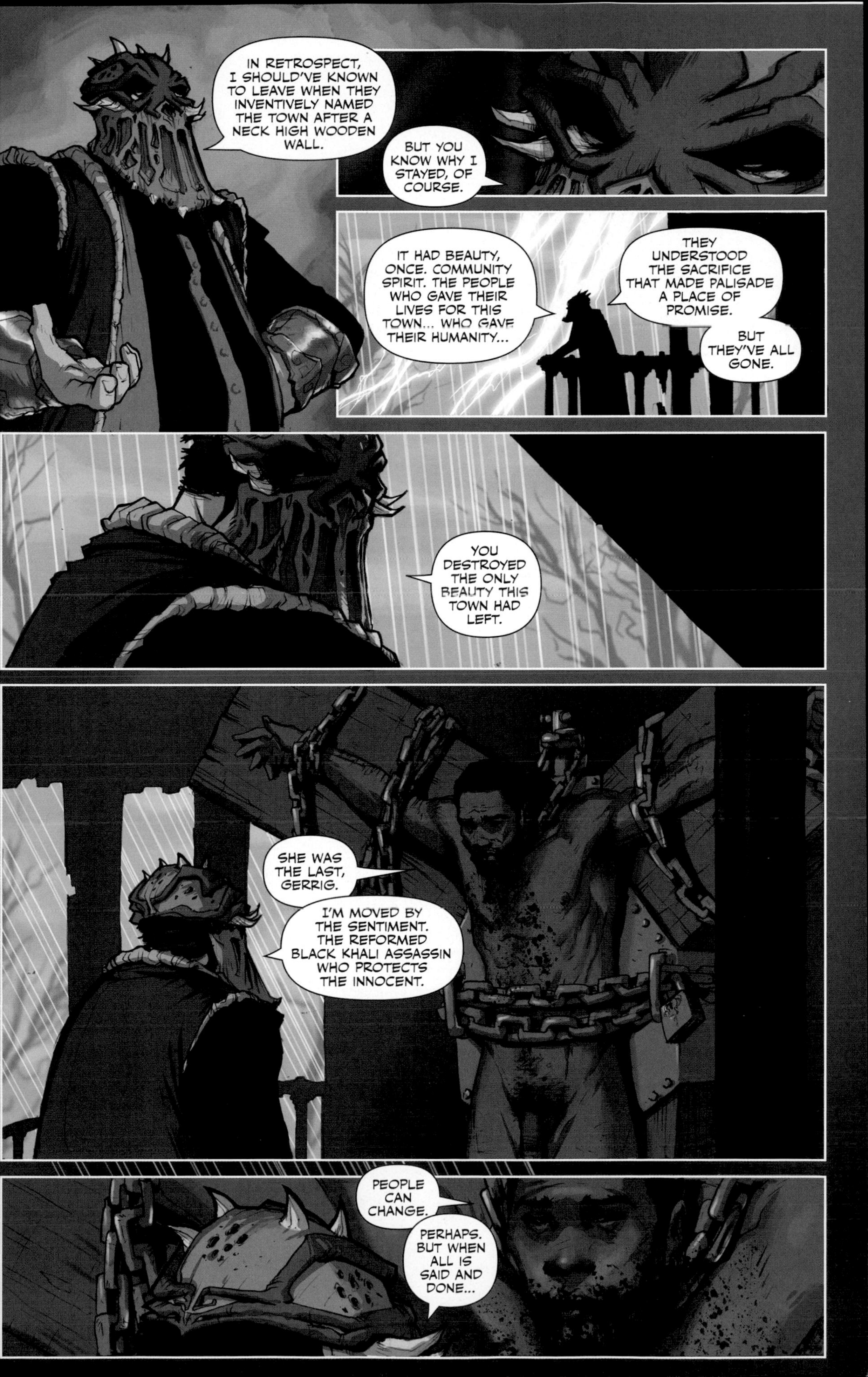
IN RETROSPECT, I SHOULD'VE KNOWN TO LEAVE WHEN THEY INVENTIVELY NAMED THE TOWN AFTER A NECK HIGH WOODEN WALL.
BUT YOU KNOW WHY I STAYED, OF COURSE.
IT HAD BEAUTY, ONCE. COMMUNITY SPIRIT. THE PEOPLE WHO GAVE THEIR LIVES FOR THIS TOWN... WHO GAVE THEIR HUMANITY...
THEY UNDERSTOOD THE SACRIFICE THAT MADE PALISADE A PLACE OF PROMISE.
BUT THEY'VE ALL GONE.
YOU DESTROYED THE ONLY BEAUTY THIS TOWN HAD LEFT.
SHE WAS THE LAST, GERRIG.
I'M MOVED BY THE SENTIMENT. THE REFORMED BLACK KHALI ASSASSIN WHO PROTECTS THE INNOCENT.
PEOPLE CAN CHANGE.
PERHAPS. BUT WHEN ALL IS SAID AND DONE...

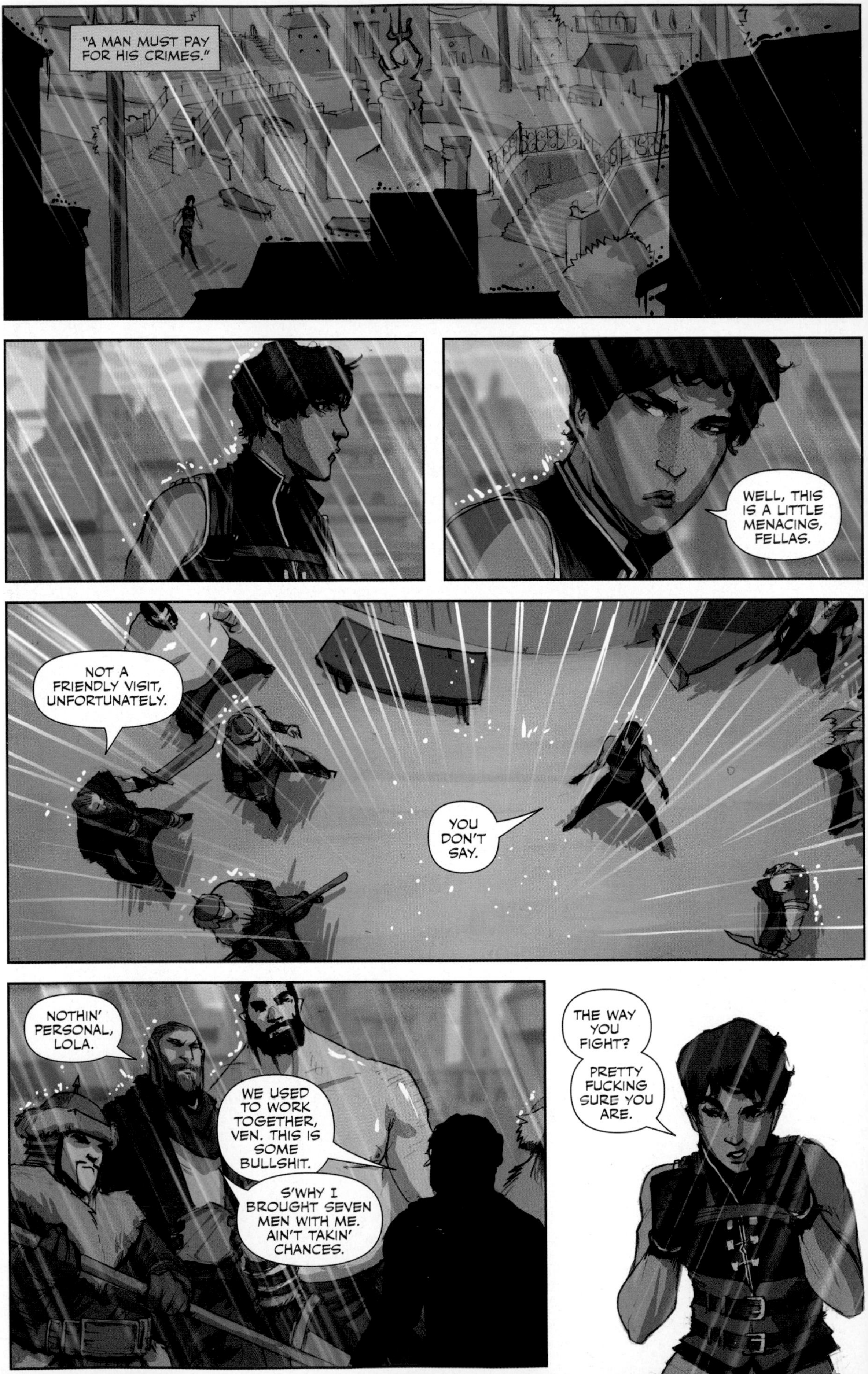
"A MAN MUST PAY FOR HIS CRIMES."
WELL, THIS IS A LITTLE MENACING, FELLAS.
NOT A FRIENDLY VISIT, UNFORTUNATELY.
YOU DON'T SAY.
NOTHIN' PERSONAL, LOLA.
WE USED TO WORK TOGETHER, VEN. THIS IS SOME BULLSHIT.
S'WHY I BROUGHT SEVEN MEN WITH ME. AIN'T TAKIN' CHANCES.
THE WAY YOU FIGHT?
PRETTY FUCKING SURE YOU ARE.

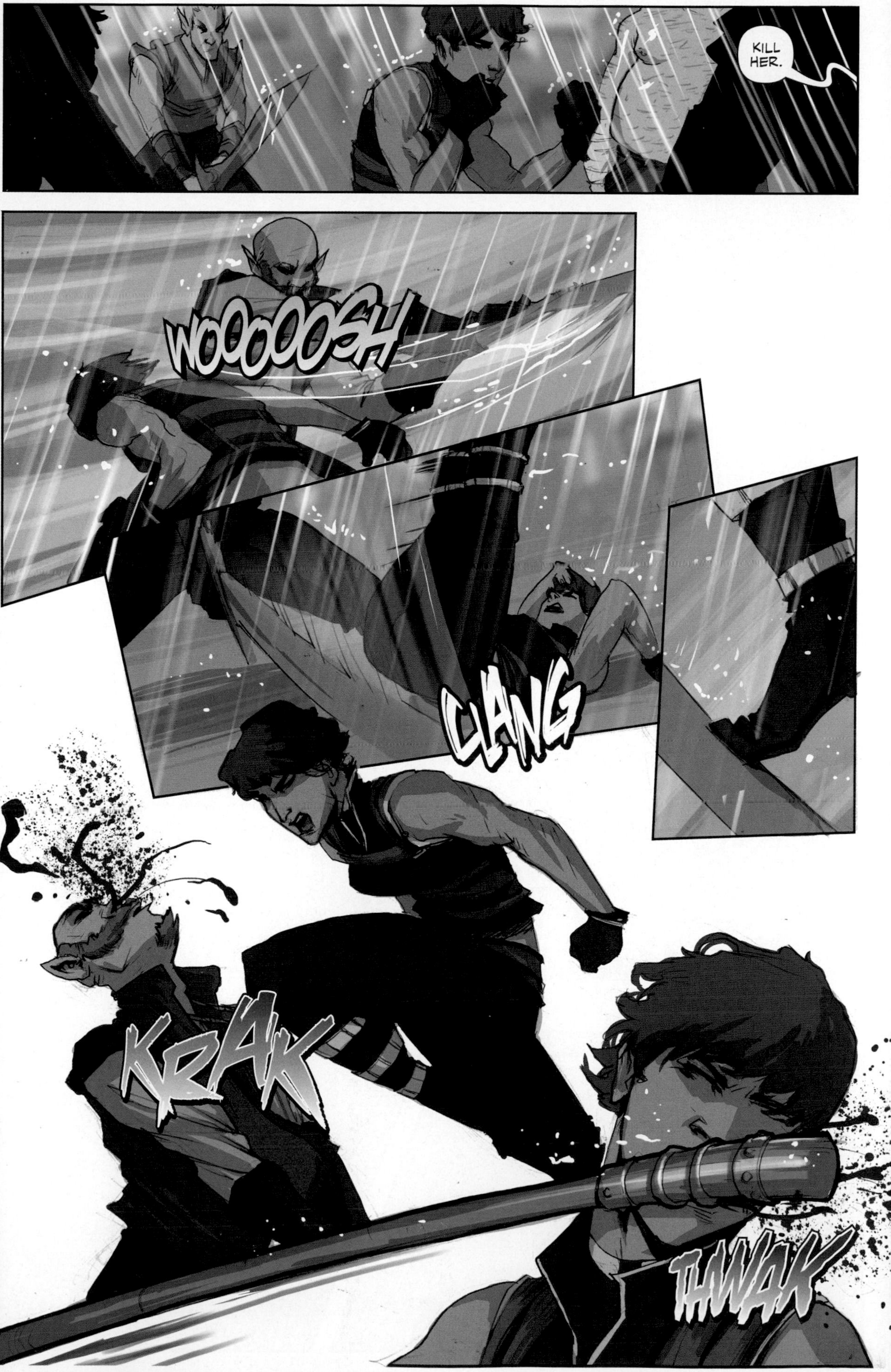

KILL HER.
WOOOOOSH
CLANG
KRAK
THWAK

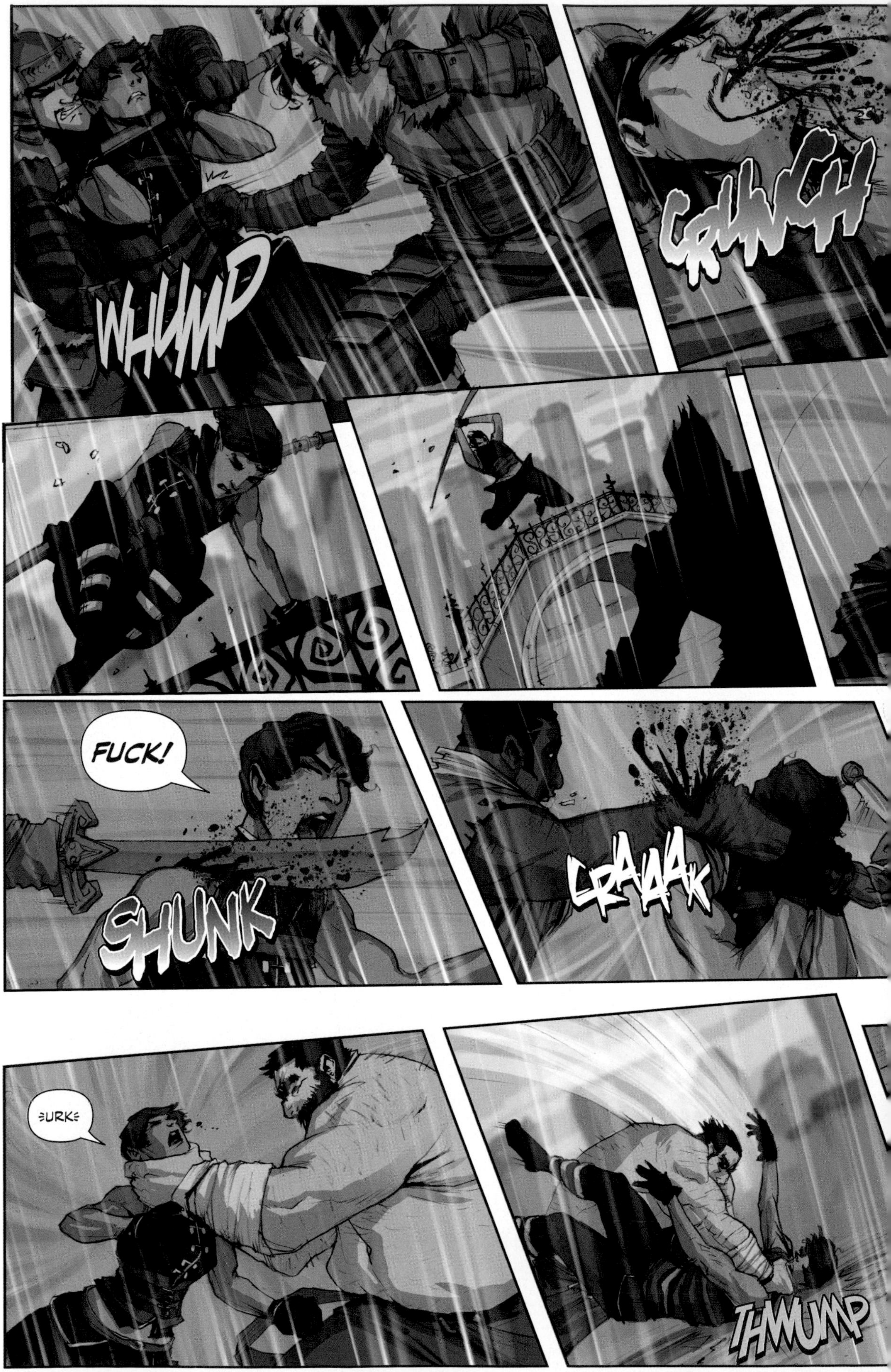
WHUMP
CRUNCH
FUCK!
SHUNK
CRAAAK
URK
THMUMP

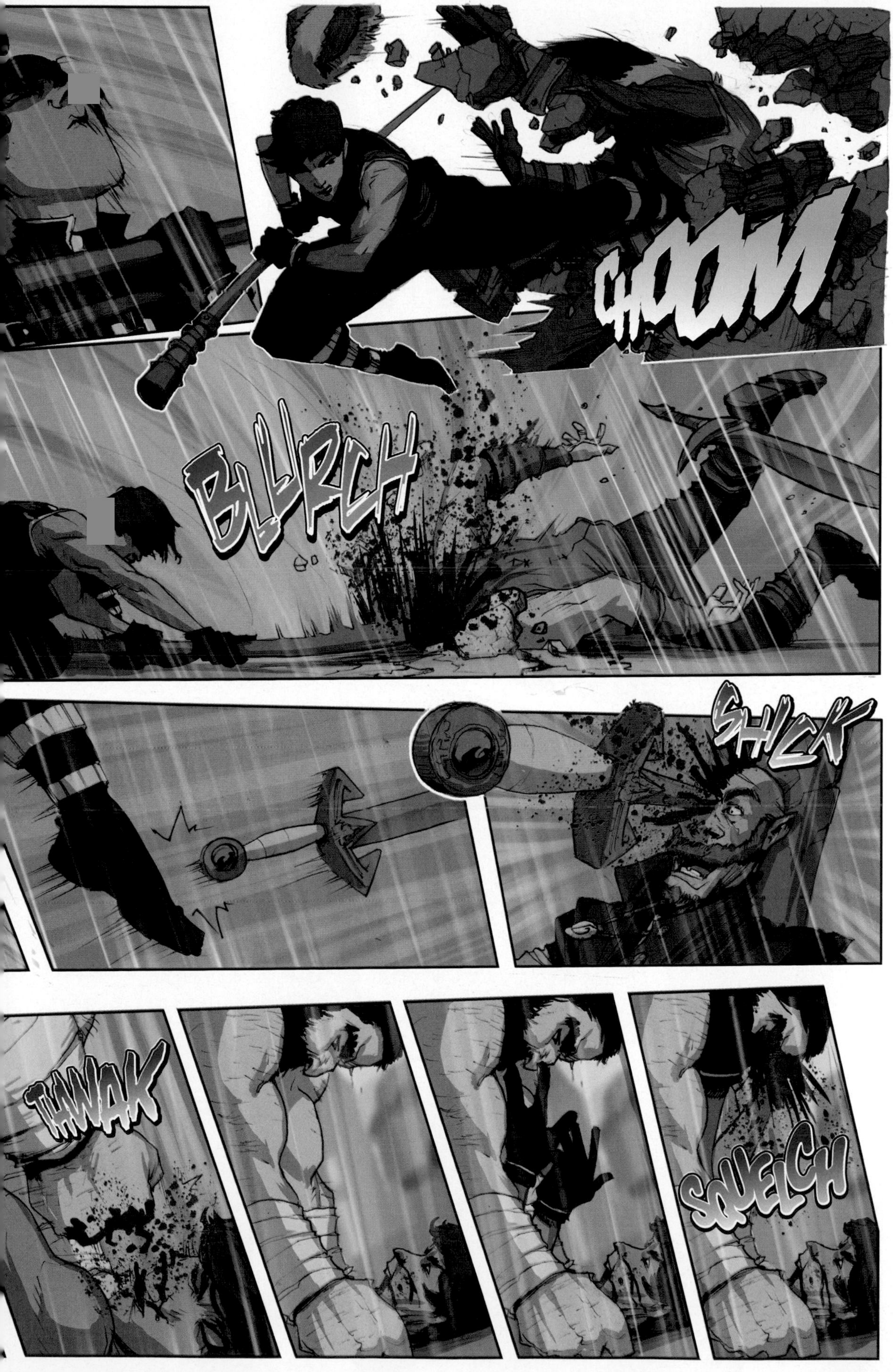
GOOM
BLURCH
SHICK
THWAK
SQUELCH

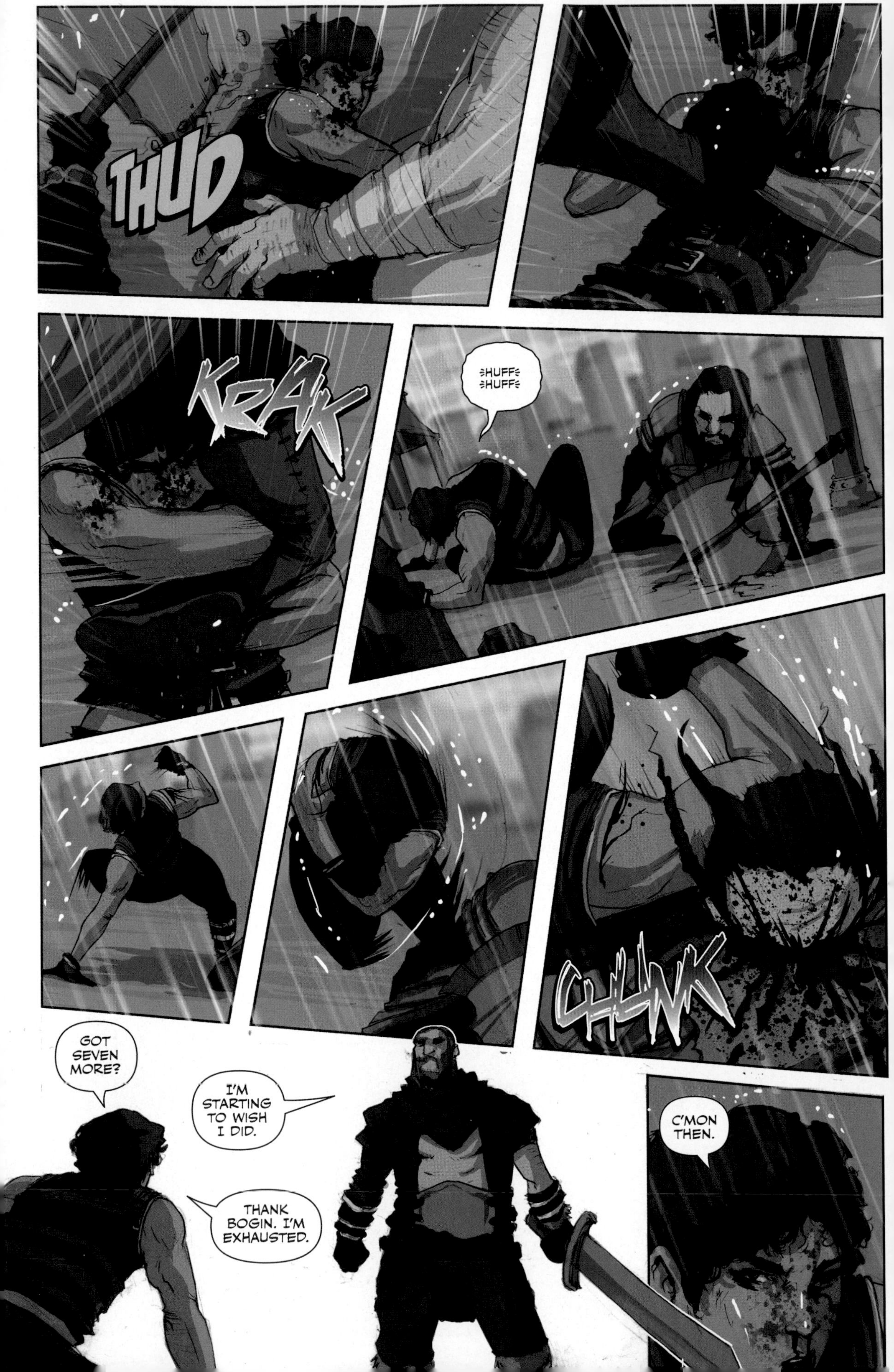
THUD
KRAK
HUFF HUFF
CHUNK
GOT SEVEN MORE?
I'M STARTING TO WISH I DID.
THANK BOGIN. I'M EXHAUSTED.
C'MON THEN.

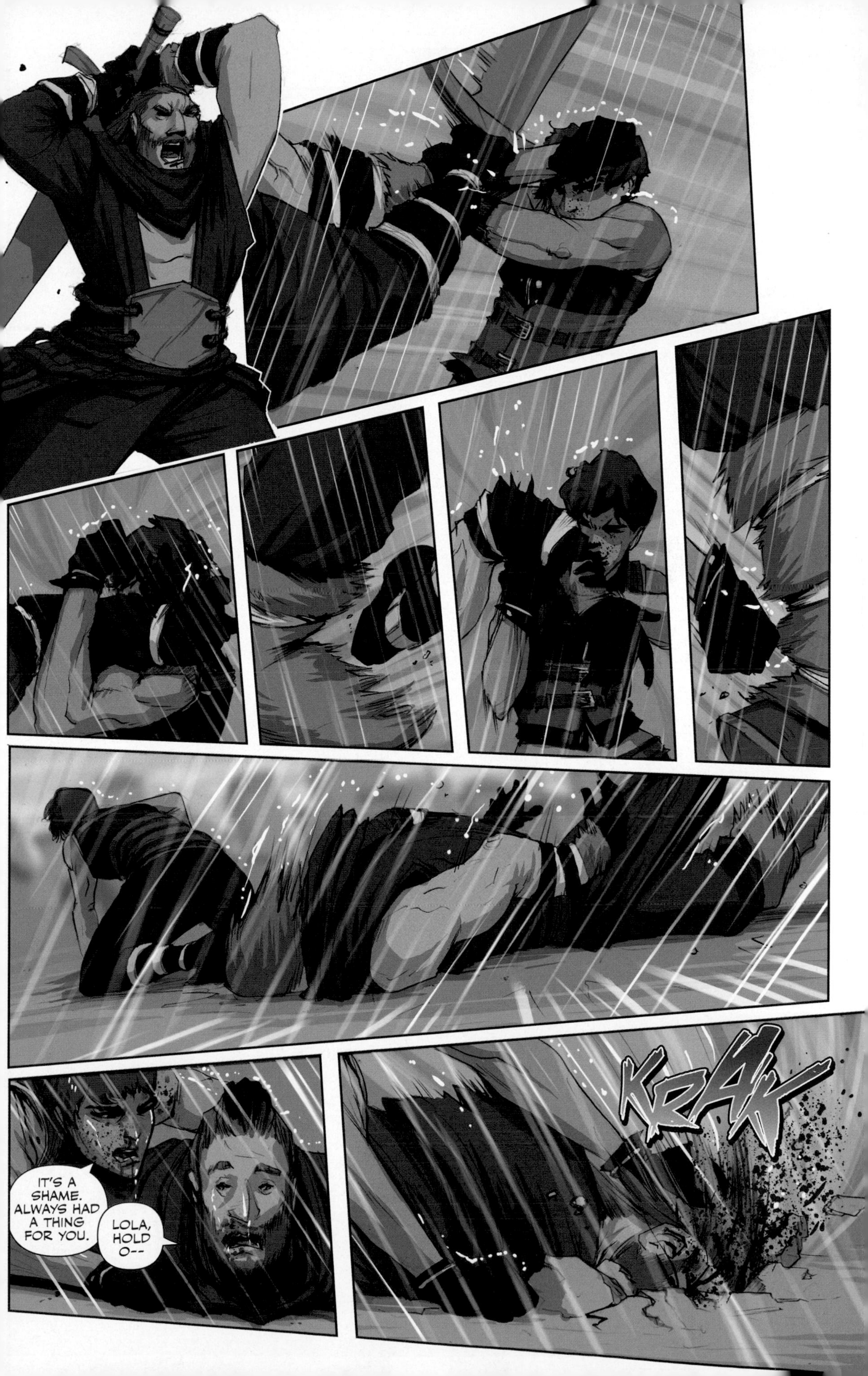
IT'S A SHAME. ALWAYS HAD A THING FOR YOU.
LOLA, HOLD O--
KRAK

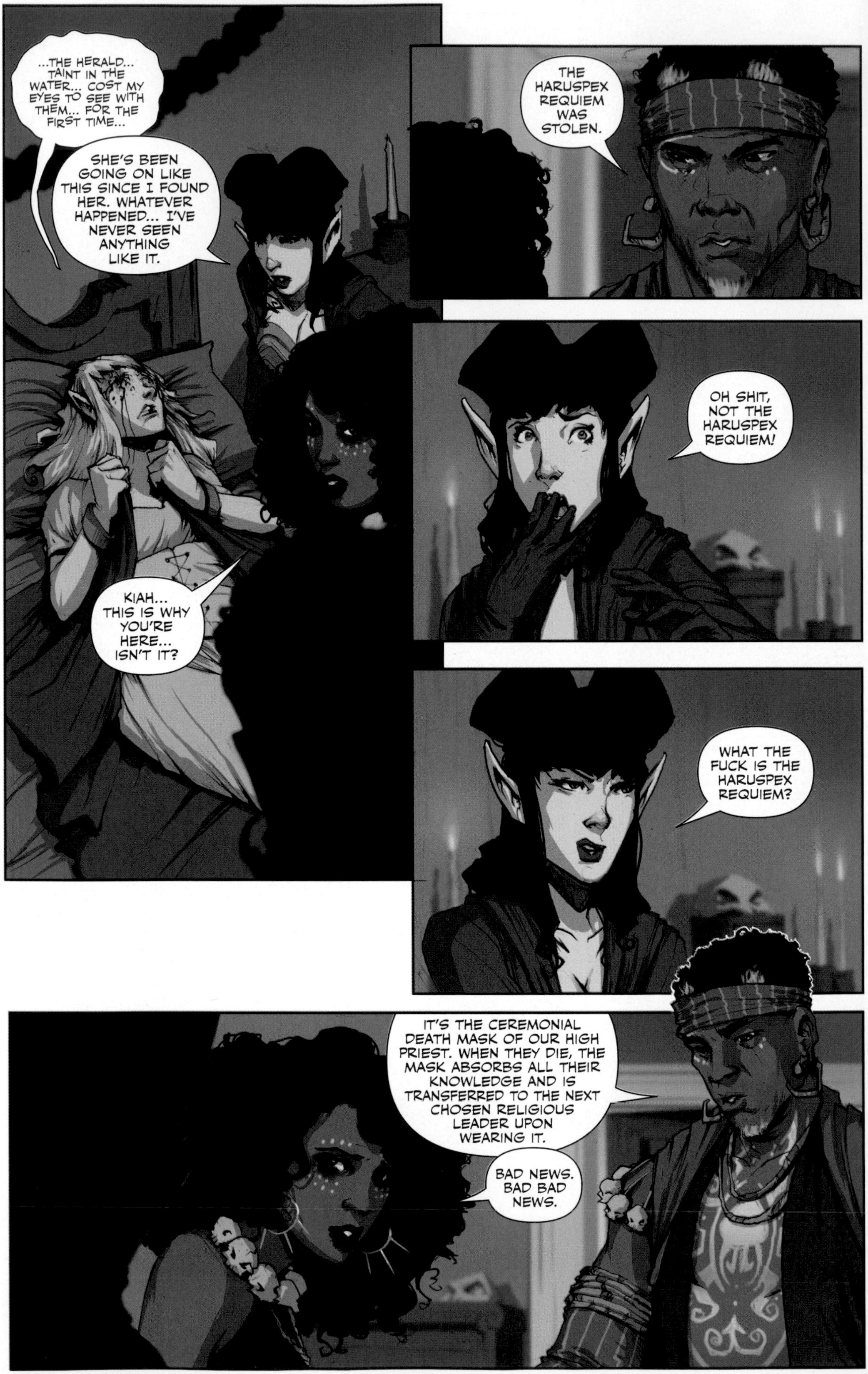
...THE HERALD... TAINT IN THE WATER... COST MY EYES TO SEE WITH THEM... FOR THE FIRST TIME...
SHE'S BEEN GOING ON LIKE THIS SINCE I FOUND HER. WHATEVER HAPPENED... I'VE NEVER SEEN ANYTHING LIKE IT.
KIAH... THIS IS WHY YOU'RE HERE... ISN'T IT?
THE HARUSPEX REQUIEM WAS STOLEN.
OH SHIT, NOT THE HARUSPEX REQUIEM!
WHAT THE FUCK IS THE HARUSPEX REQUIEM?
IT'S THE CEREMONIAL DEATH MASK OF OUR HIGH PRIEST. WHEN THEY DIE, THE MASK ABSORBS ALL THEIR KNOWLEDGE AND IS TRANSFERRED TO THE NEXT CHOSEN RELIGIOUS LEADER UPON WEARING IT.
BAD NEWS. BAD BAD NEWS.

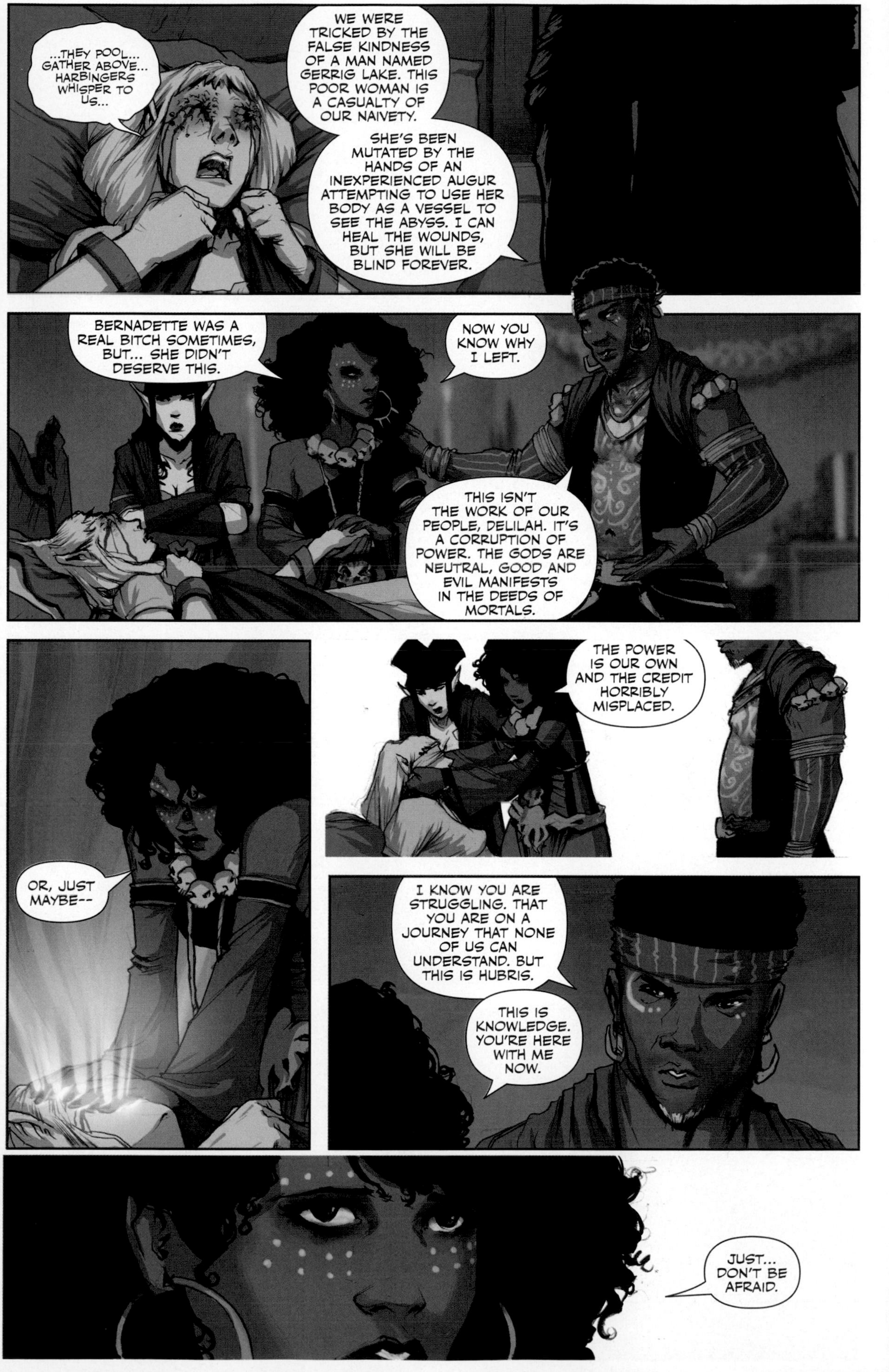
...THEY POOL... GATHER ABOVE... HARBINGERS WHISPER TO US...
WE WERE TRICKED BY THE FALSE KINDNESS OF A MAN NAMED GERRIG LAKE. THIS POOR WOMAN IS A CASUALTY OF OUR NAIVETY.
SHE'S BEEN MUTATED BY THE HANDS OF AN INEXPERIENCED AUGUR ATTEMPTING TO USE HER BODY AS A VESSEL TO SEE THE ABYSS. I CAN HEAL THE WOUNDS, BUT SHE WILL BE BLIND FOREVER.
BERNADETTE WAS A REAL BITCH SOMETIMES, BUT... SHE DIDN'T DESERVE THIS.
NOW YOU KNOW WHY I LEFT.
THIS ISN'T THE WORK OF OUR PEOPLE, DELILAH. IT'S A CORRUPTION OF POWER. THE GODS ARE NEUTRAL, GOOD AND EVIL MANIFESTS IN THE DEEDS OF MORTALS.
THE POWER IS OUR OWN AND THE CREDIT HORRIBLY MISPLACED.
OR, JUST MAYBE--
I KNOW YOU ARE STRUGGLING. THAT YOU ARE ON A JOURNEY THAT NONE OF US CAN UNDERSTAND. BUT THIS IS HUBRIS.
THIS IS KNOWLEDGE. YOU'RE HERE WITH ME NOW.
JUST... DON'T BE AFRAID.

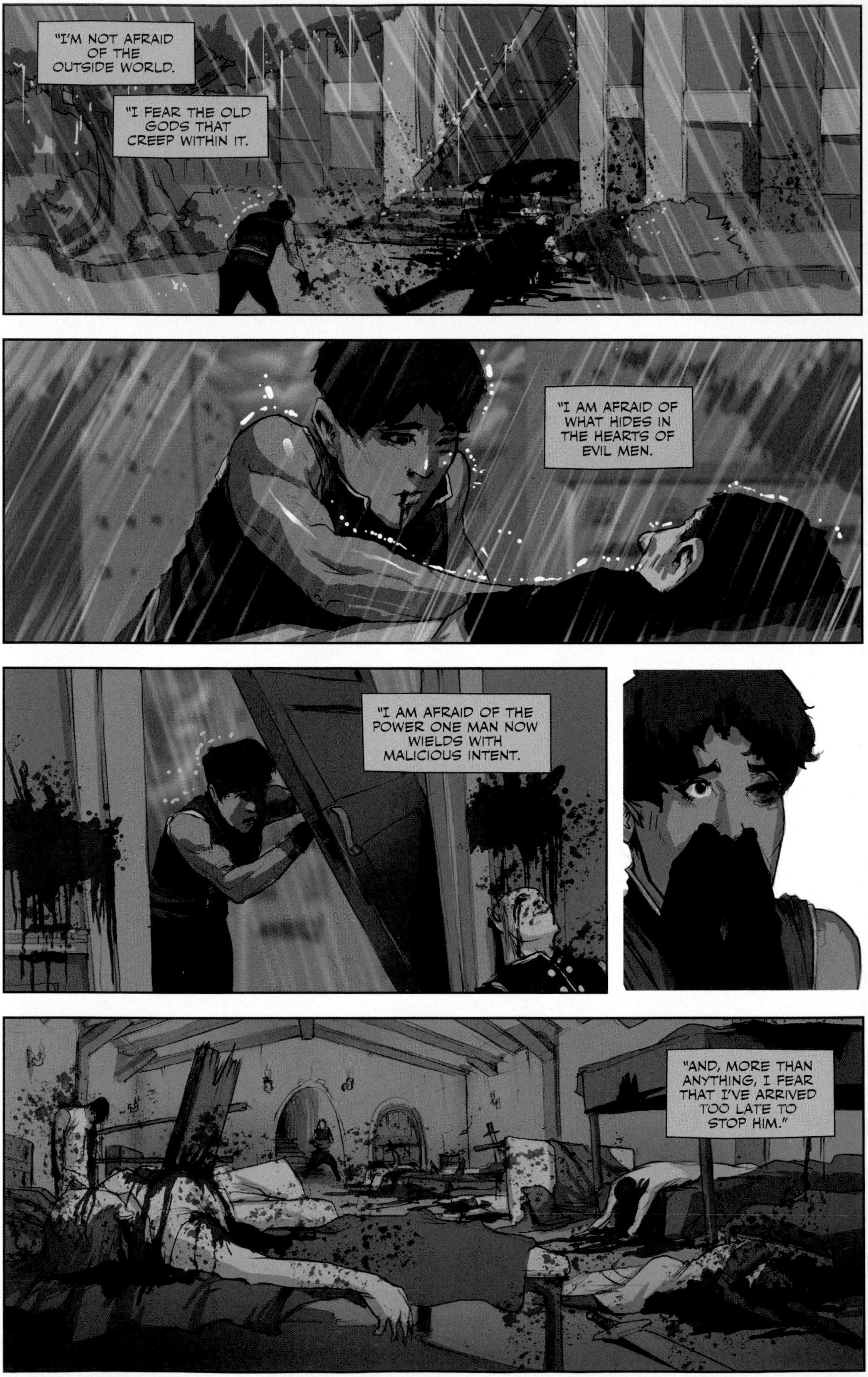
"I'M NOT AFRAID OF THE OUTSIDE WORLD.
"I FEAR THE OLD GODS THAT CREEP WITHIN IT.
"I AM AFRAID OF WHAT HIDES IN THE HEARTS OF EVIL MEN.
"I AM AFRAID OF THE POWER ONE MAN NOW WIELDS WITH MALICIOUS INTENT.
"AND, MORE THAN ANYTHING, I FEAR THAT I'VE ARRIVED TOO LATE TO STOP HIM."

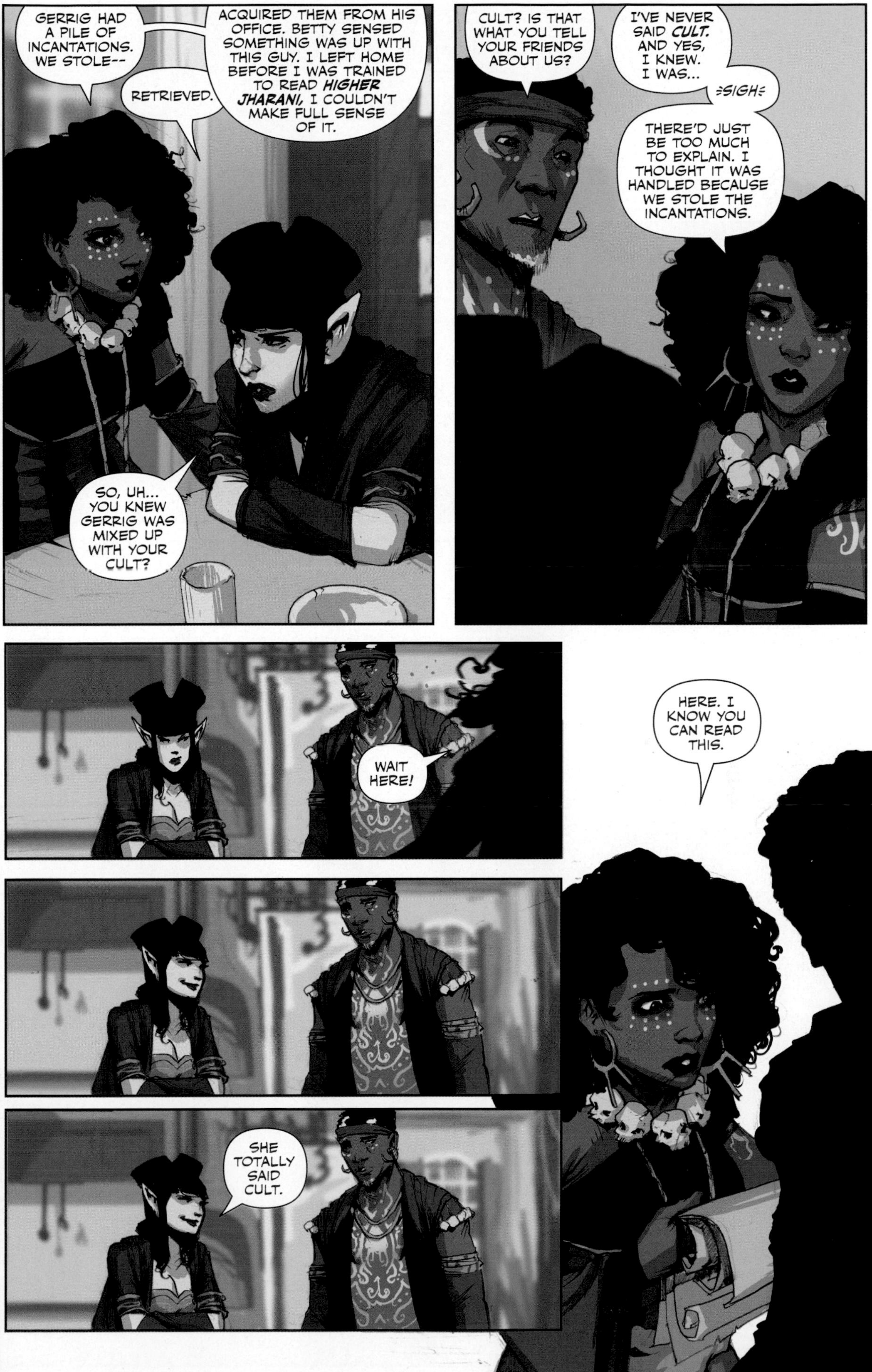
GERRIG HAD A PILE OF INCANTATIONS. WE STOLE--
RETRIEVED.
ACQUIRED THEM FROM HIS OFFICE. BETTY SENSED SOMETHING WAS UP WITH THIS GUY. I LEFT HOME BEFORE I WAS TRAINED TO READ HIGHER JHARANI, I COULDN'T MAKE FULL SENSE OF IT.
SO, UH... YOU KNEW GERRIG WAS MIXED UP WITH YOUR CULT?
CULT? IS THAT WHAT YOU TELL YOUR FRIENDS ABOUT US?
I'VE NEVER SAID CULT. AND YES, I KNEW. I WAS...
SIGH
THERE'D JUST BE TOO MUCH TO EXPLAIN. I THOUGHT IT WAS HANDLED BECAUSE WE STOLE THE INCANTATIONS.
WAIT HERE!
SHE TOTALLY SAID CULT.
HERE. I KNOW YOU CAN READ THIS.

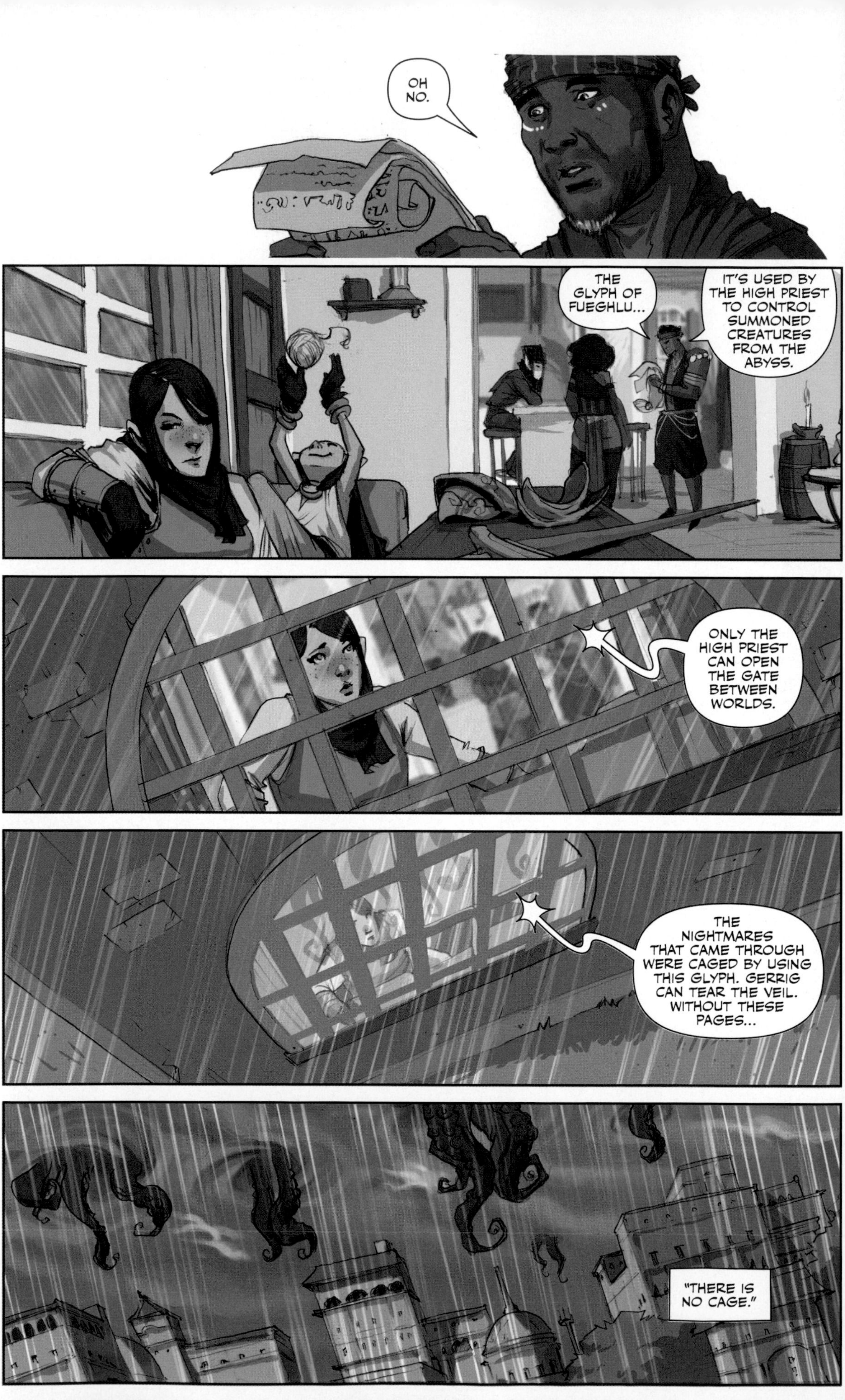
OH NO.
THE GLYPH OF FUEGHLU...
IT'S USED BY THE HIGH PRIEST TO CONTROL SUMMONED CREATURES FROM THE ABYSS.
ONLY THE HIGH PRIEST CAN OPEN THE GATE BETWEEN WORLDS.
THE NIGHTMARES THAT CAME THROUGH WERE CAGED BY USING THIS GLYPH. GERRIG CAN TEAR THE VEIL. WITHOUT THESE PAGES...
"THERE IS NO CAGE."

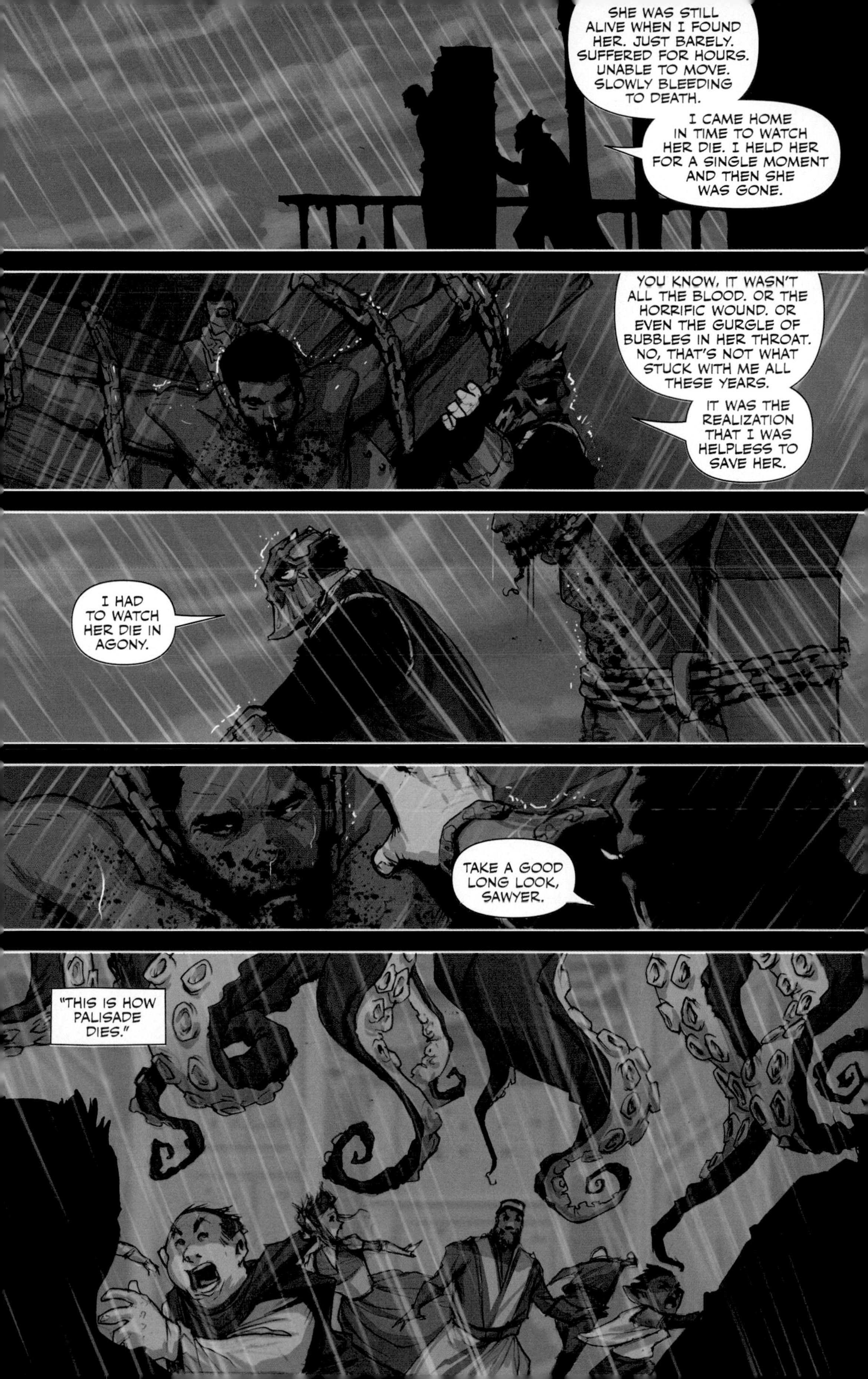
SHE WAS STILL ALIVE WHEN I FOUND HER. JUST BARELY. SUFFERED FOR HOURS. UNABLE TO MOVE. SLOWLY BLEEDING TO DEATH.
I CAME HOME IN TIME TO WATCH HER DIE. I HELD HER FOR A SINGLE MOMENT AND THEN SHE WAS GONE.
YOU KNOW, IT WASN'T ALL THE BLOOD. OR THE HORRIFIC WOUND. OR EVEN THE GURGLE OF BUBBLES IN HER THROAT. NO, THAT'S NOT WHAT STUCK WITH ME ALL THESE YEARS.
IT WAS THE REALIZATION THAT I WAS HELPLESS TO SAVE HER.
I HAD TO WATCH HER DIE IN AGONY.
TAKE A GOOD LONG LOOK, SAWYER.
"THIS IS HOW PALISADE DIES."

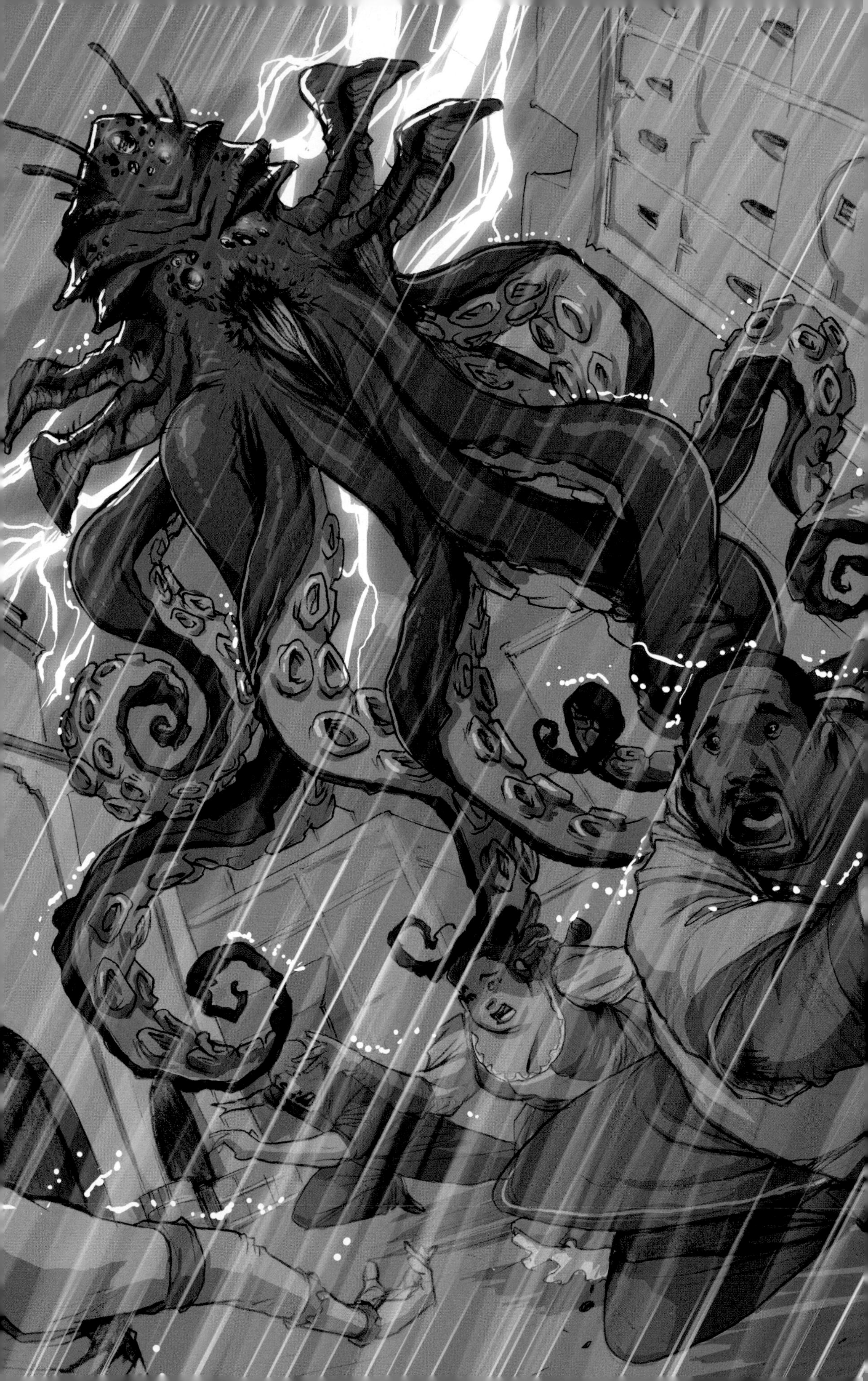

CHAPTER EIGHT

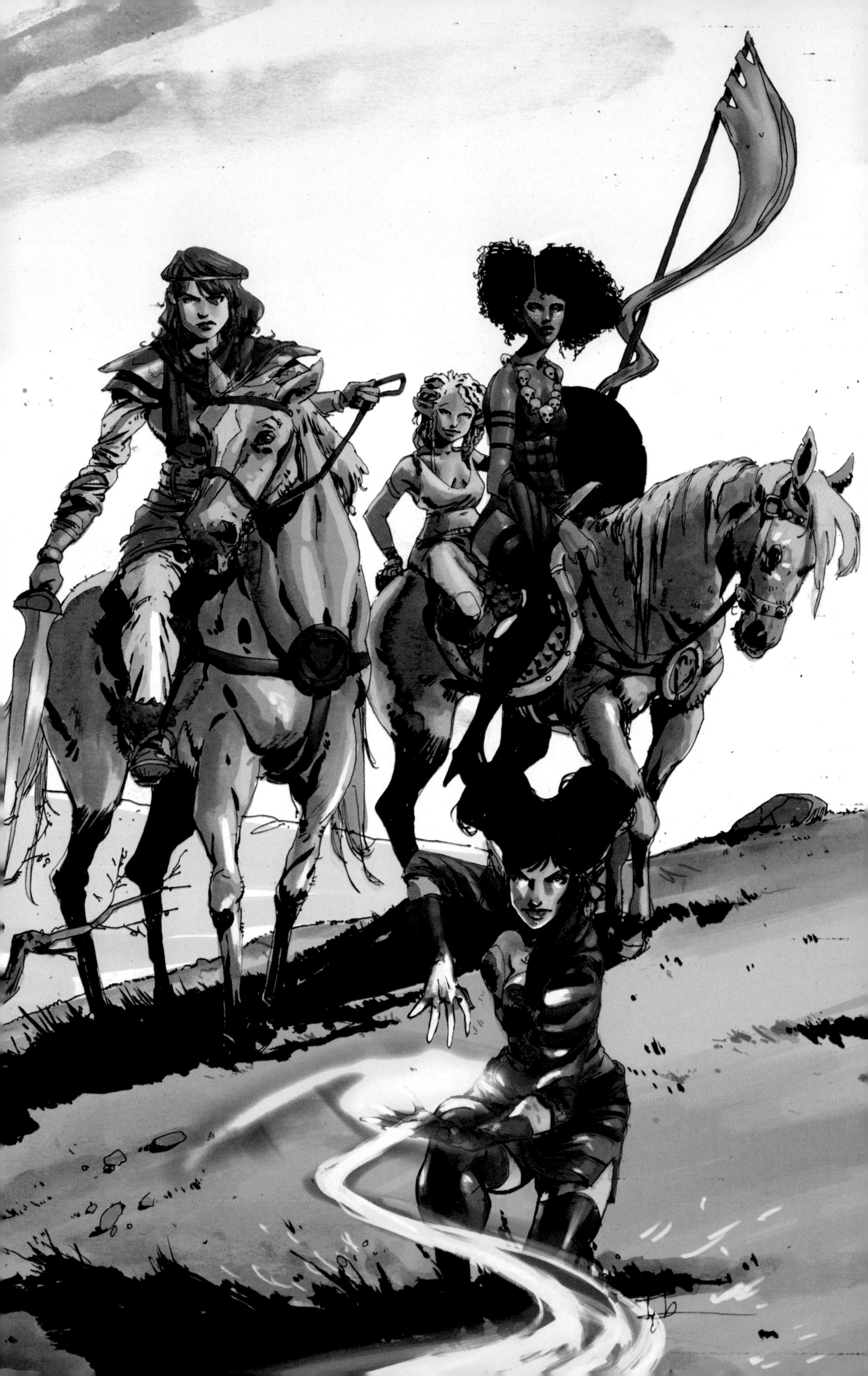

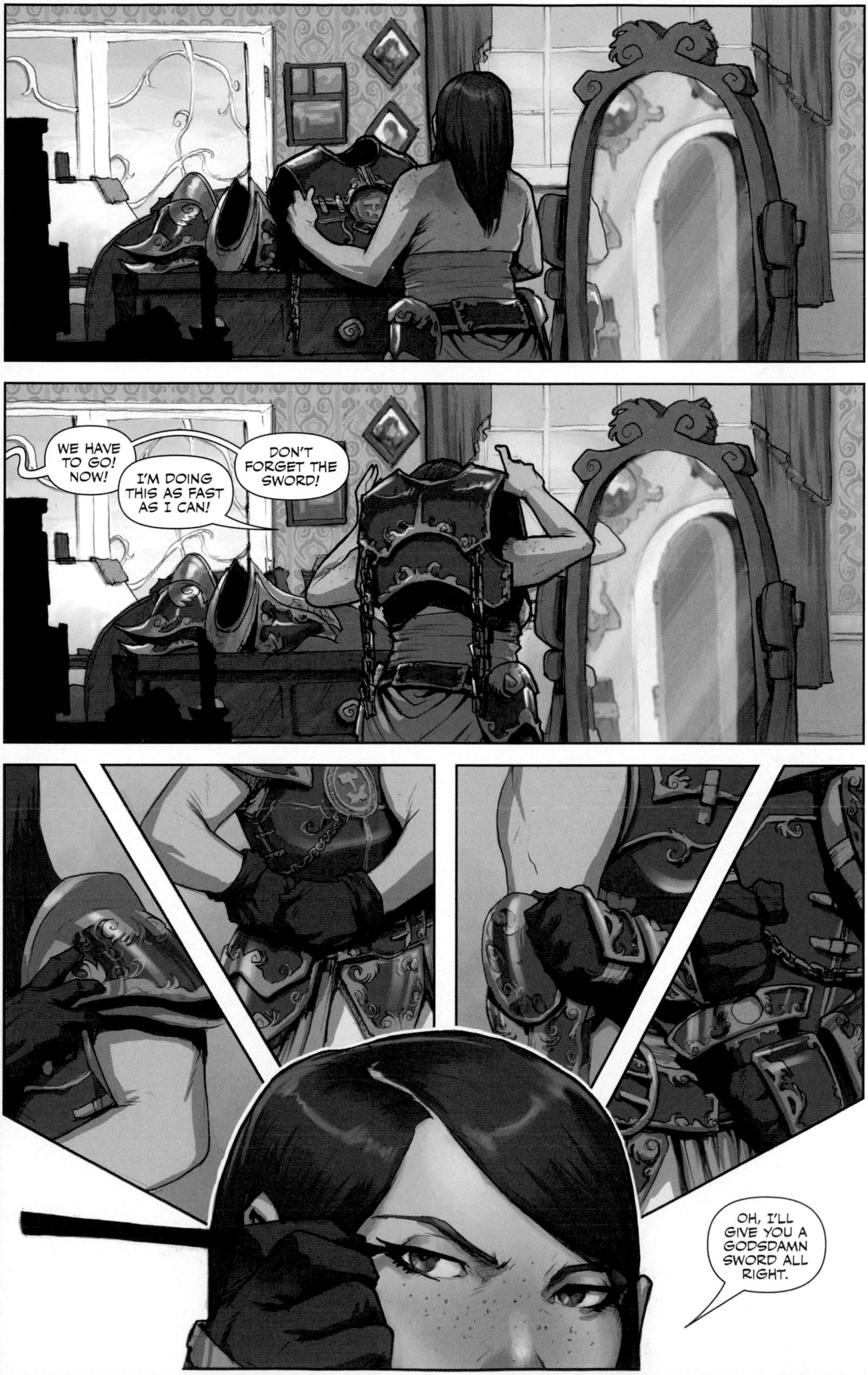
WE HAVE TO GO! NOW!
I'M DOING THIS AS FAST AS I CAN!
DON'T FORGET THE SWORD!
OH, I'LL GIVE YOU A GODSDAMN SWORD ALL RIGHT.

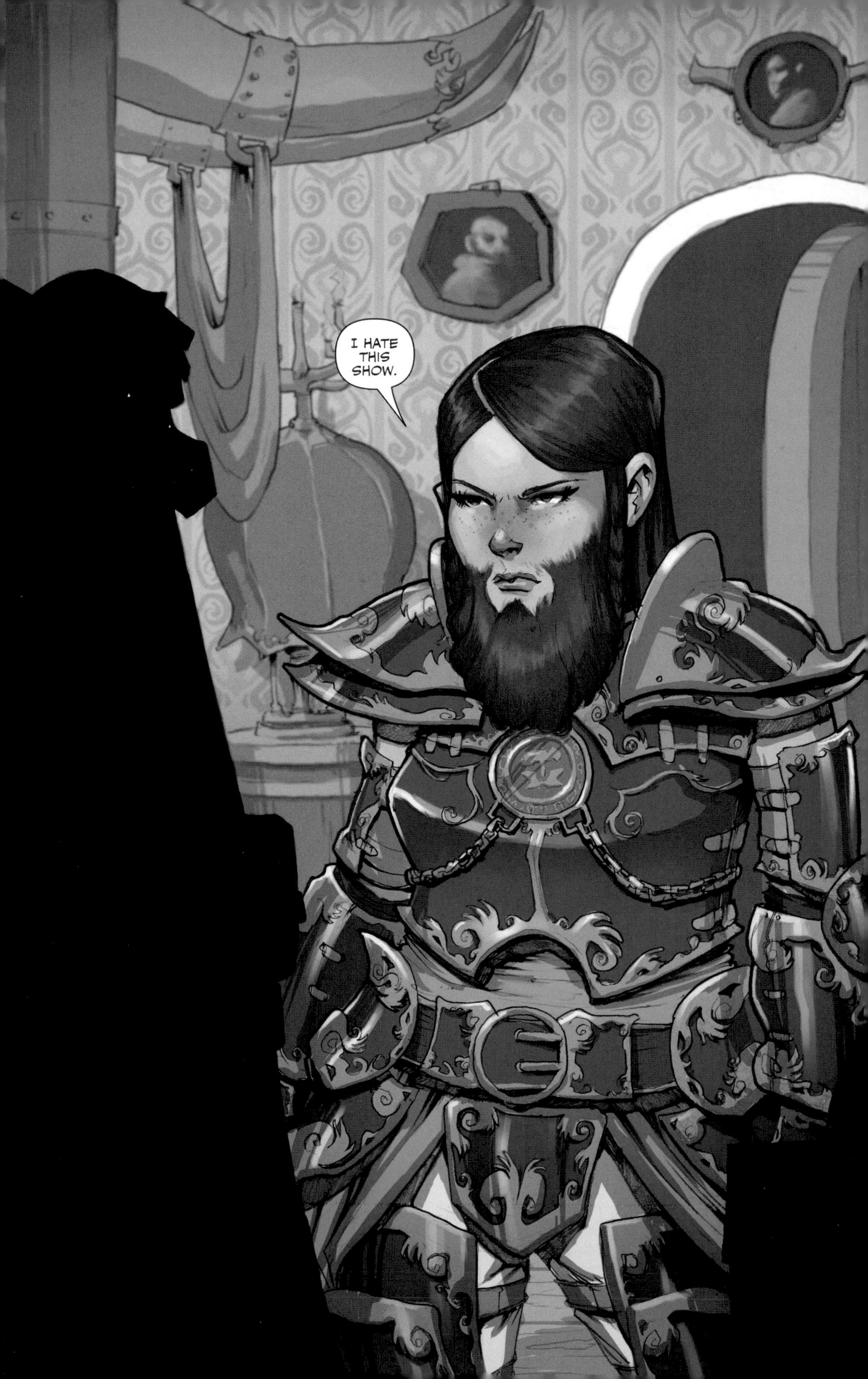
I HATE THIS SHOW.

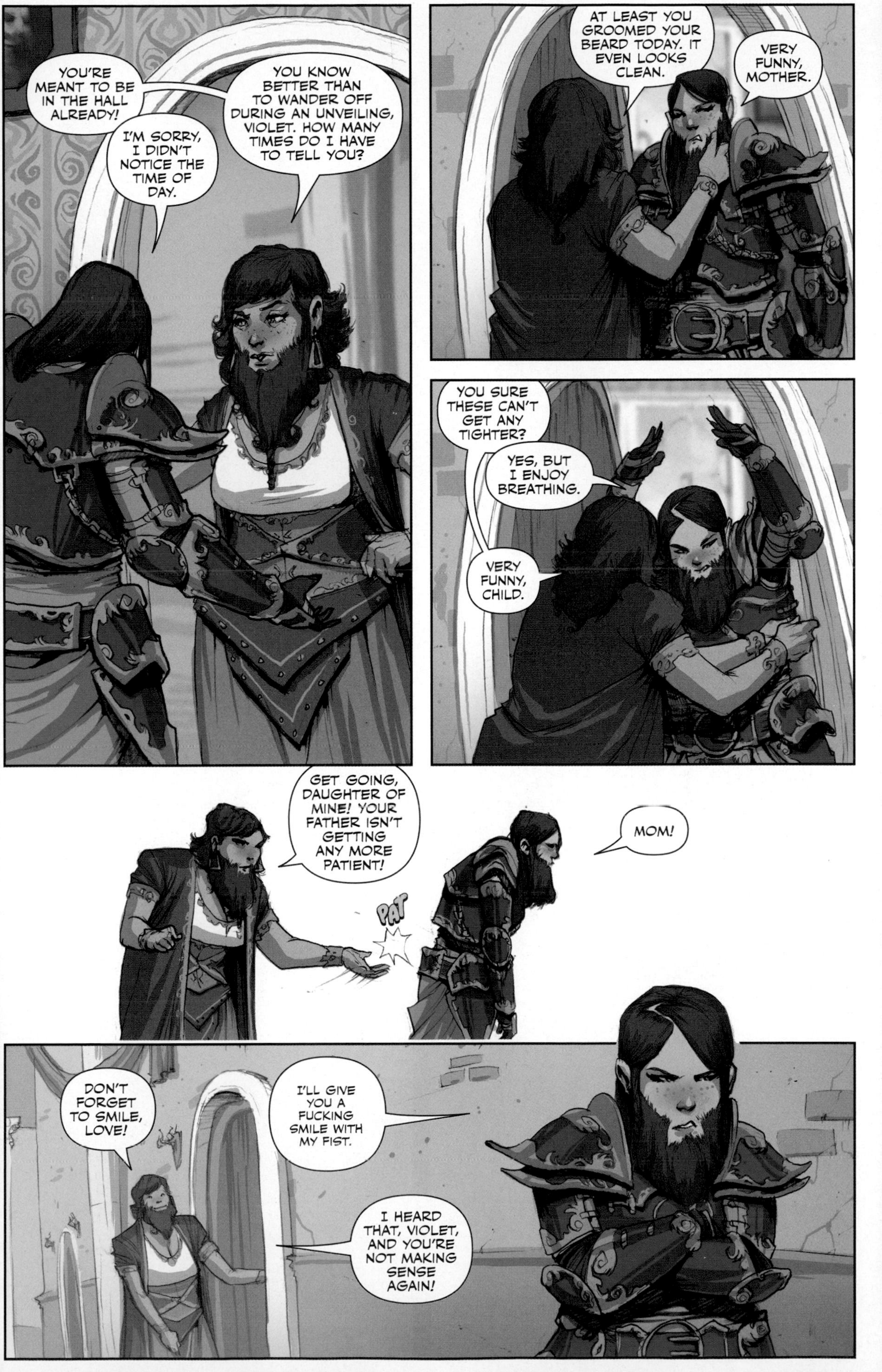
YOU'RE MEANT TO BE IN THE HALL ALREADY!
YOU KNOW BETTER THAN TO WANDER OFF DURING AN UNVEILING, VIOLET. HOW MANY TIMES DO I HAVE TO TELL YOU?
I'M SORRY, I DIDN'T NOTICE THE TIME OF DAY.
AT LEAST YOU GROOMED YOUR BEARD TODAY. IT EVEN LOOKS CLEAN.
VERY FUNNY, MOTHER.
YOU SURE THESE CAN'T GET ANY TIGHTER?
YES, BUT I ENJOY BREATHING.
VERY FUNNY, CHILD.
GET GOING, DAUGHTER OF MINE! YOUR FATHER ISN'T GETTING ANY MORE PATIENT!
PAT
MOM!
DON'T FORGET TO SMILE, LOVE!
I'LL GIVE YOU A FUCKING SMILE WITH MY FIST.
I HEARD THAT, VIOLET, AND YOU'RE NOT MAKING SENSE AGAIN!

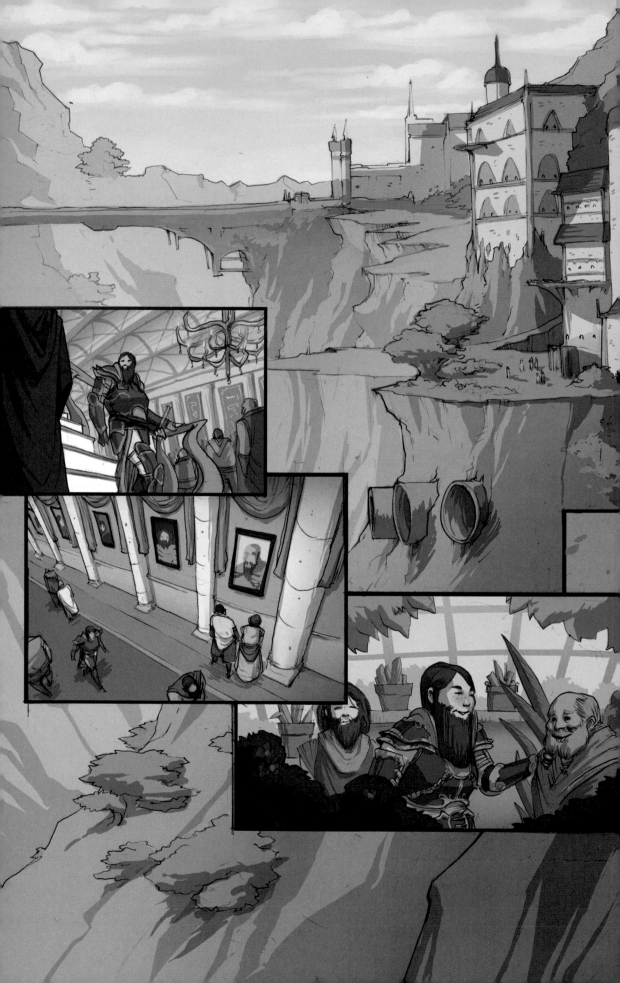

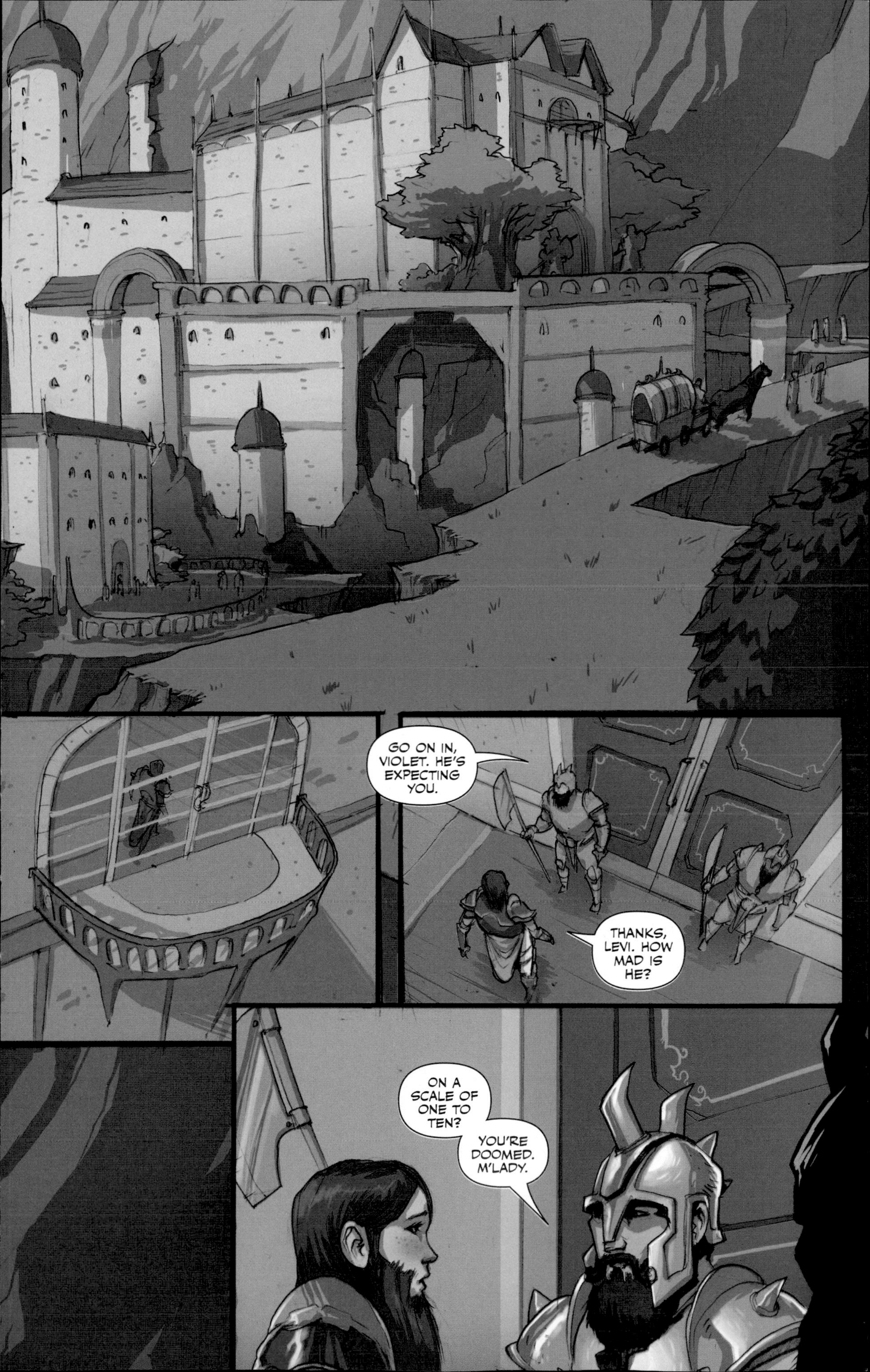
GO ON IN, VIOLET. HE'S EXPECTING YOU.
THANKS, LEVI. HOW MAD IS HE?
ON A SCALE OF ONE TO TEN?
YOU'RE DOOMED. M'LADY.

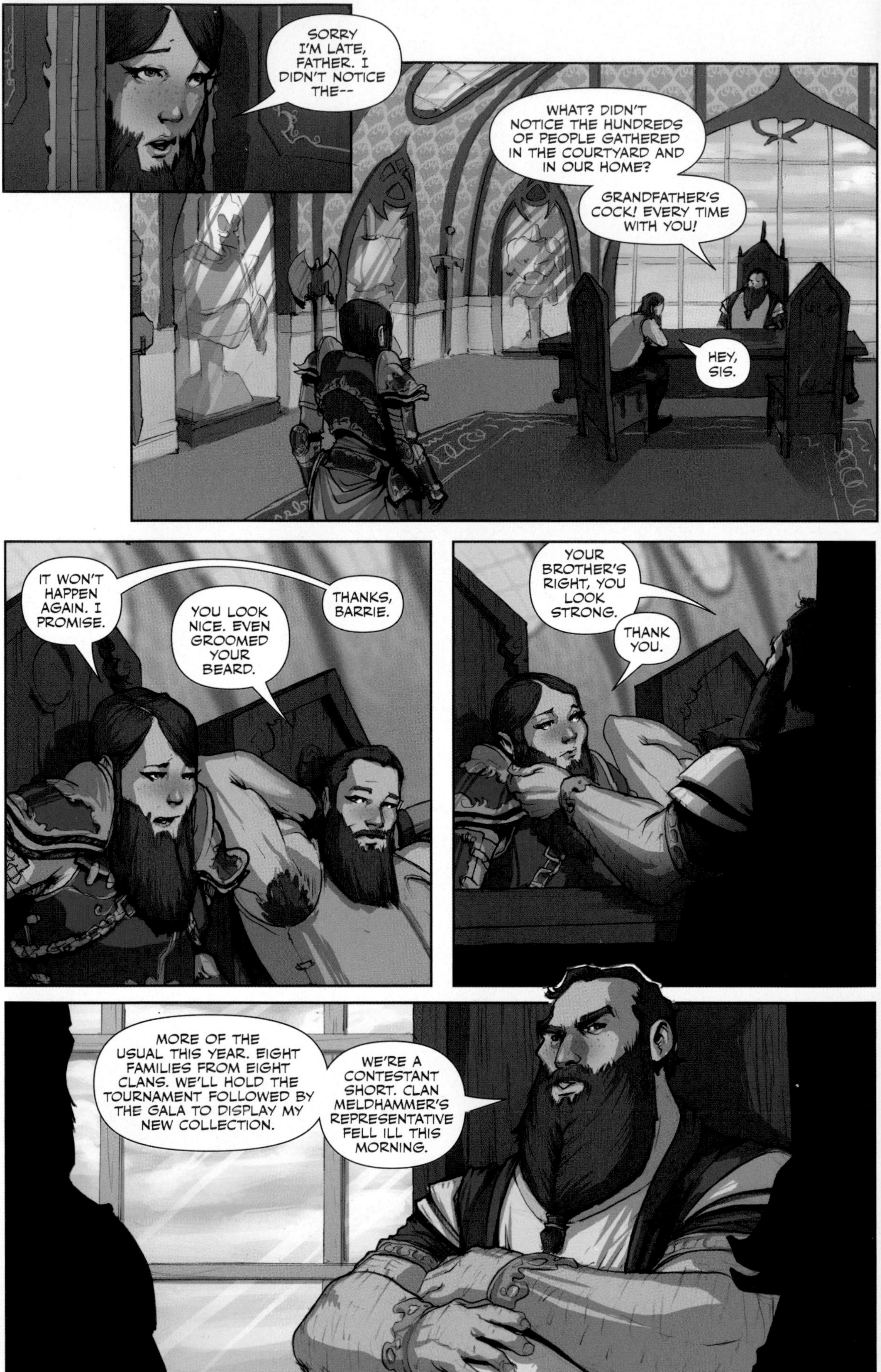
SORRY I'M LATE, FATHER. I DIDN'T NOTICE THE--
WHAT? DIDN'T NOTICE THE HUNDREDS OF PEOPLE GATHERED IN THE COURTYARD AND IN OUR HOME?
GRANDFATHER'S COCK! EVERY TIME WITH YOU!
HEY, SIS.
IT WON'T HAPPEN AGAIN. I PROMISE.
YOU LOOK NICE. EVEN GROOMED YOUR BEARD.
THANKS, BARRIE.
YOUR BROTHER'S RIGHT, YOU LOOK STRONG.
THANK YOU.
MORE OF THE USUAL THIS YEAR. EIGHT FAMILIES FROM EIGHT CLANS. WE'LL HOLD THE TOURNAMENT FOLLOWED BY THE GALA TO DISPLAY MY NEW COLLECTION.
WE'RE A CONTESTANT SHORT. CLAN MELDHAMMER'S REPRESENTATIVE FELL ILL THIS MORNING.

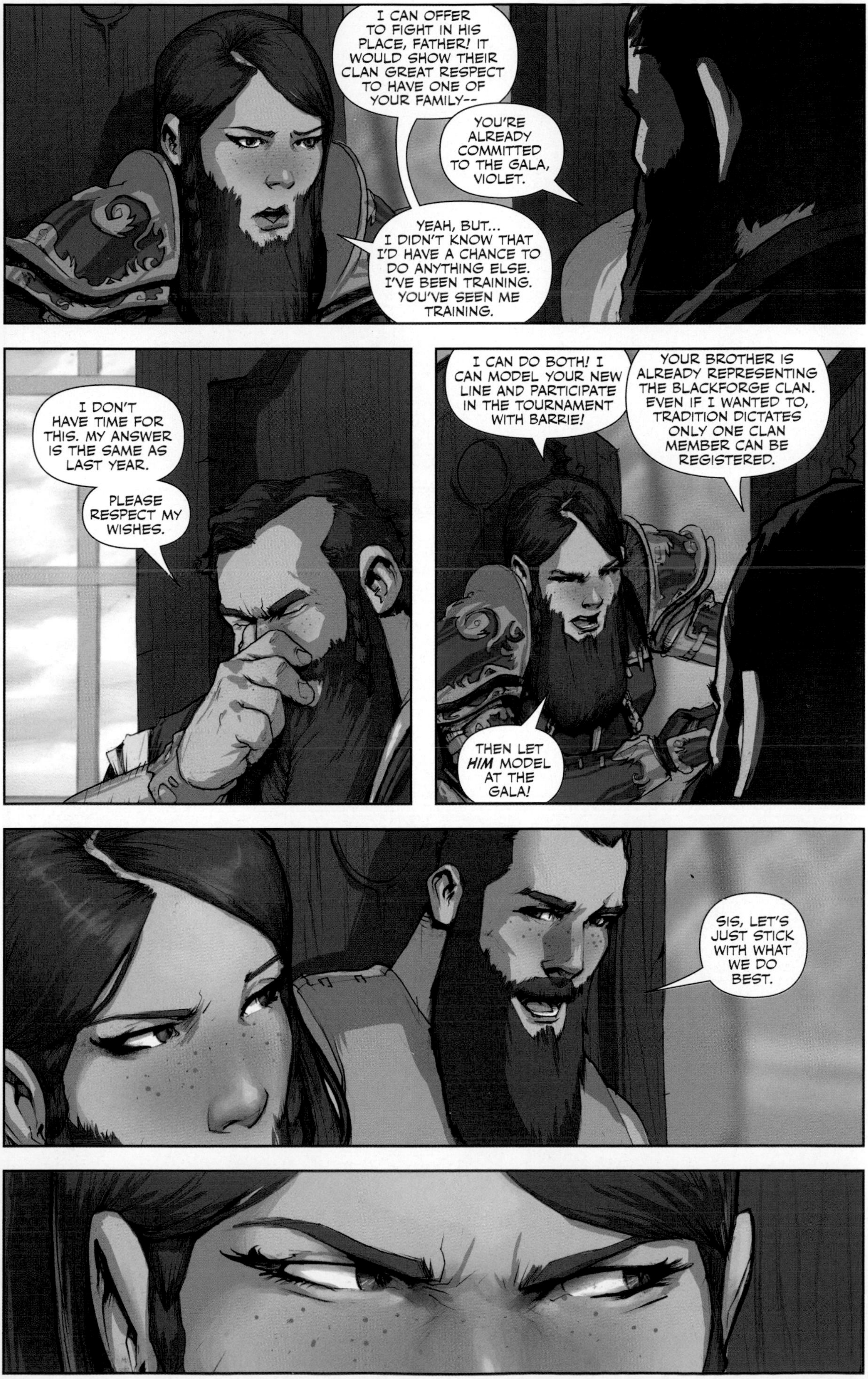
I CAN OFFER TO FIGHT IN HIS PLACE, FATHER! IT WOULD SHOW THEIR CLAN GREAT RESPECT TO HAVE ONE OF YOUR FAMILY--
YOU'RE ALREADY COMMITTED TO THE GALA, VIOLET.
YEAH, BUT... I DIDN'T KNOW THAT I'D HAVE A CHANCE TO DO ANYTHING ELSE. I'VE BEEN TRAINING. YOU'VE SEEN ME TRAINING.
I DON'T HAVE TIME FOR THIS. MY ANSWER IS THE SAME AS LAST YEAR.
PLEASE RESPECT MY WISHES.
I CAN DO BOTH! I CAN MODEL YOUR NEW LINE AND PARTICIPATE IN THE TOURNAMENT WITH BARRIE!
YOUR BROTHER IS ALREADY REPRESENTING THE BLACKFORGE CLAN. EVEN IF I WANTED TO, TRADITION DICTATES ONLY ONE CLAN MEMBER CAN BE REGISTERED.
THEN LET HIM MODEL AT THE GALA!
SIS, LET'S JUST STICK WITH WHAT WE DO BEST.

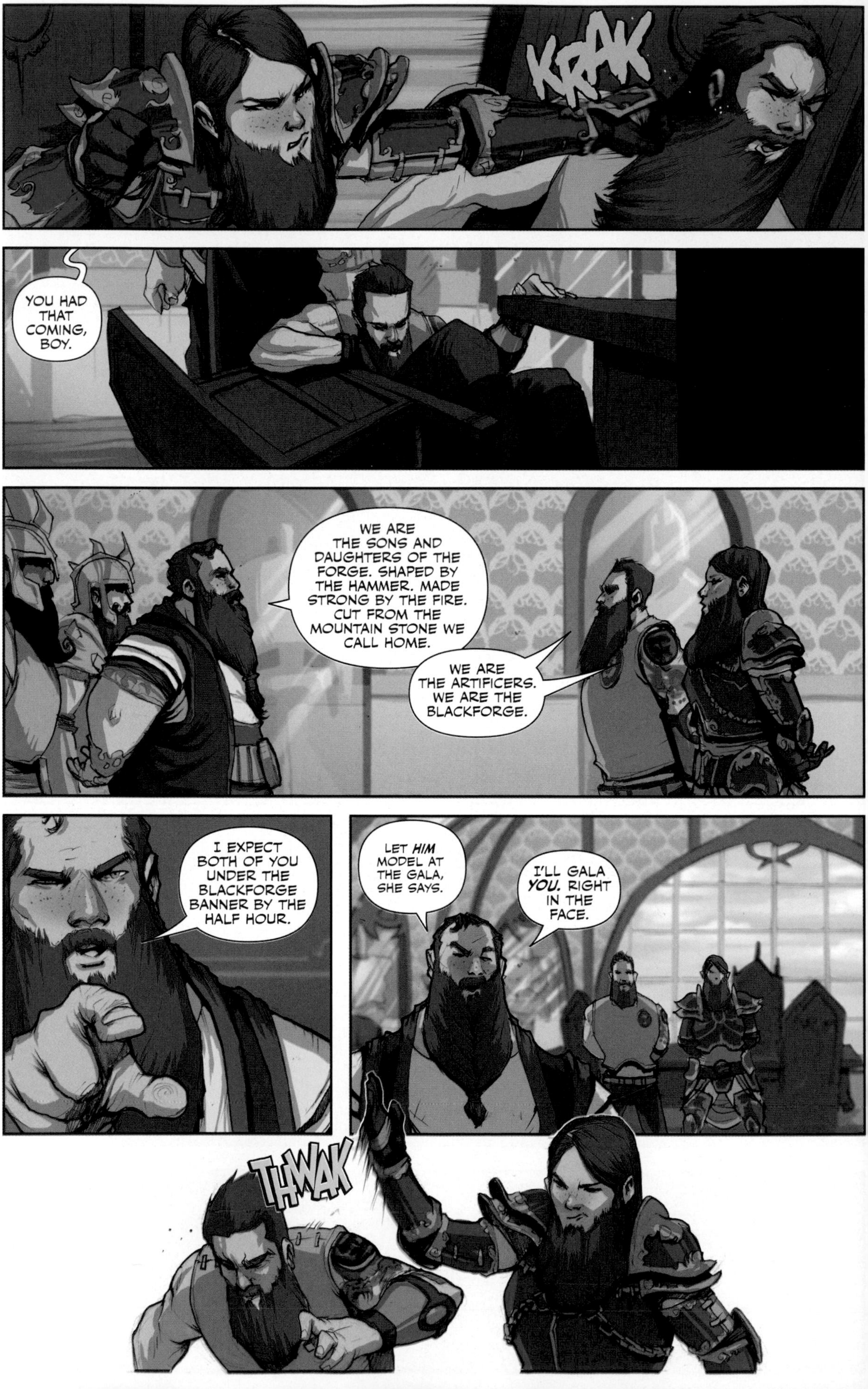
KRAK
YOU HAD THAT COMING, BOY.
WE ARE THE SONS AND DAUGHTERS OF THE FORGE. SHAPED BY THE HAMMER. MADE STRONG BY THE FIRE. CUT FROM THE MOUNTAIN STONE WE CALL HOME.
WE ARE THE ARTIFICERS. WE ARE THE BLACKFORGE.
I EXPECT BOTH OF YOU UNDER THE BLACKFORGE BANNER BY THE HALF HOUR.
LET *HIM* MODEL AT THE GALA, SHE SAYS.
I'LL GALA *YOU.* RIGHT IN THE FACE.
THWAK

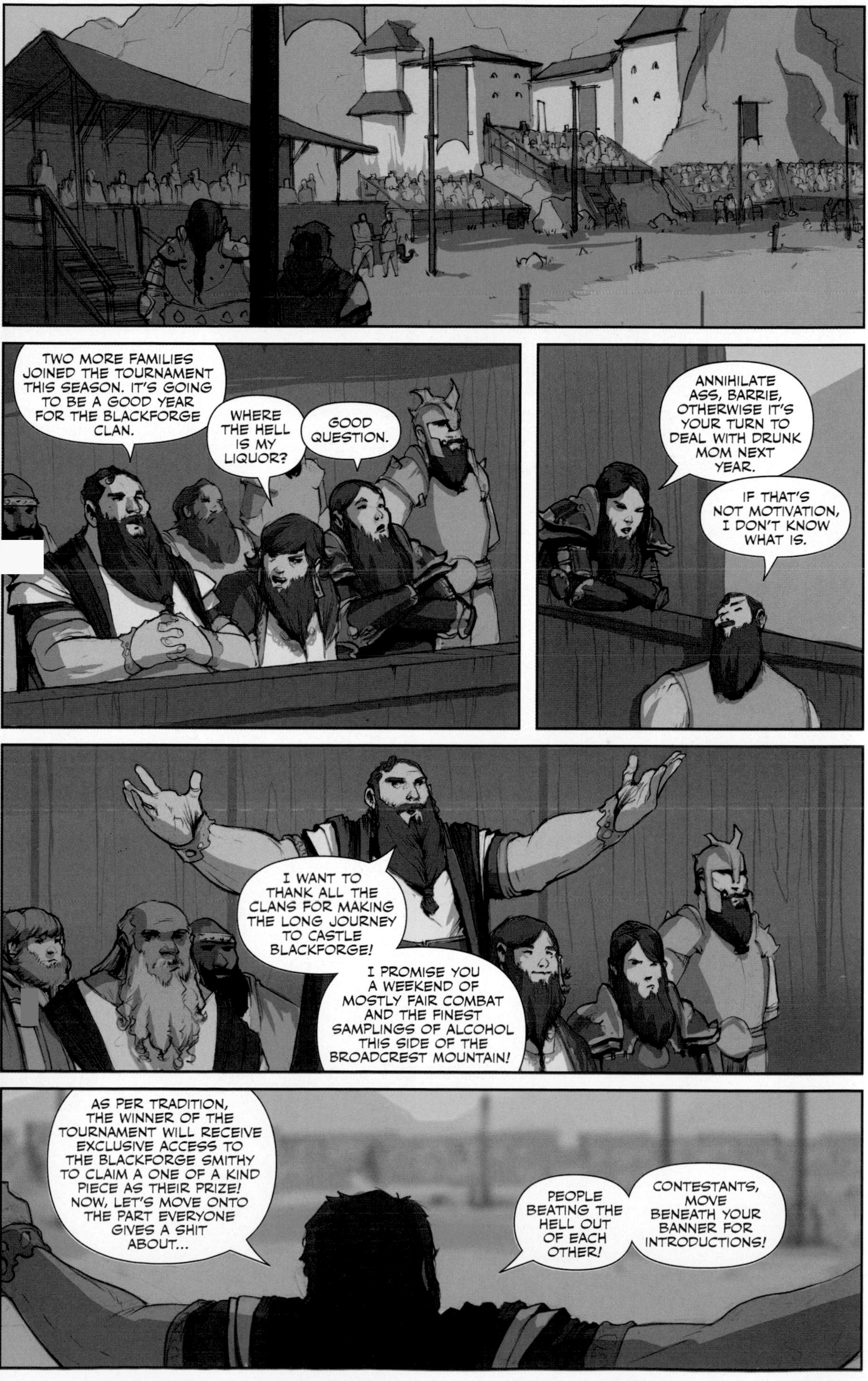
TWO MORE FAMILIES JOINED THE TOURNAMENT THIS SEASON. IT'S GOING TO BE A GOOD YEAR FOR THE BLACKFORGE CLAN.
WHERE THE HELL IS MY LIQUOR?
GOOD QUESTION.
ANNIHILATE ASS, BARRIE, OTHERWISE IT'S YOUR TURN TO DEAL WITH DRUNK MOM NEXT YEAR.
IF THAT'S NOT MOTIVATION, I DON'T KNOW WHAT IS.
I WANT TO THANK ALL THE CLANS FOR MAKING THE LONG JOURNEY TO CASTLE BLACKFORGE!
I PROMISE YOU A WEEKEND OF MOSTLY FAIR COMBAT AND THE FINEST SAMPLINGS OF ALCOHOL THIS SIDE OF THE BROADCREST MOUNTAIN!
AS PER TRADITION, THE WINNER OF THE TOURNAMENT WILL RECEIVE EXCLUSIVE ACCESS TO THE BLACKFORGE SMITHY TO CLAIM A ONE OF A KIND PIECE AS THEIR PRIZE! NOW, LET'S MOVE ONTO THE PART EVERYONE GIVES A SHIT ABOUT...
PEOPLE BEATING THE HELL OUT OF EACH OTHER!
CONTESTANTS, MOVE BENEATH YOUR BANNER FOR INTRODUCTIONS!

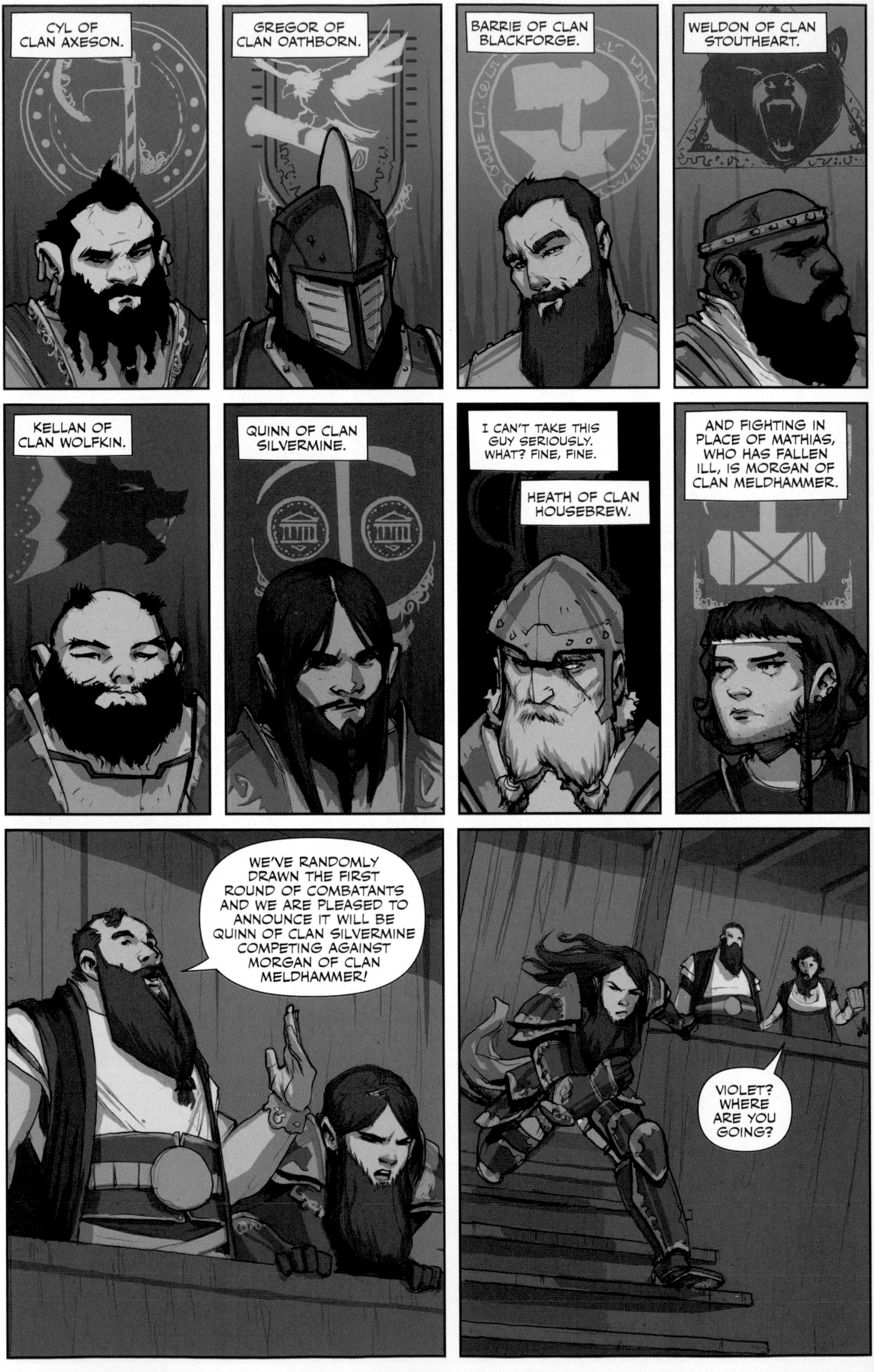

CYL OF CLAN AXESON.
GREGOR OF CLAN OATHBORN.
BARRIE OF CLAN BLACKFORGE.
WELDON OF CLAN STOUTHEART.
KELLAN OF CLAN WOLFKIN.
QUINN OF CLAN SILVERMINE.
I CAN'T TAKE THIS GUY SERIOUSLY. WHAT? FINE, FINE.
HEATH OF CLAN HOUSEBREW.
AND FIGHTING IN PLACE OF MATHIAS, WHO HAS FALLEN ILL, IS MORGAN OF CLAN MELDHAMMER.
WE'VE RANDOMLY DRAWN THE FIRST ROUND OF COMBATANTS AND WE ARE PLEASED TO ANNOUNCE IT WILL BE QUINN OF CLAN SILVERMINE COMPETING AGAINST MORGAN OF CLAN MELDHAMMER!
VIOLET? WHERE ARE YOU GOING?

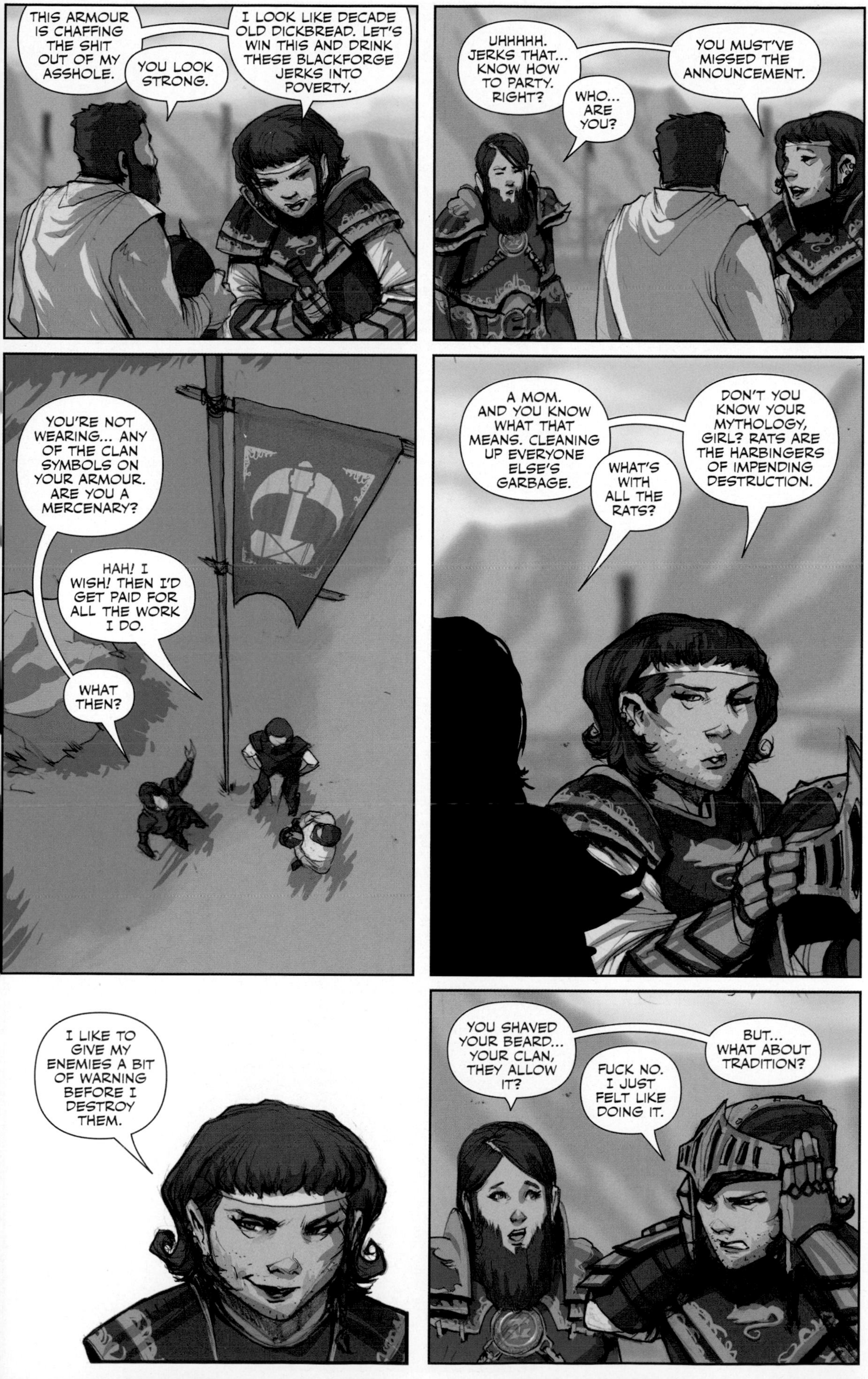
THIS ARMOUR IS CHAFFING THE SHIT OUT OF MY ASSHOLE.
YOU LOOK STRONG.
I LOOK LIKE DECADE OLD DICKBREAD. LET'S WIN THIS AND DRINK THESE BLACKFORGE JERKS INTO POVERTY.
UHHHHH. JERKS THAT... KNOW HOW TO PARTY. RIGHT?
WHO... ARE YOU?
YOU MUST'VE MISSED THE ANNOUNCEMENT.
YOU'RE NOT WEARING... ANY OF THE CLAN SYMBOLS ON YOUR ARMOUR. ARE YOU A MERCENARY?
HAH! I WISH! THEN I'D GET PAID FOR ALL THE WORK I DO.
WHAT THEN?
A MOM. AND YOU KNOW WHAT THAT MEANS. CLEANING UP EVERYONE ELSE'S GARBAGE.
WHAT'S WITH ALL THE RATS?
DON'T YOU KNOW YOUR MYTHOLOGY, GIRL? RATS ARE THE HARBINGERS OF IMPENDING DESTRUCTION.
I LIKE TO GIVE MY ENEMIES A BIT OF WARNING BEFORE I DESTROY THEM.
YOU SHAVED YOUR BEARD... YOUR CLAN, THEY ALLOW IT?
FUCK NO. I JUST FELT LIKE DOING IT.
BUT... WHAT ABOUT TRADITION?

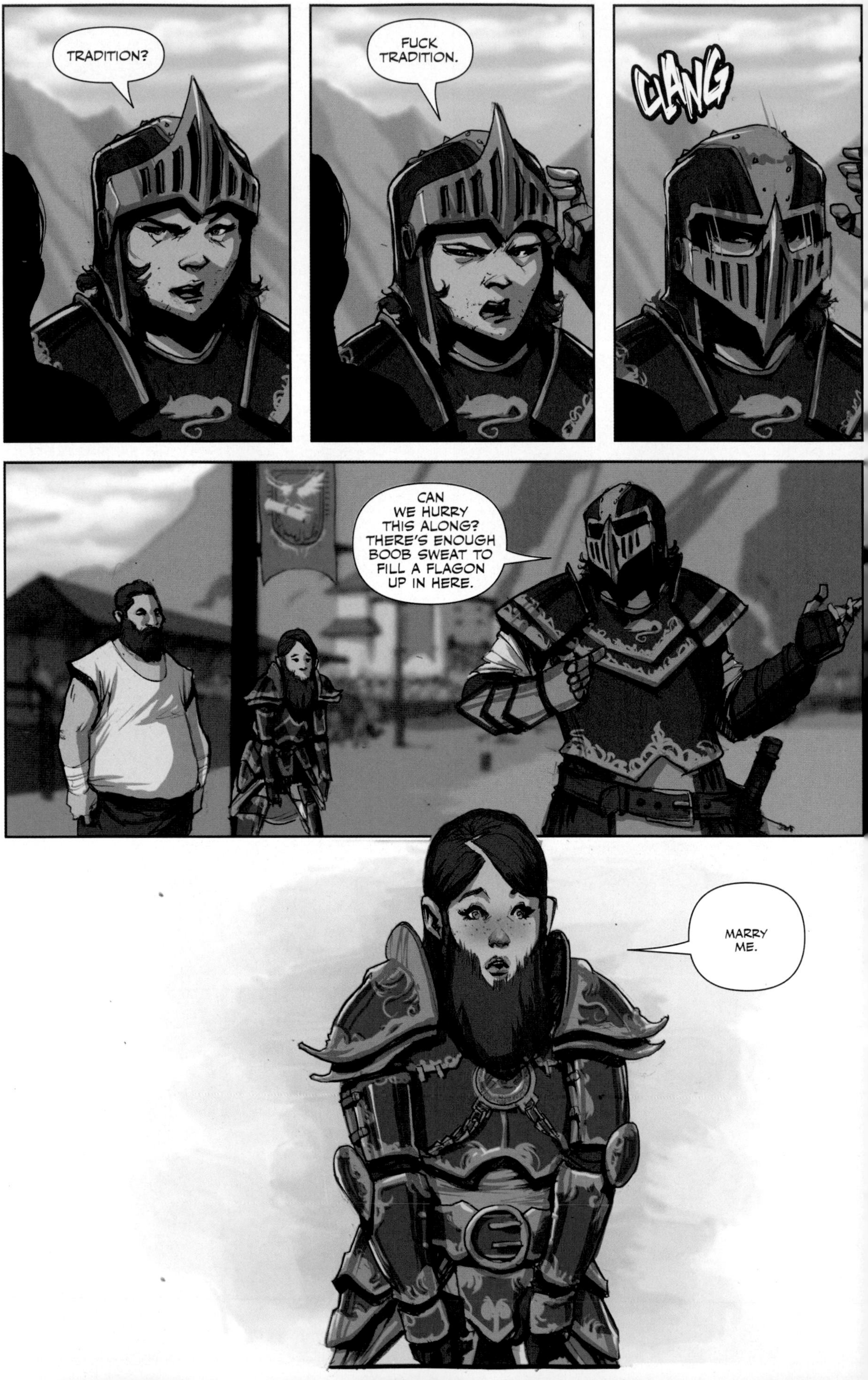
TRADITION?
FUCK TRADITION.
CLANG
CAN WE HURRY THIS ALONG? THERE'S ENOUGH BOOB SWEAT TO FILL A FLAGON UP IN HERE.
MARRY ME.

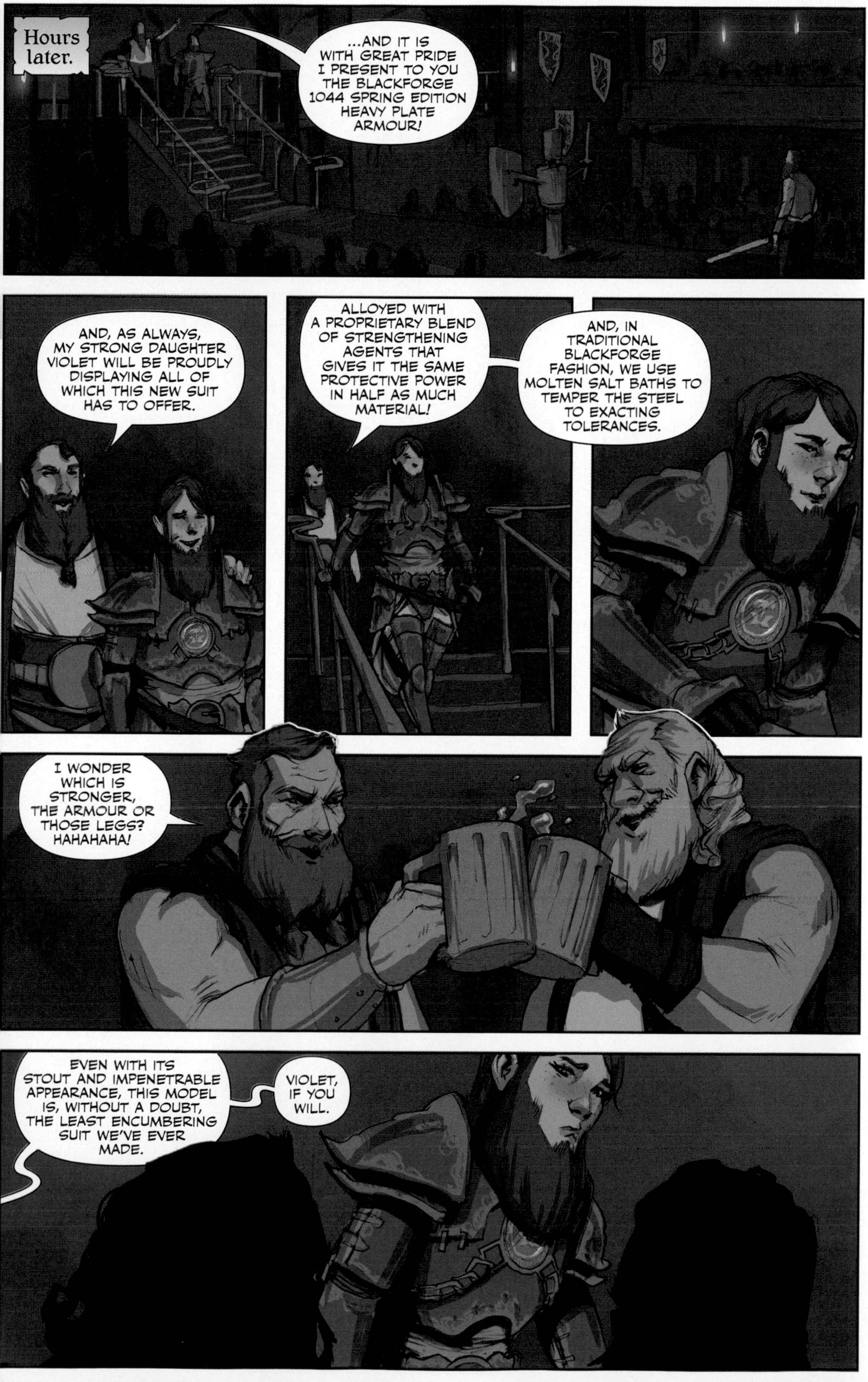
Hours later.
...AND IT IS WITH GREAT PRIDE I PRESENT TO YOU THE BLACKFORGE 1044 SPRING EDITION HEAVY PLATE ARMOUR!
AND, AS ALWAYS, MY STRONG DAUGHTER VIOLET WILL BE PROUDLY DISPLAYING ALL OF WHICH THIS NEW SUIT HAS TO OFFER.
ALLOYED WITH A PROPRIETARY BLEND OF STRENGTHENING AGENTS THAT GIVES IT THE SAME PROTECTIVE POWER IN HALF AS MUCH MATERIAL!
AND, IN TRADITIONAL BLACKFORGE FASHION, WE USE MOLTEN SALT BATHS TO TEMPER THE STEEL TO EXACTING TOLERANCES.
I WONDER WHICH IS STRONGER, THE ARMOUR OR THOSE LEGS? HAHAHAHA!
EVEN WITH ITS STOUT AND IMPENETRABLE APPEARANCE, THIS MODEL IS, WITHOUT A DOUBT, THE LEAST ENCUMBERING SUIT WE'VE EVER MADE.
VIOLET, IF YOU WILL.

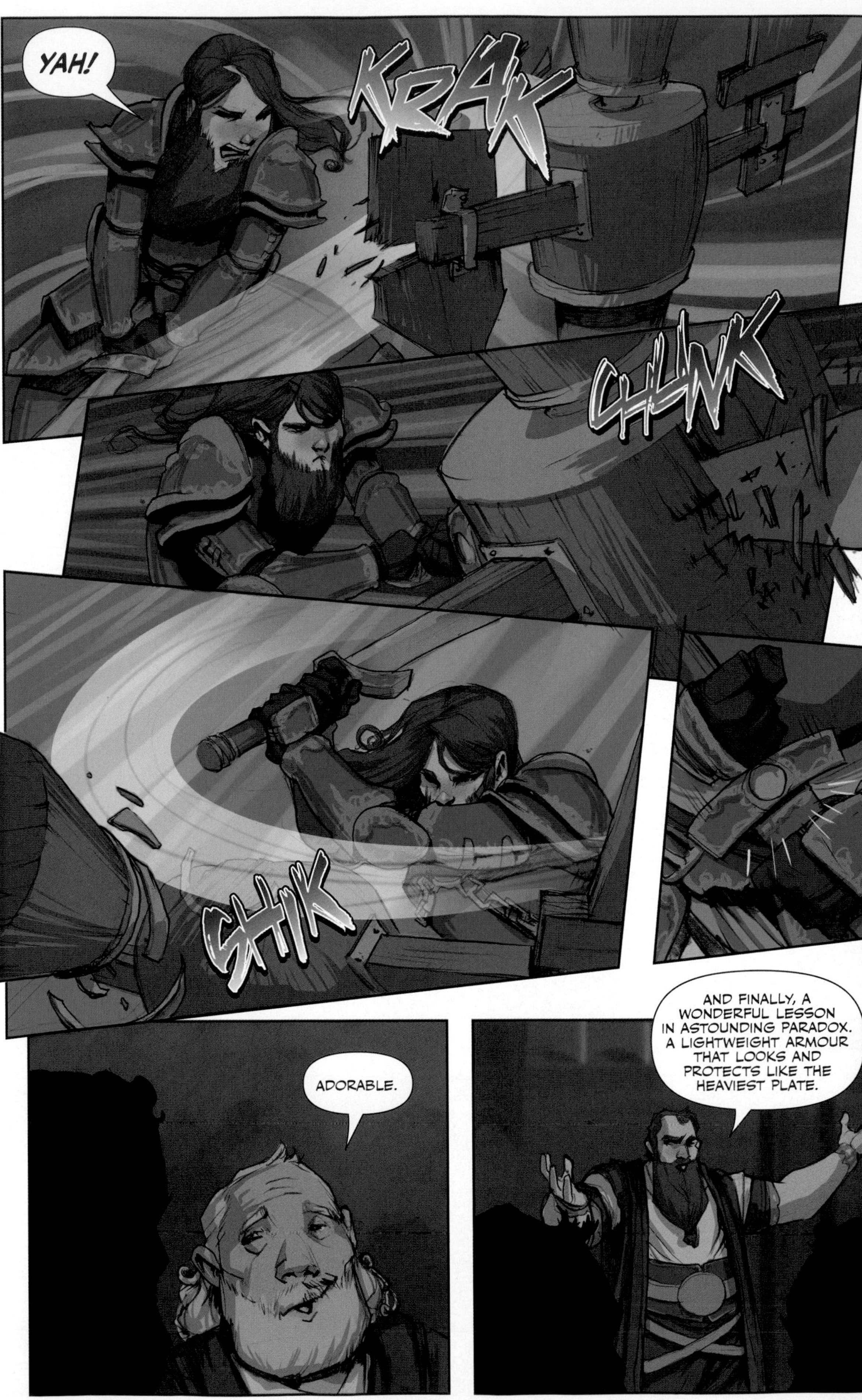
YAH!
KRAK
CHUNK
CHIK
ADORABLE.
AND FINALLY, A WONDERFUL LESSON IN ASTOUNDING PARADOX. A LIGHTWEIGHT ARMOUR THAT LOOKS AND PROTECTS LIKE THE HEAVIEST PLATE.

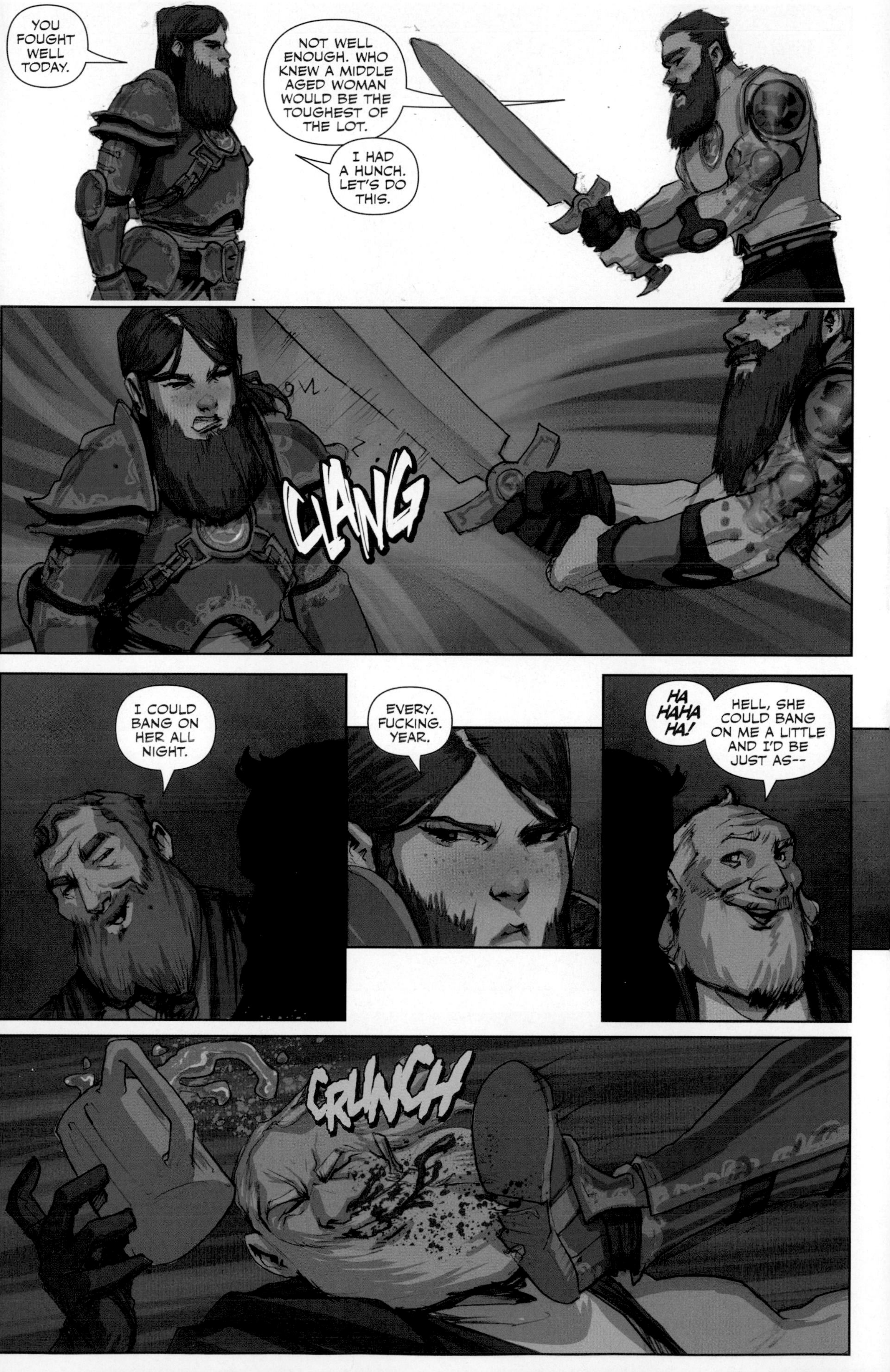
YOU FOUGHT WELL TODAY.
NOT WELL ENOUGH. WHO KNEW A MIDDLE AGED WOMAN WOULD BE THE TOUGHEST OF THE LOT.
I HAD A HUNCH. LET'S DO THIS.
CLANG
I COULD BANG ON HER ALL NIGHT.
EVERY. FUCKING. YEAR.
HA HAHAHA HA!
HELL, SHE COULD BANG ON ME A LITTLE AND I'D BE JUST AS--
CRUNCH

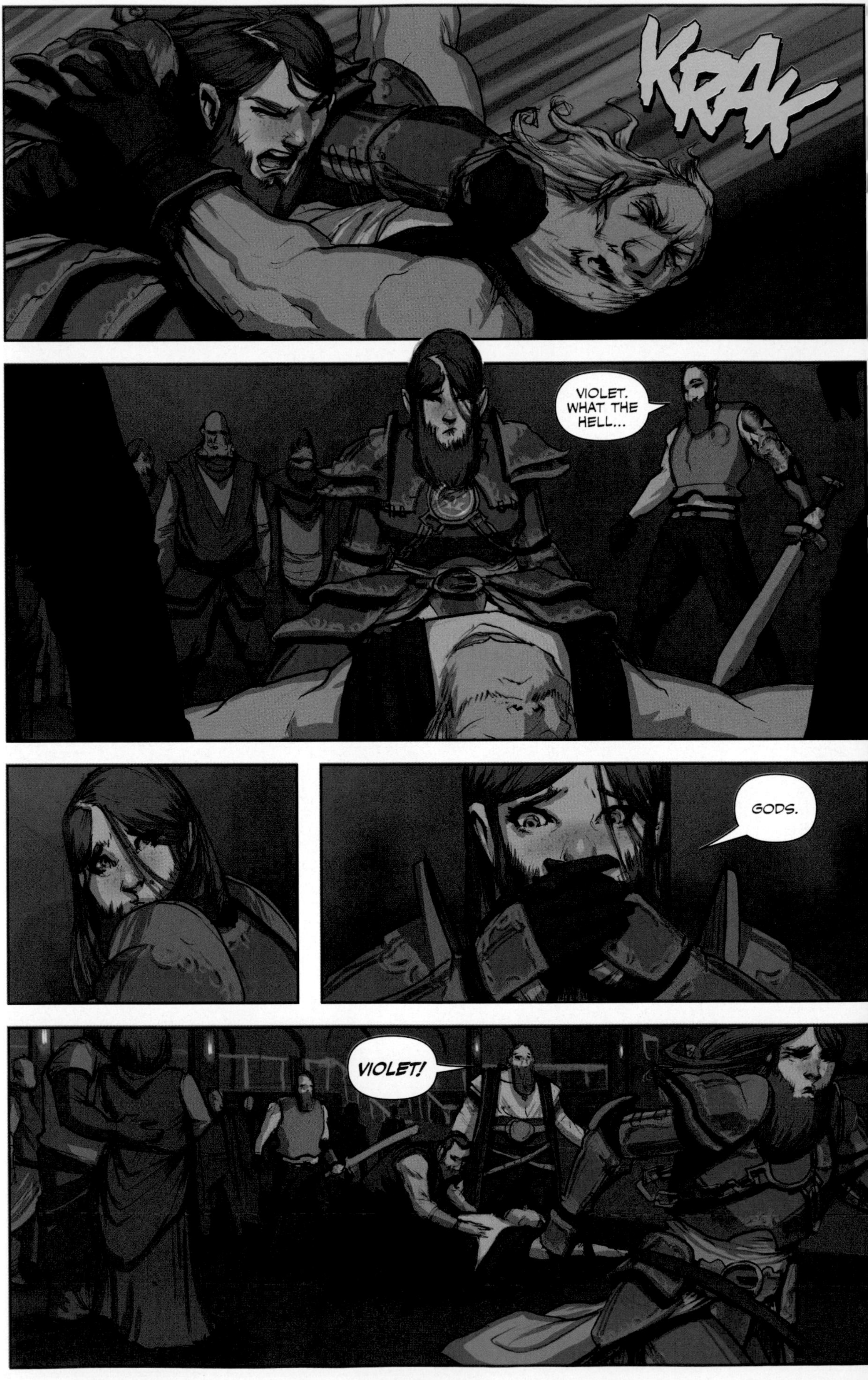
KRAK
VIOLET. WHAT THE HELL...
GODS.
VIOLET!

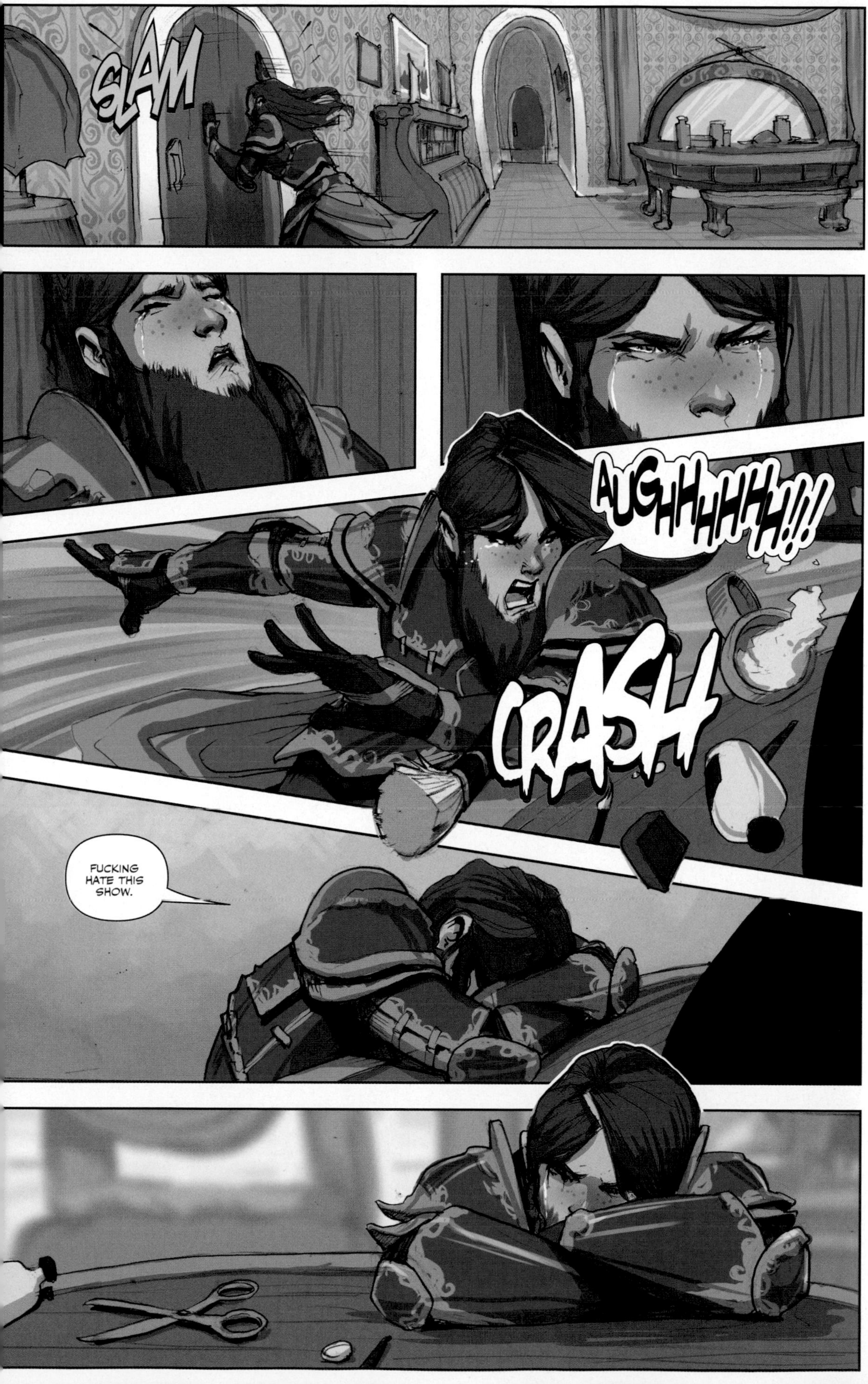
SLAM
AUGHHHHHH!!!
CRASH
FUCKING HATE THIS SHOW.

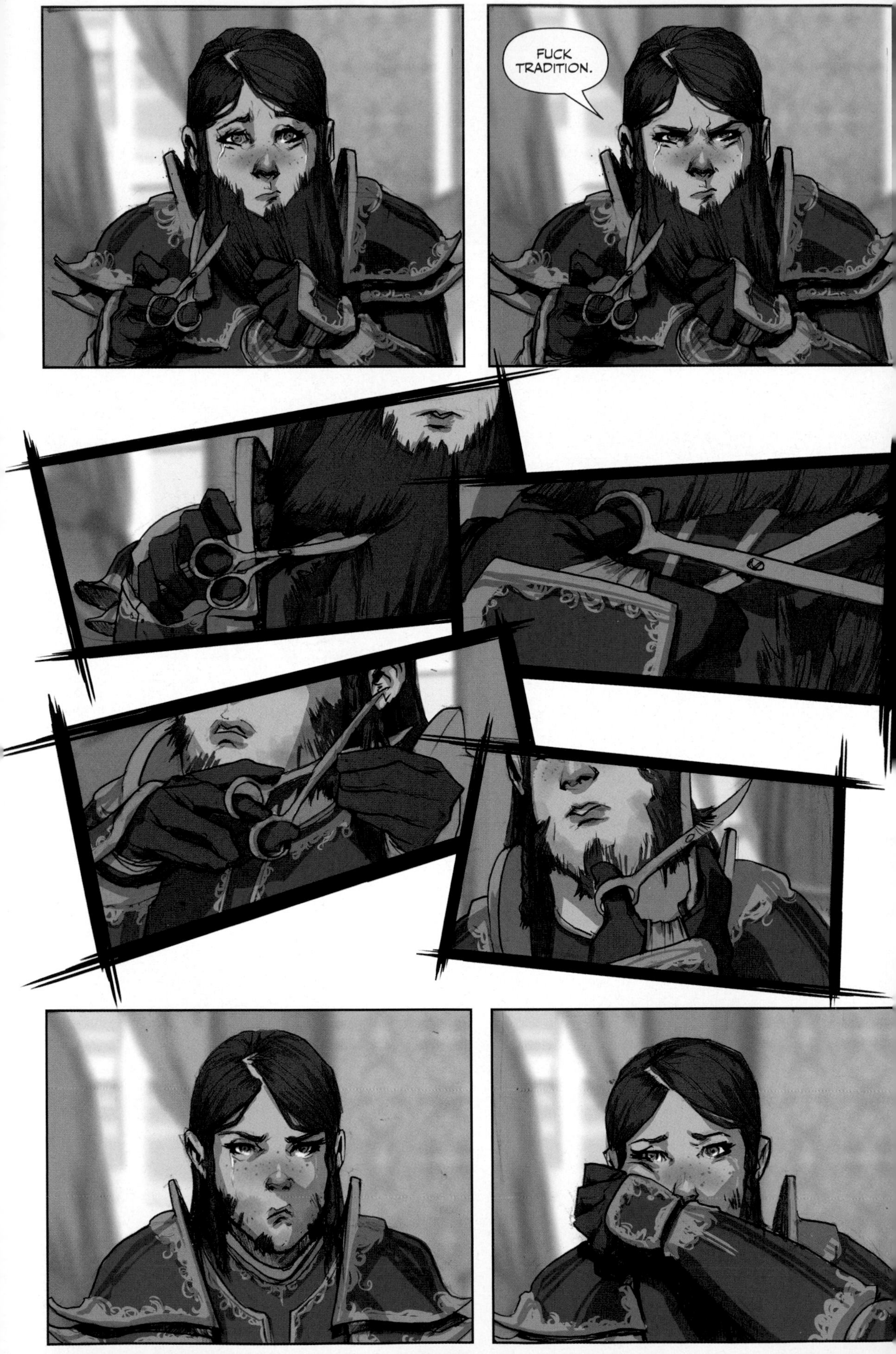
FUCK TRADITION.

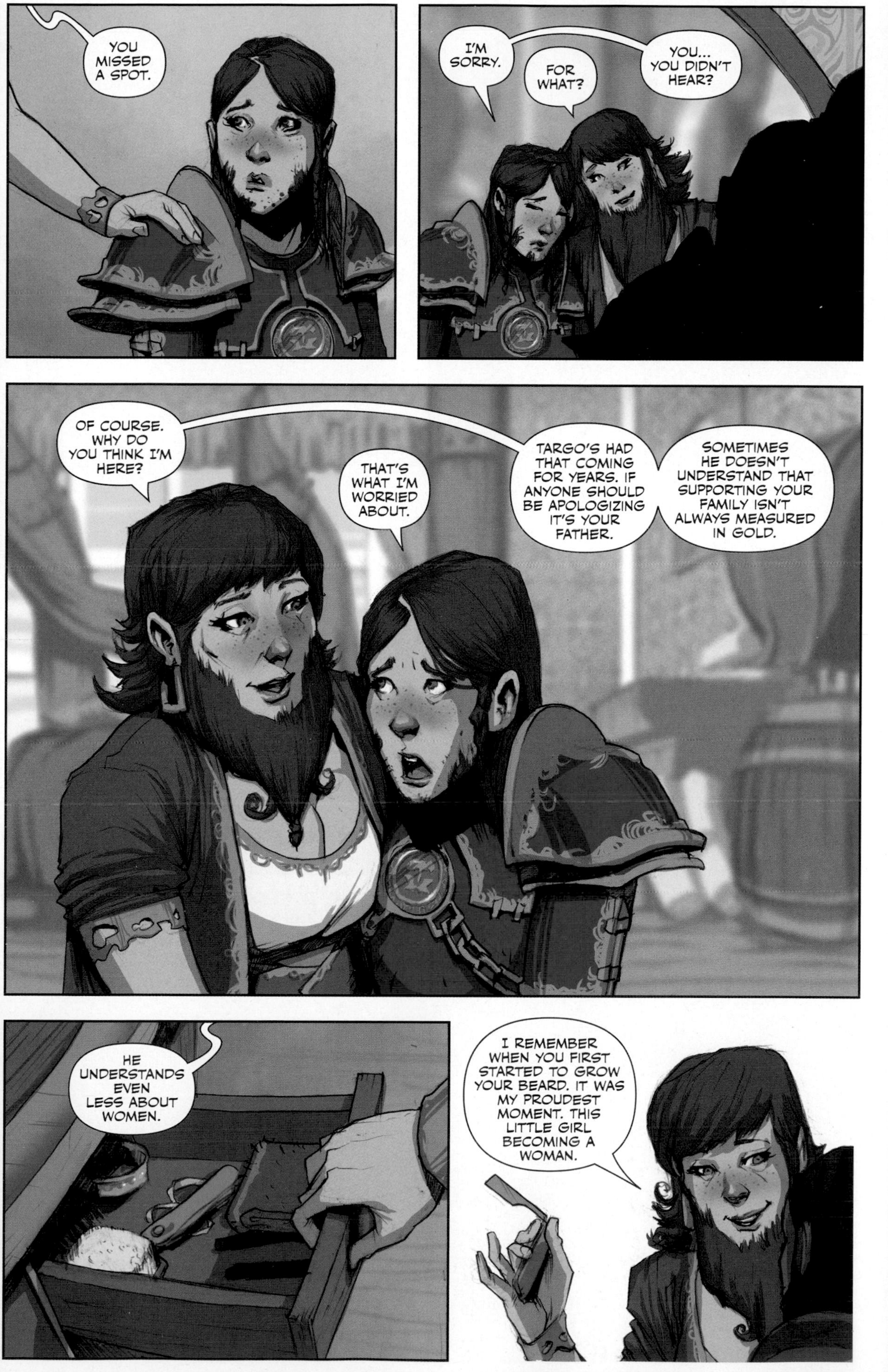
YOU MISSED A SPOT.
I'M SORRY.
FOR WHAT?
YOU... YOU DIDN'T HEAR?
OF COURSE. WHY DO YOU THINK I'M HERE?
THAT'S WHAT I'M WORRIED ABOUT.
TARGO'S HAD THAT COMING FOR YEARS. IF ANYONE SHOULD BE APOLOGIZING IT'S YOUR FATHER.
SOMETIMES HE DOESN'T UNDERSTAND THAT SUPPORTING YOUR FAMILY ISN'T ALWAYS MEASURED IN GOLD.
HE UNDERSTANDS EVEN LESS ABOUT WOMEN.
I REMEMBER WHEN YOU FIRST STARTED TO GROW YOUR BEARD. IT WAS MY PROUDEST MOMENT. THIS LITTLE GIRL BECOMING A WOMAN.

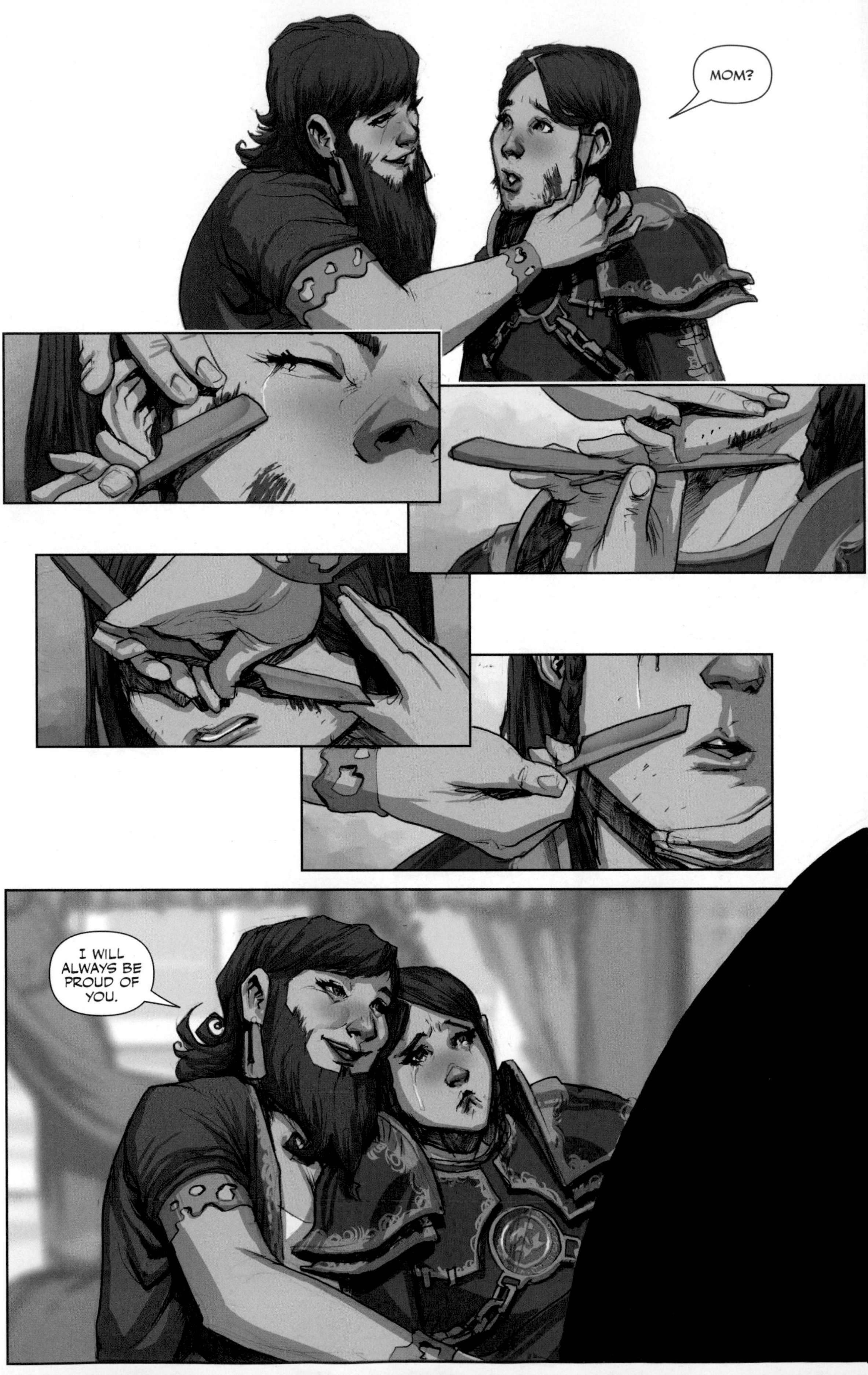
MOM?
I WILL ALWAYS BE PROUD OF YOU.

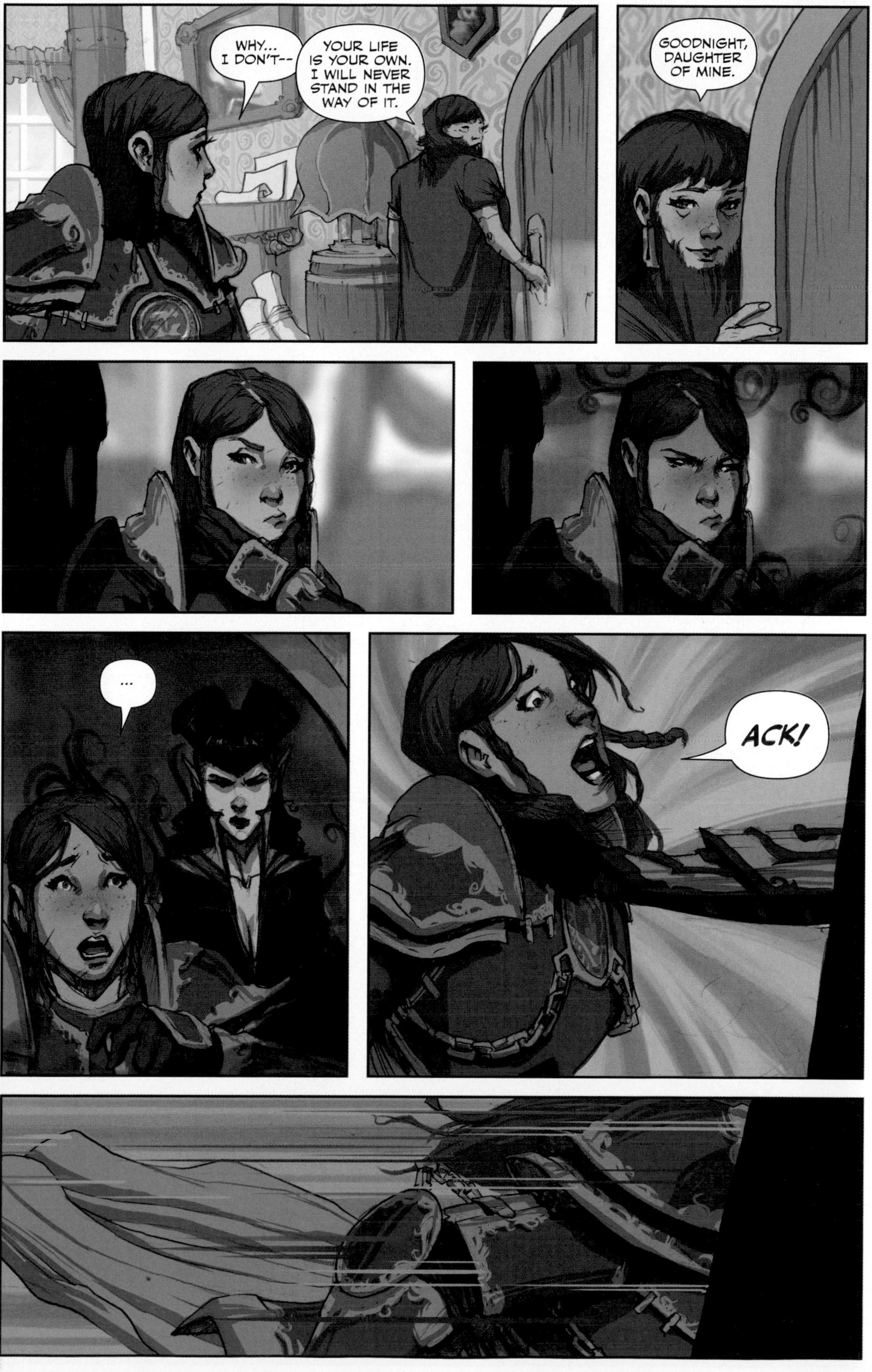
WHY... I DON'T--
YOUR LIFE IS YOUR OWN. I WILL NEVER STAND IN THE WAY OF IT.
GOODNIGHT, DAUGHTER OF MINE.
...
ACK!

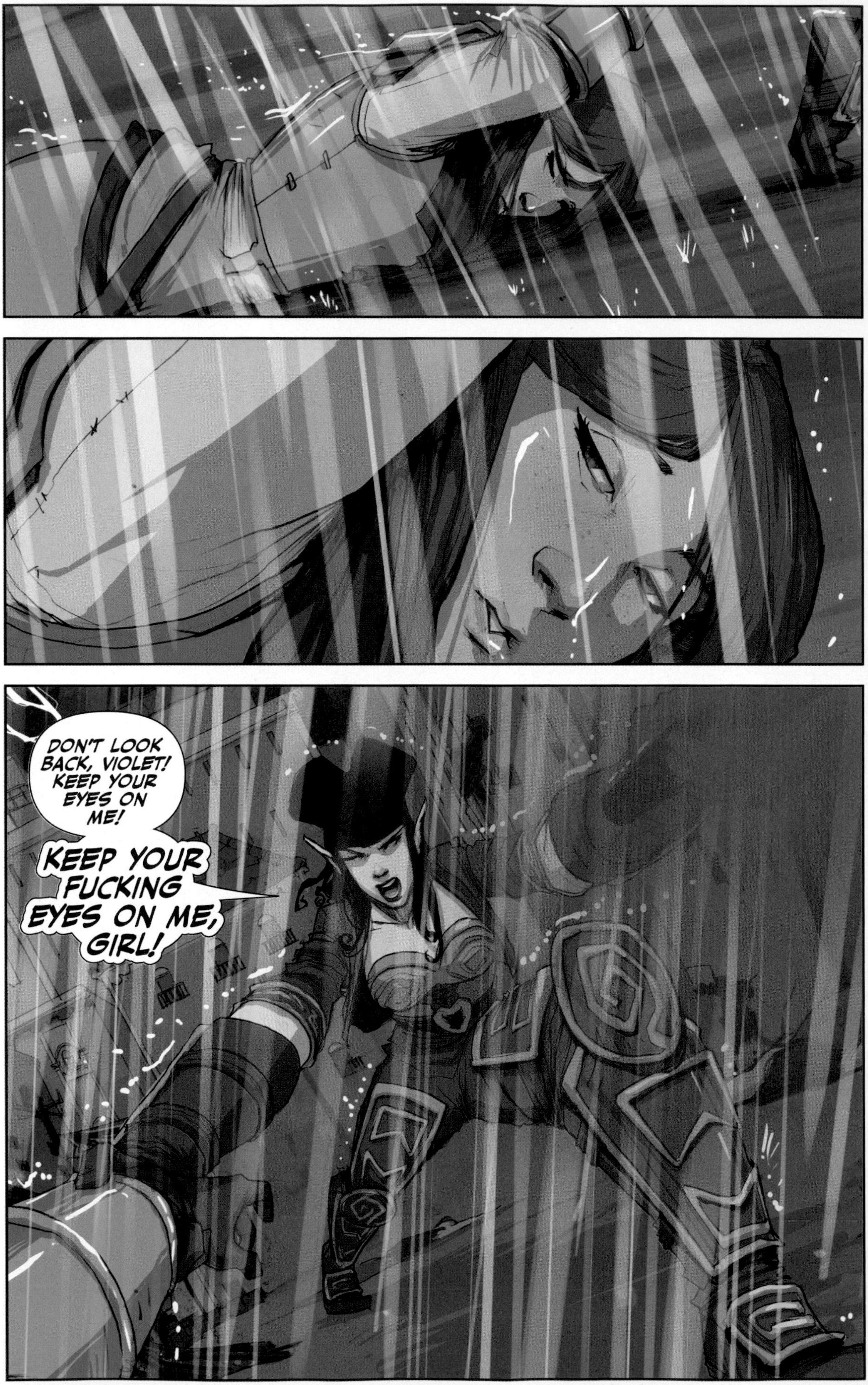
DON'T LOOK BACK, VIOLET! KEEP YOUR EYES ON ME!
KEEP YOUR FUCKING EYES ON ME, GIRL!

CHAPTER NINE

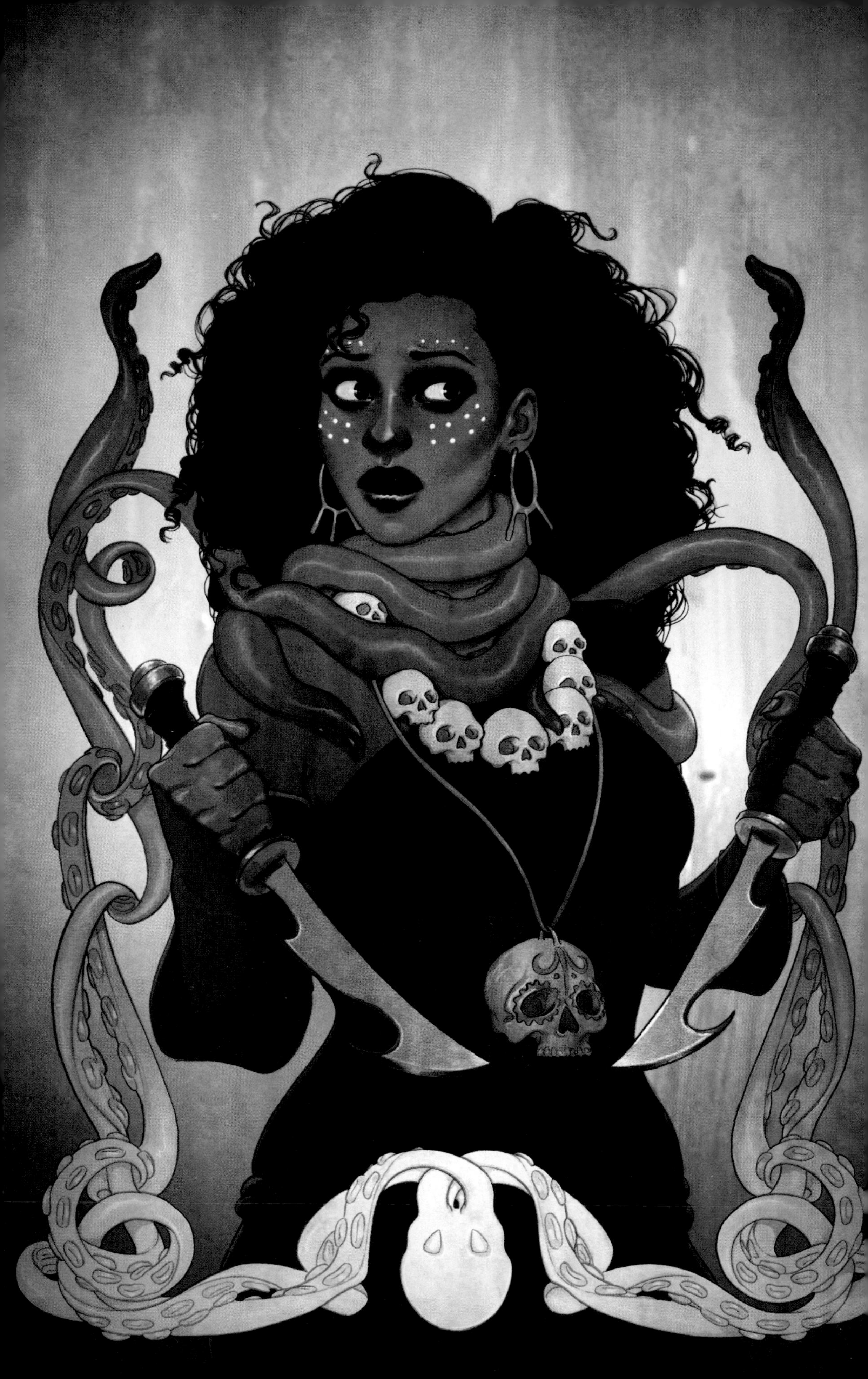

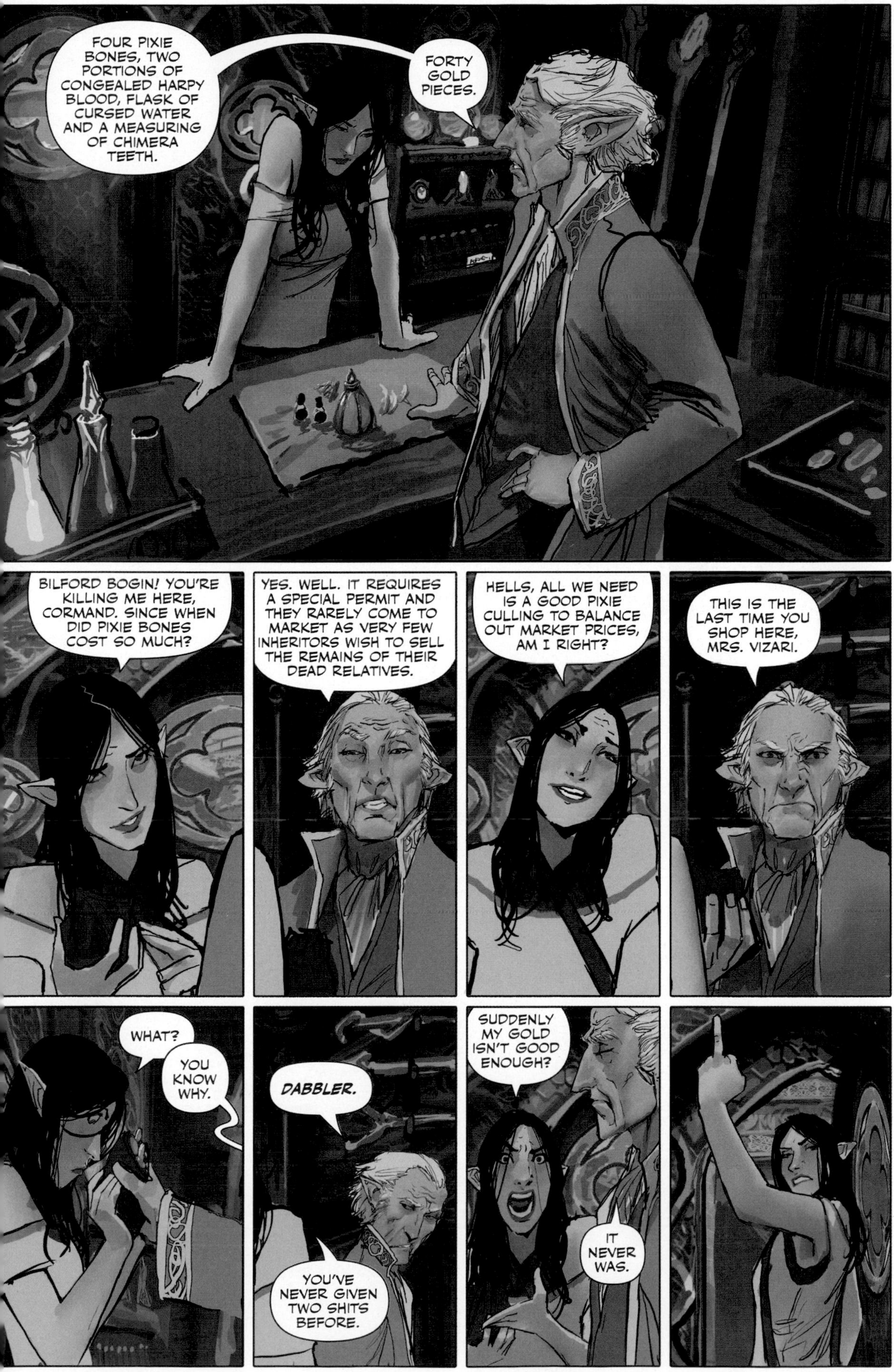
FOUR PIXIE BONES, TWO PORTIONS OF CONGEALED HARPY BLOOD, FLASK OF CURSED WATER AND A MEASURING OF CHIMERA TEETH.
FORTY GOLD PIECES.
BILFORD BOGIN! YOU'RE KILLING ME HERE, CORMAND. SINCE WHEN DID PIXIE BONES COST SO MUCH?
YES. WELL. IT REQUIRES A SPECIAL PERMIT AND THEY RARELY COME TO MARKET AS VERY FEW INHERITORS WISH TO SELL THE REMAINS OF THEIR DEAD RELATIVES.
HELLS, ALL WE NEED IS A GOOD PIXIE CULLING TO BALANCE OUT MARKET PRICES, AM I RIGHT?
THIS IS THE LAST TIME YOU SHOP HERE, MRS. VIZARI.
WHAT?
YOU KNOW WHY.
DABBLER.
YOU'VE NEVER GIVEN TWO SHITS BEFORE.
SUDDENLY MY GOLD ISN'T GOOD ENOUGH?
IT NEVER WAS.

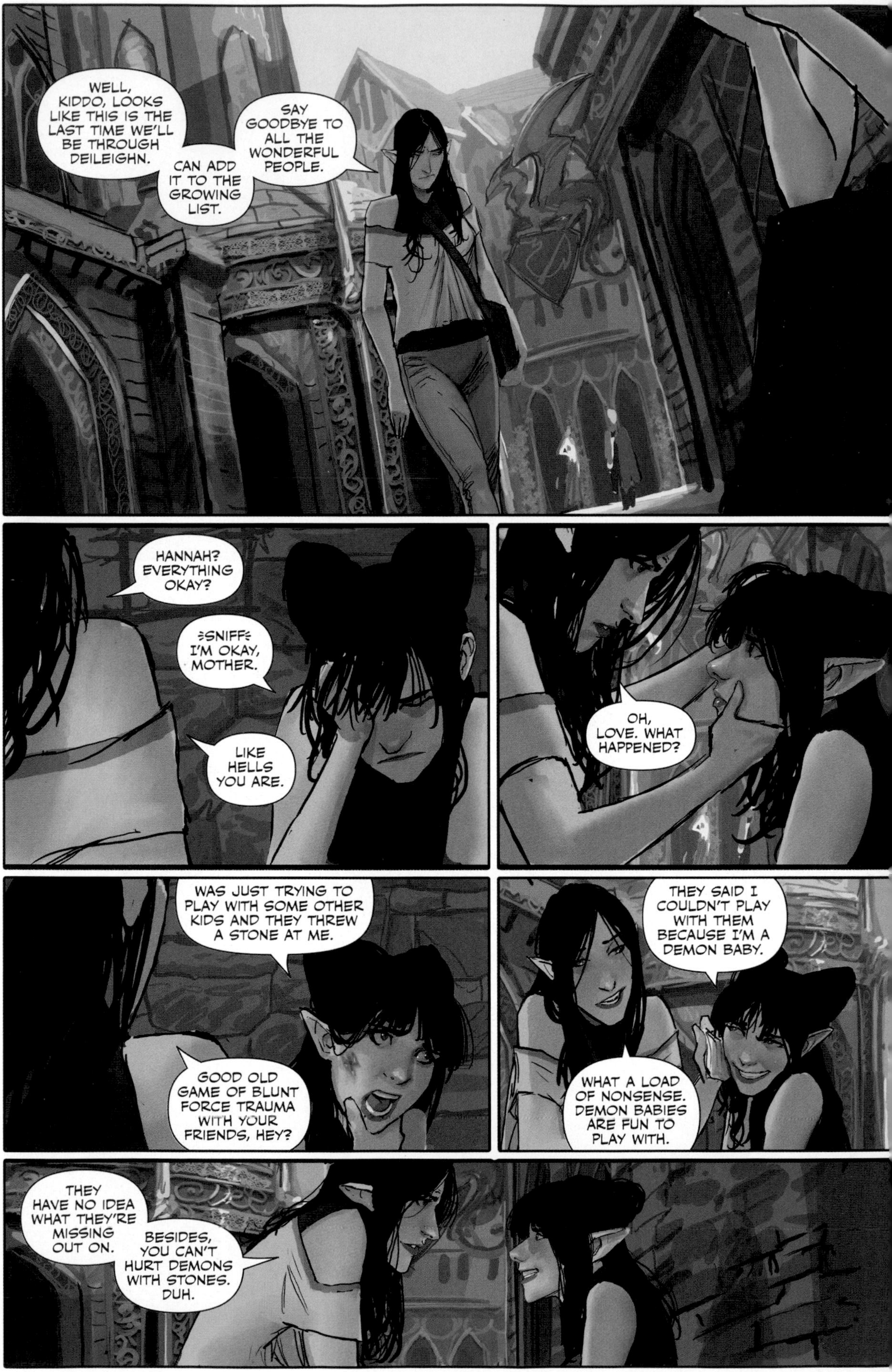
WELL, KIDDO, LOOKS LIKE THIS IS THE LAST TIME WE'LL BE THROUGH DEILEIGHN.
CAN ADD IT TO THE GROWING LIST.
SAY GOODBYE TO ALL THE WONDERFUL PEOPLE.
HANNAH? EVERYTHING OKAY?
≈SNIFF≈ I'M OKAY, MOTHER.
LIKE HELLS YOU ARE.
OH, LOVE. WHAT HAPPENED?
WAS JUST TRYING TO PLAY WITH SOME OTHER KIDS AND THEY THREW A STONE AT ME.
GOOD OLD GAME OF BLUNT FORCE TRAUMA WITH YOUR FRIENDS, HEY?
THEY SAID I COULDN'T PLAY WITH THEM BECAUSE I'M A DEMON BABY.
WHAT A LOAD OF NONSENSE. DEMON BABIES ARE FUN TO PLAY WITH.
THEY HAVE NO IDEA WHAT THEY'RE MISSING OUT ON.
BESIDES, YOU CAN'T HURT DEMONS WITH STONES. DUH.

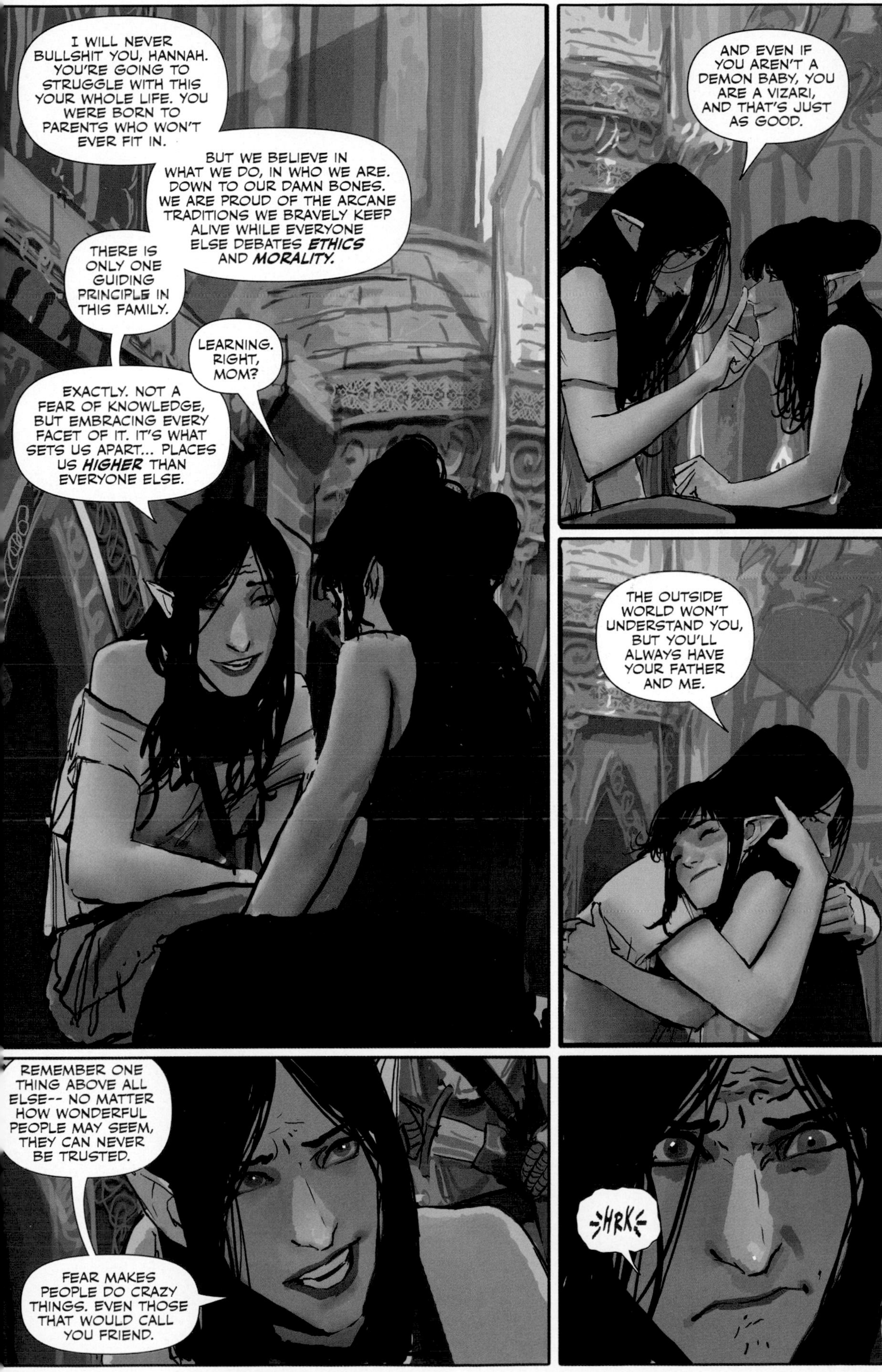
I WILL NEVER BULLSHIT YOU, HANNAH. YOU'RE GOING TO STRUGGLE WITH THIS YOUR WHOLE LIFE. YOU WERE BORN TO PARENTS WHO WON'T EVER FIT IN.
BUT WE BELIEVE IN WHAT WE DO, IN WHO WE ARE. DOWN TO OUR DAMN BONES. WE ARE PROUD OF THE ARCANE TRADITIONS WE BRAVELY KEEP ALIVE WHILE EVERYONE ELSE DEBATES ***ETHICS*** AND ***MORALITY.***
THERE IS ONLY ONE GUIDING PRINCIPLE IN THIS FAMILY.
LEARNING. RIGHT, MOM?
EXACTLY. NOT A FEAR OF KNOWLEDGE, BUT EMBRACING EVERY FACET OF IT. IT'S WHAT SETS US APART... PLACES US ***HIGHER*** THAN EVERYONE ELSE.
AND EVEN IF YOU AREN'T A DEMON BABY, YOU ARE A VIZARI, AND THAT'S JUST AS GOOD.
THE OUTSIDE WORLD WON'T UNDERSTAND YOU, BUT YOU'LL ALWAYS HAVE YOUR FATHER AND ME.
REMEMBER ONE THING ABOVE ALL ELSE-- NO MATTER HOW WONDERFUL PEOPLE MAY SEEM, THEY CAN NEVER BE TRUSTED.
FEAR MAKES PEOPLE DO CRAZY THINGS. EVEN THOSE THAT WOULD CALL YOU FRIEND.
HRK

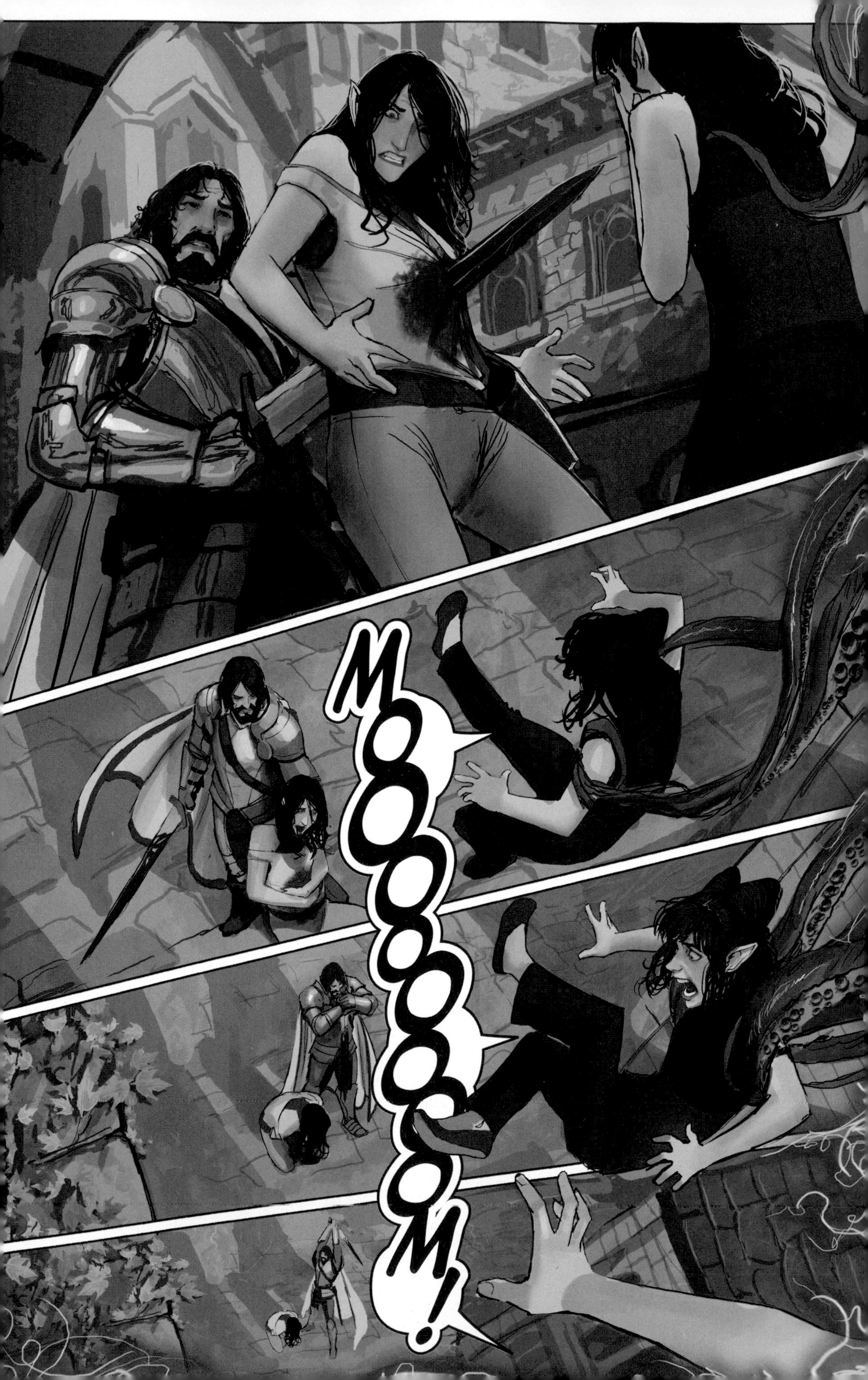
MOOOOOOOOM!

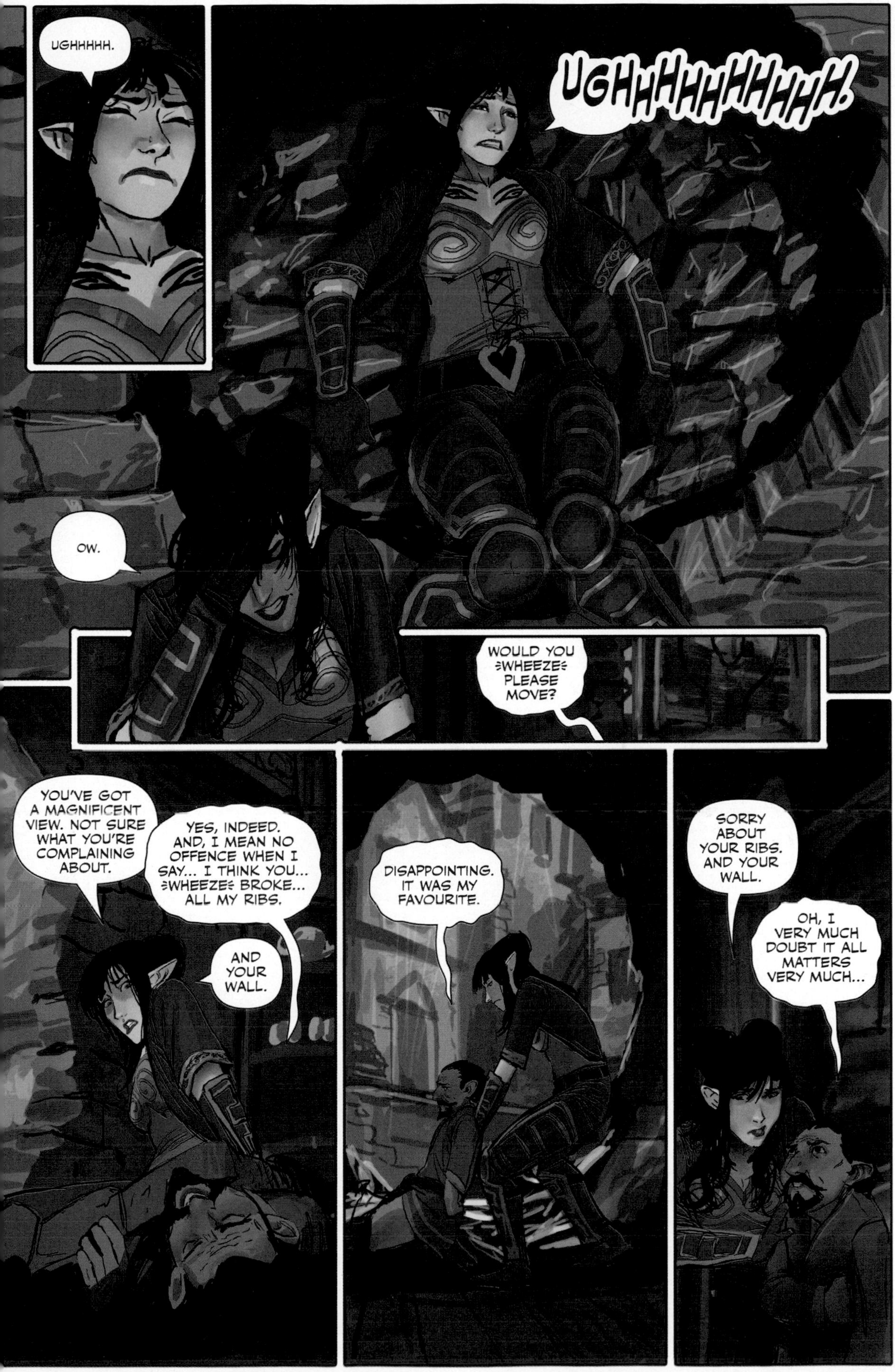
UGHHHHH.
UGHHHHHHHHHH.
OW.
WOULD YOU ≈WHEEZE≈ PLEASE MOVE?
YOU'VE GOT A MAGNIFICENT VIEW. NOT SURE WHAT YOU'RE COMPLAINING ABOUT.
YES, INDEED. AND, I MEAN NO OFFENCE WHEN I SAY... I THINK YOU... ≈WHEEZE≈ BROKE... ALL MY RIBS.
AND YOUR WALL.
DISAPPOINTING. IT WAS MY FAVOURITE.
SORRY ABOUT YOUR RIBS. AND YOUR WALL.
OH, I VERY MUCH DOUBT IT ALL MATTERS VERY MUCH...

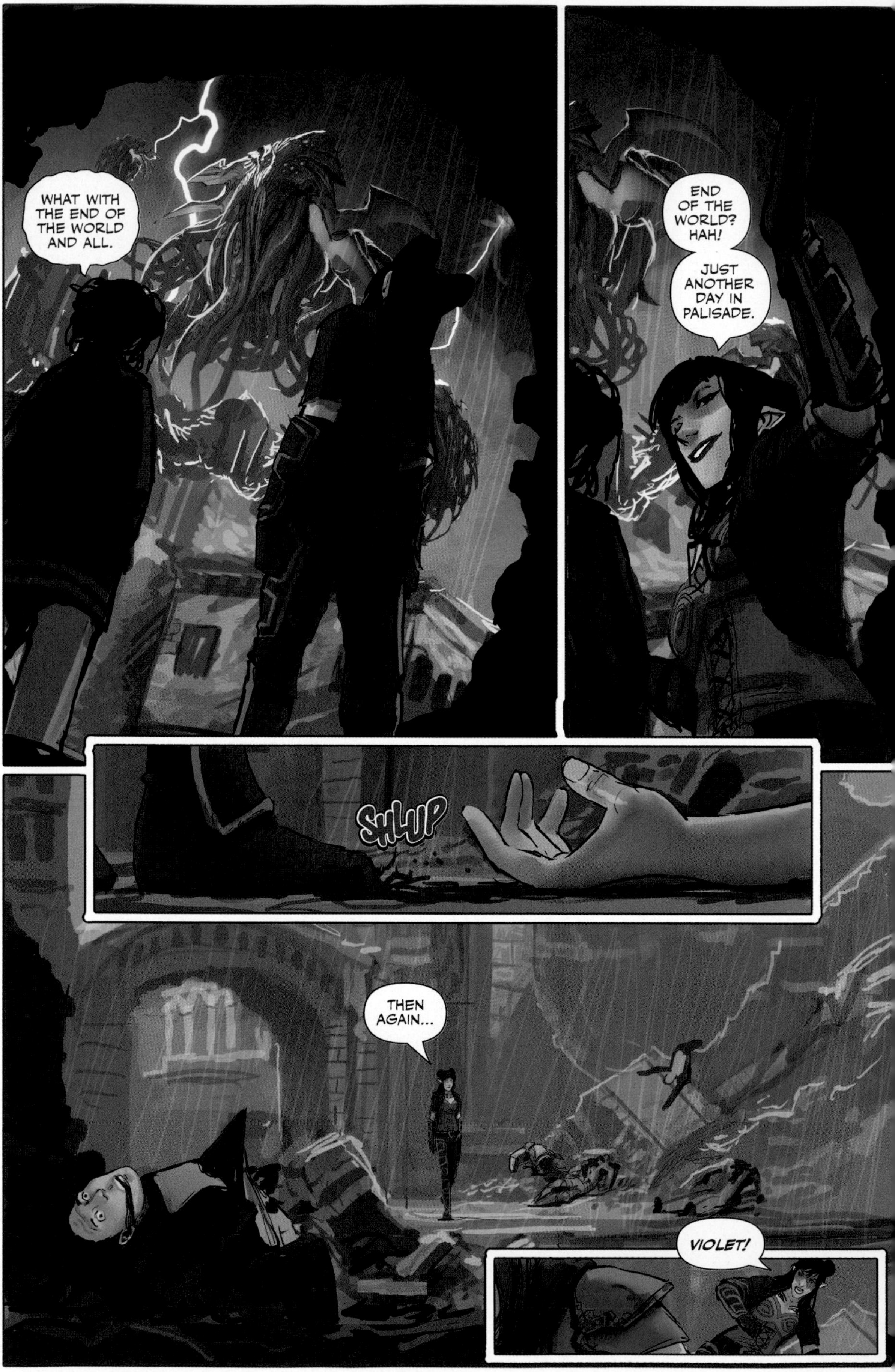
WHAT WITH THE END OF THE WORLD AND ALL.
END OF THE WORLD? HAH!
JUST ANOTHER DAY IN PALISADE.
SHLUP
THEN AGAIN...
VIOLET!

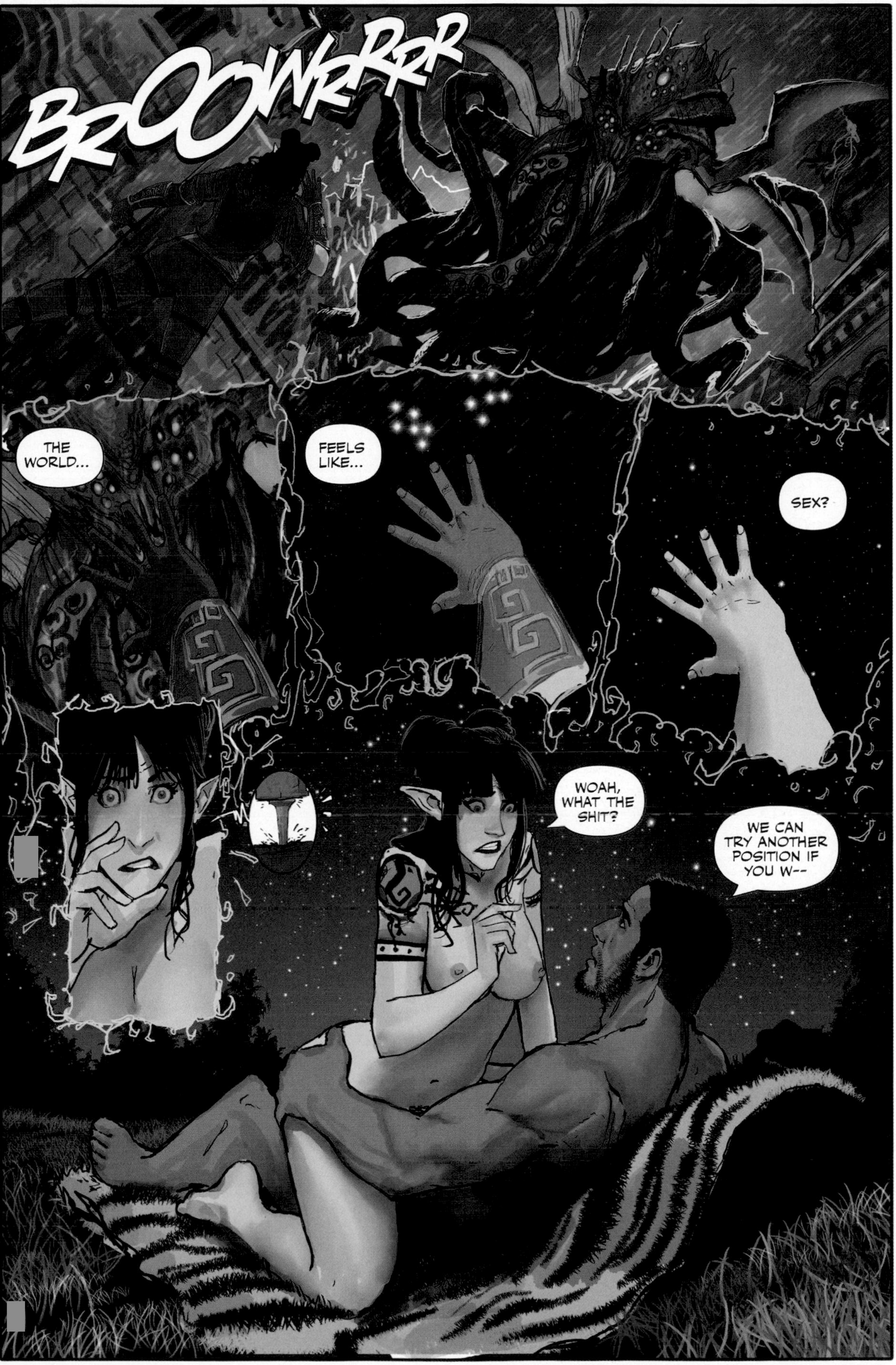
BROOOWRRRR
THE WORLD...
FEELS LIKE...
SEX?
WOAH, WHAT THE SHIT?
WE CAN TRY ANOTHER POSITION IF YOU W--

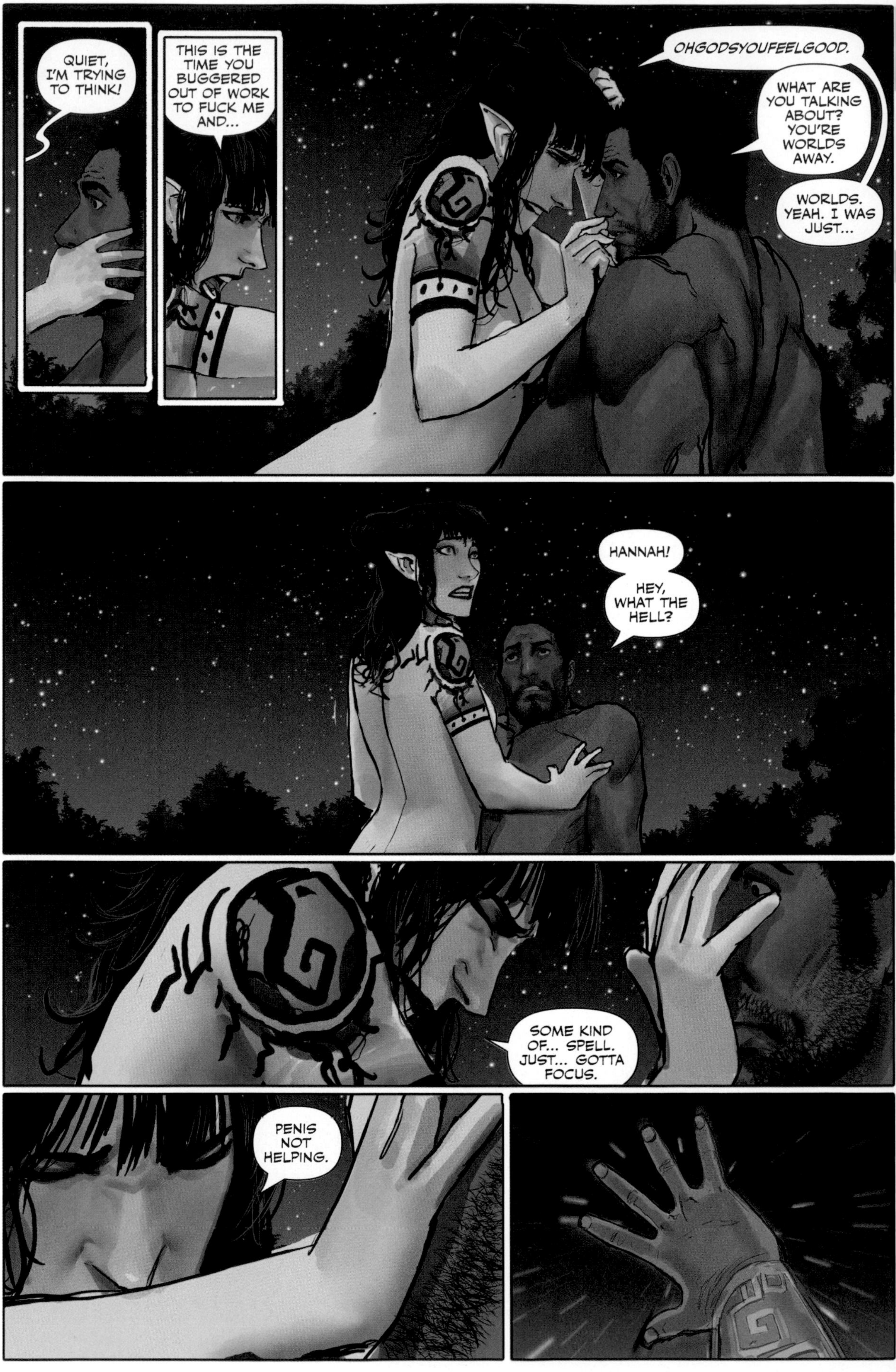
QUIET, I'M TRYING TO THINK!
THIS IS THE TIME YOU BUGGERED OUT OF WORK TO FUCK ME AND...
OHGODSYOUFEELGOOD.
WHAT ARE YOU TALKING ABOUT? YOU'RE WORLDS AWAY.
WORLDS. YEAH. I WAS JUST...
HANNAH!
HEY, WHAT THE HELL?
SOME KIND OF... SPELL. JUST... GOTTA FOCUS.
PENIS NOT HELPING.

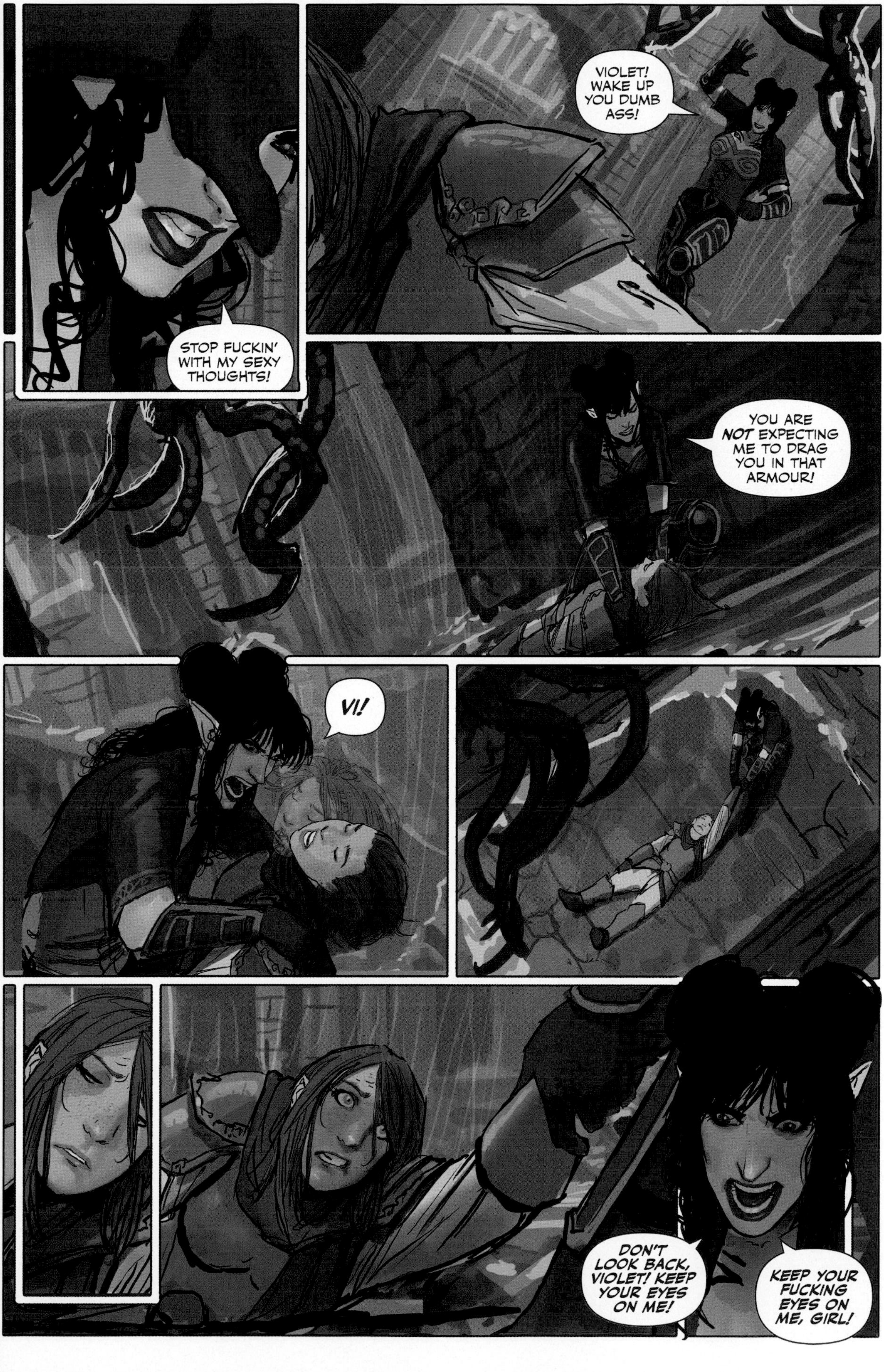
STOP FUCKIN' WITH MY SEXY THOUGHTS!
VIOLET! WAKE UP YOU DUMB ASS!
YOU ARE NOT EXPECTING ME TO DRAG YOU IN THAT ARMOUR!
VI!
DON'T LOOK BACK, VIOLET! KEEP YOUR EYES ON ME!
KEEP YOUR FUCKING EYES ON ME, GIRL!

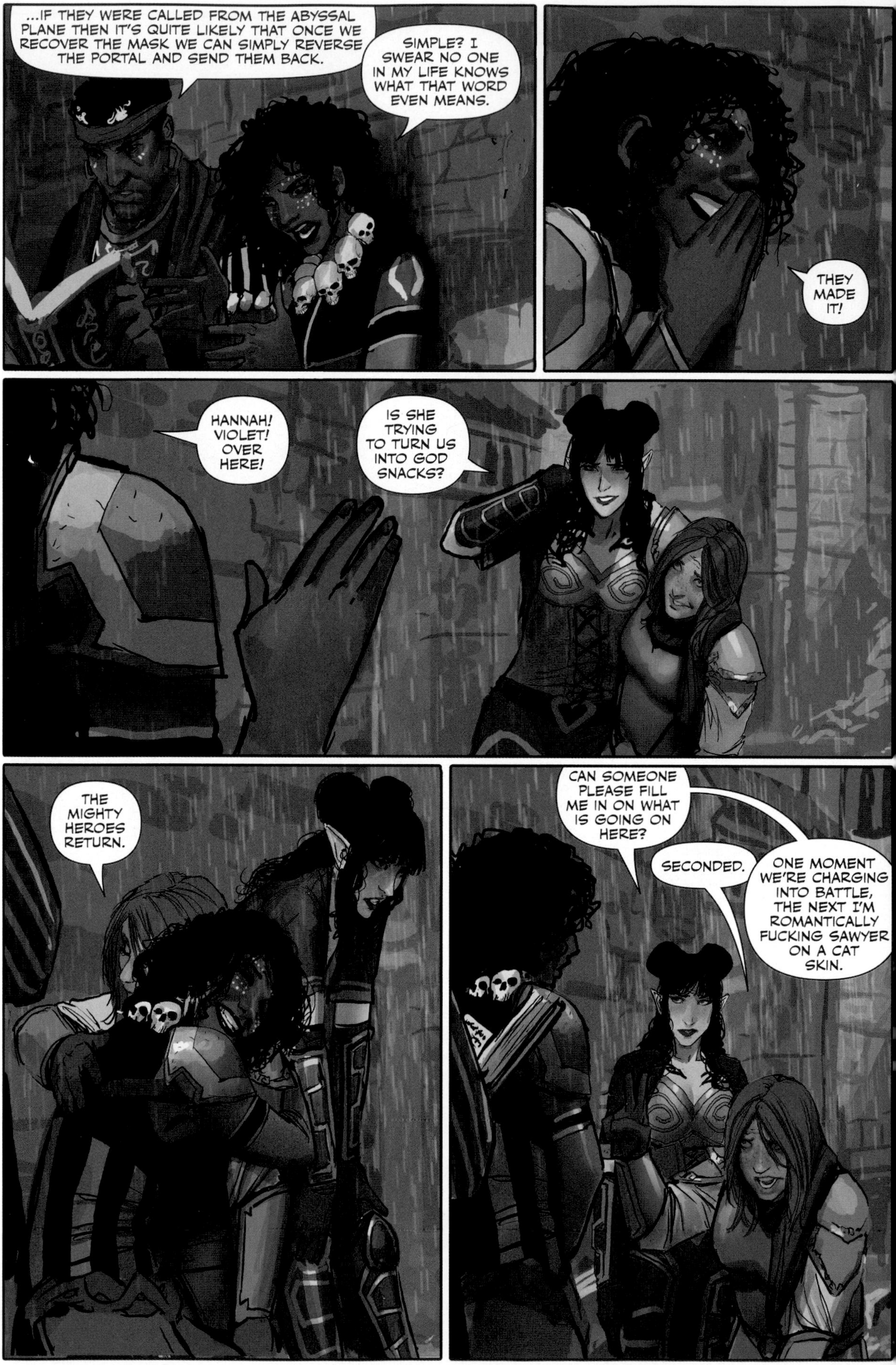
...IF THEY WERE CALLED FROM THE ABYSSAL PLANE THEN IT'S QUITE LIKELY THAT ONCE WE RECOVER THE MASK WE CAN SIMPLY REVERSE THE PORTAL AND SEND THEM BACK.
SIMPLE? I SWEAR NO ONE IN MY LIFE KNOWS WHAT THAT WORD EVEN MEANS.
THEY MADE IT!
HANNAH! VIOLET! OVER HERE!
IS SHE TRYING TO TURN US INTO GOD SNACKS?
THE MIGHTY HEROES RETURN.
CAN SOMEONE PLEASE FILL ME IN ON WHAT IS GOING ON HERE?
SECONDED.
ONE MOMENT WE'RE CHARGING INTO BATTLE, THE NEXT I'M ROMANTICALLY FUCKING SAWYER ON A CAT SKIN.

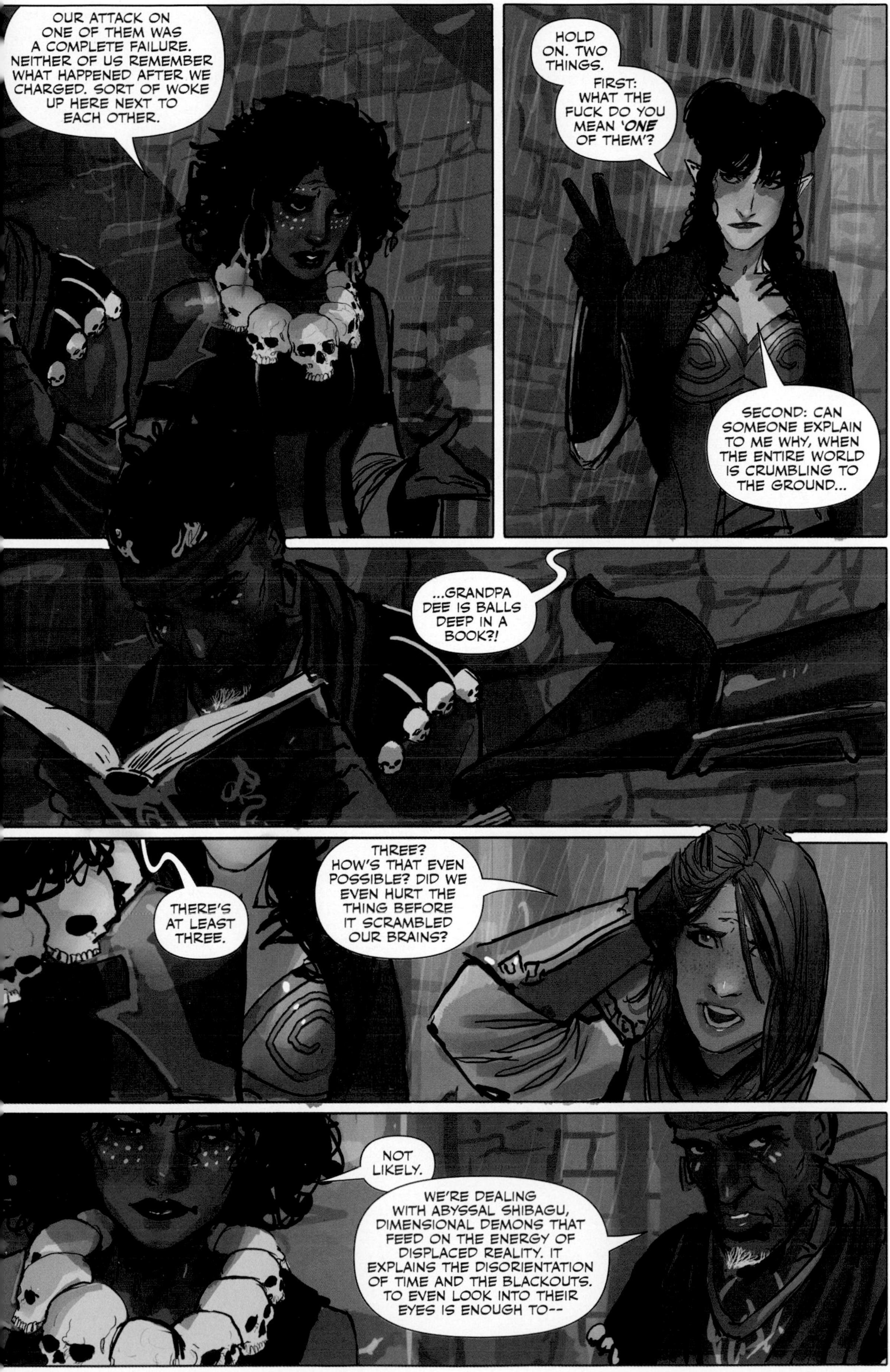
OUR ATTACK ON ONE OF THEM WAS A COMPLETE FAILURE. NEITHER OF US REMEMBER WHAT HAPPENED AFTER WE CHARGED. SORT OF WOKE UP HERE NEXT TO EACH OTHER.
HOLD ON. TWO THINGS.
FIRST: WHAT THE FUCK DO YOU MEAN 'ONE OF THEM'?
SECOND: CAN SOMEONE EXPLAIN TO ME WHY, WHEN THE ENTIRE WORLD IS CRUMBLING TO THE GROUND...
...GRANDPA DEE IS BALLS DEEP IN A BOOK?!
THERE'S AT LEAST THREE.
THREE? HOW'S THAT EVEN POSSIBLE? DID WE EVEN HURT THE THING BEFORE IT SCRAMBLED OUR BRAINS?
NOT LIKELY.
WE'RE DEALING WITH ABYSSAL SHIBAGU, DIMENSIONAL DEMONS THAT FEED ON THE ENERGY OF DISPLACED REALITY. IT EXPLAINS THE DISORIENTATION OF TIME AND THE BLACKOUTS. TO EVEN LOOK INTO THEIR EYES IS ENOUGH TO--

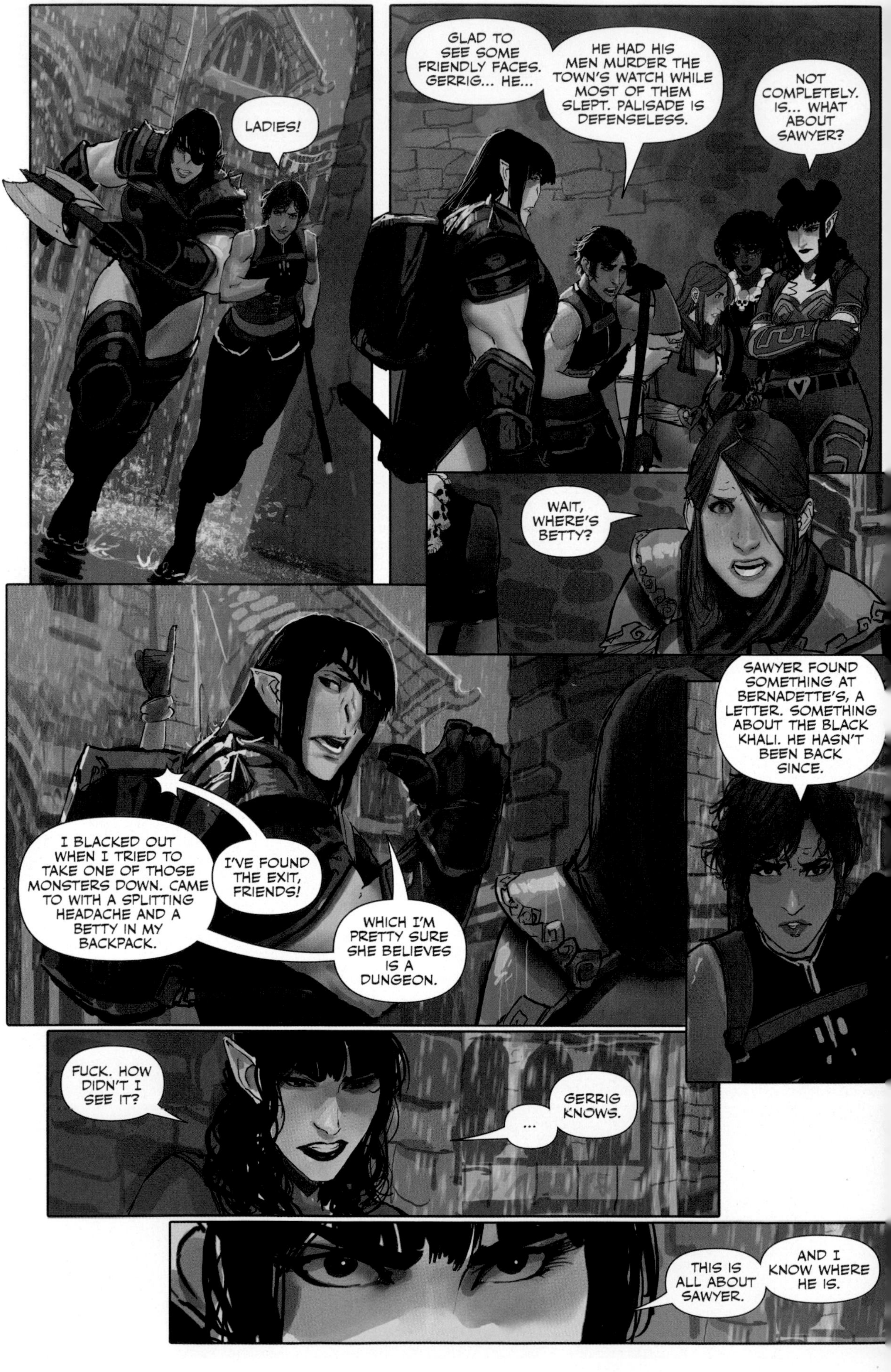
LADIES!
GLAD TO SEE SOME FRIENDLY FACES. GERRIG... HE...
HE HAD HIS MEN MURDER THE TOWN'S WATCH WHILE MOST OF THEM SLEPT. PALISADE IS DEFENSELESS.
NOT COMPLETELY. IS... WHAT ABOUT SAWYER?
WAIT, WHERE'S BETTY?
I'VE FOUND THE EXIT, FRIENDS!
I BLACKED OUT WHEN I TRIED TO TAKE ONE OF THOSE MONSTERS DOWN. CAME TO WITH A SPLITTING HEADACHE AND A BETTY IN MY BACKPACK.
WHICH I'M PRETTY SURE SHE BELIEVES IS A DUNGEON.
SAWYER FOUND SOMETHING AT BERNADETTE'S, A LETTER. SOMETHING ABOUT THE BLACK KHALI. HE HASN'T BEEN BACK SINCE.
FUCK. HOW DIDN'T I SEE IT?
...
GERRIG KNOWS.
THIS IS ALL ABOUT SAWYER.
AND I KNOW WHERE HE IS.

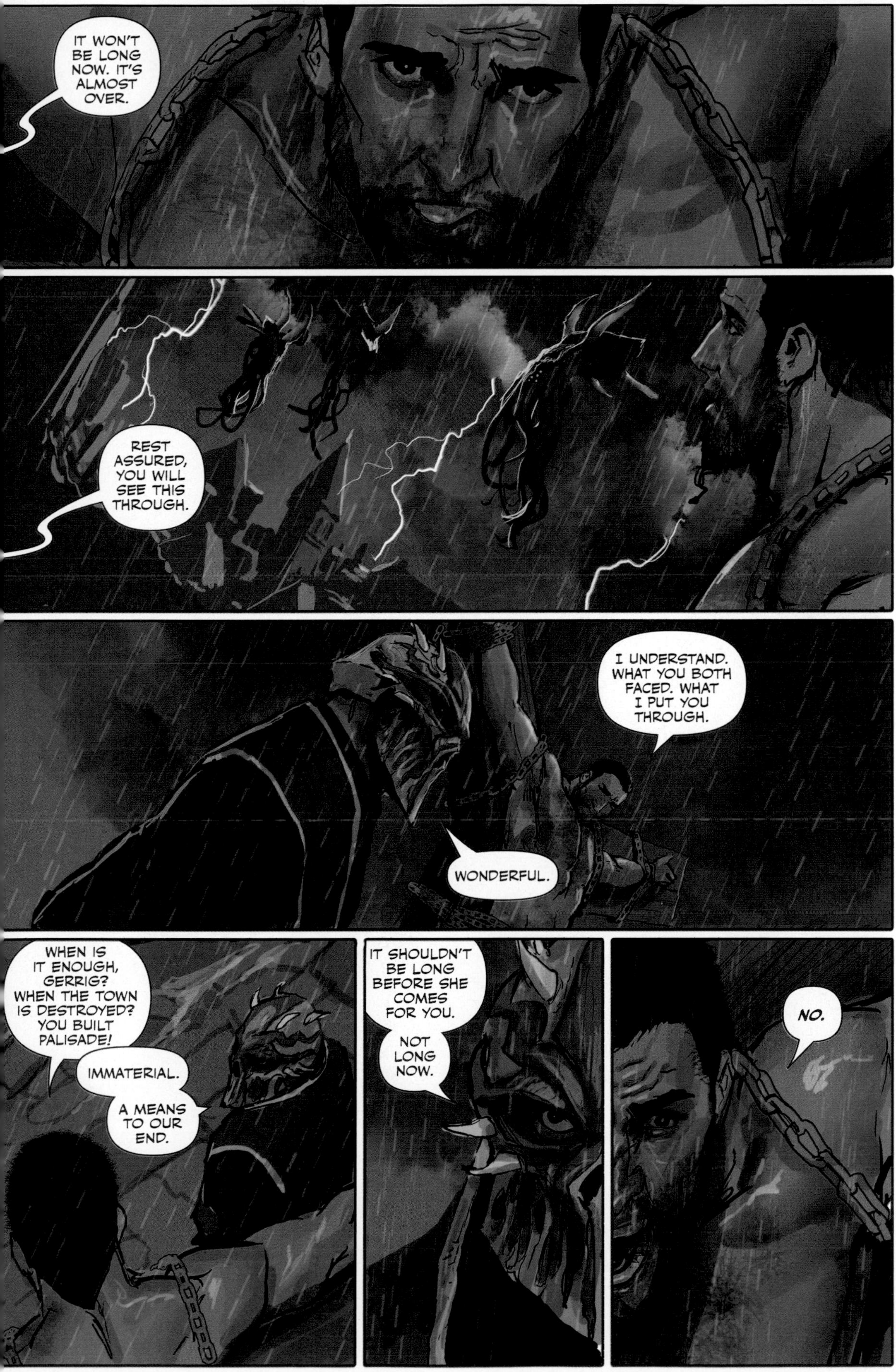
IT WON'T BE LONG NOW. IT'S ALMOST OVER.
REST ASSURED, YOU WILL SEE THIS THROUGH.
I UNDERSTAND. WHAT YOU BOTH FACED. WHAT I PUT YOU THROUGH.
WONDERFUL.
WHEN IS IT ENOUGH, GERRIG? WHEN THE TOWN IS DESTROYED? YOU BUILT PALISADE!
IMMATERIAL.
A MEANS TO OUR END.
IT SHOULDN'T BE LONG BEFORE SHE COMES FOR YOU.
NOT LONG NOW.
NO.

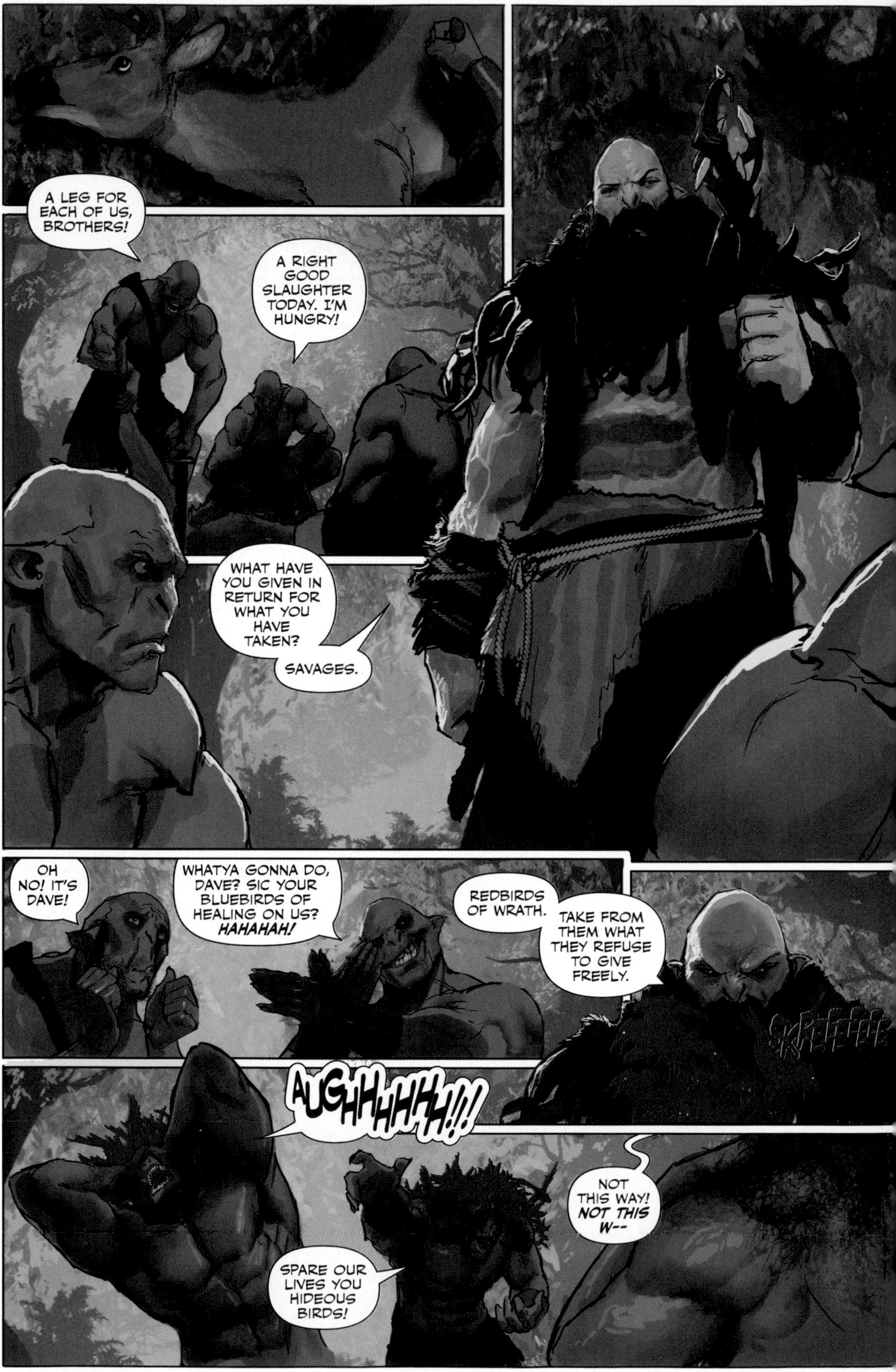

A LEG FOR EACH OF US, BROTHERS!
A RIGHT GOOD SLAUGHTER TODAY. I'M HUNGRY!
WHAT HAVE YOU GIVEN IN RETURN FOR WHAT YOU HAVE TAKEN?
SAVAGES.
OH NO! IT'S DAVE!
WHATYA GONNA DO, DAVE? SIC YOUR BLUEBIRDS OF HEALING ON US? *HAHAHAH!*
REDBIRDS OF WRATH.
TAKE FROM THEM WHAT THEY REFUSE TO GIVE FREELY.
SKREEEEEE
AUGHHHHHH!!!
NOT THIS WAY! *NOT THIS W--*
SPARE OUR LIVES YOU HIDEOUS BIRDS!

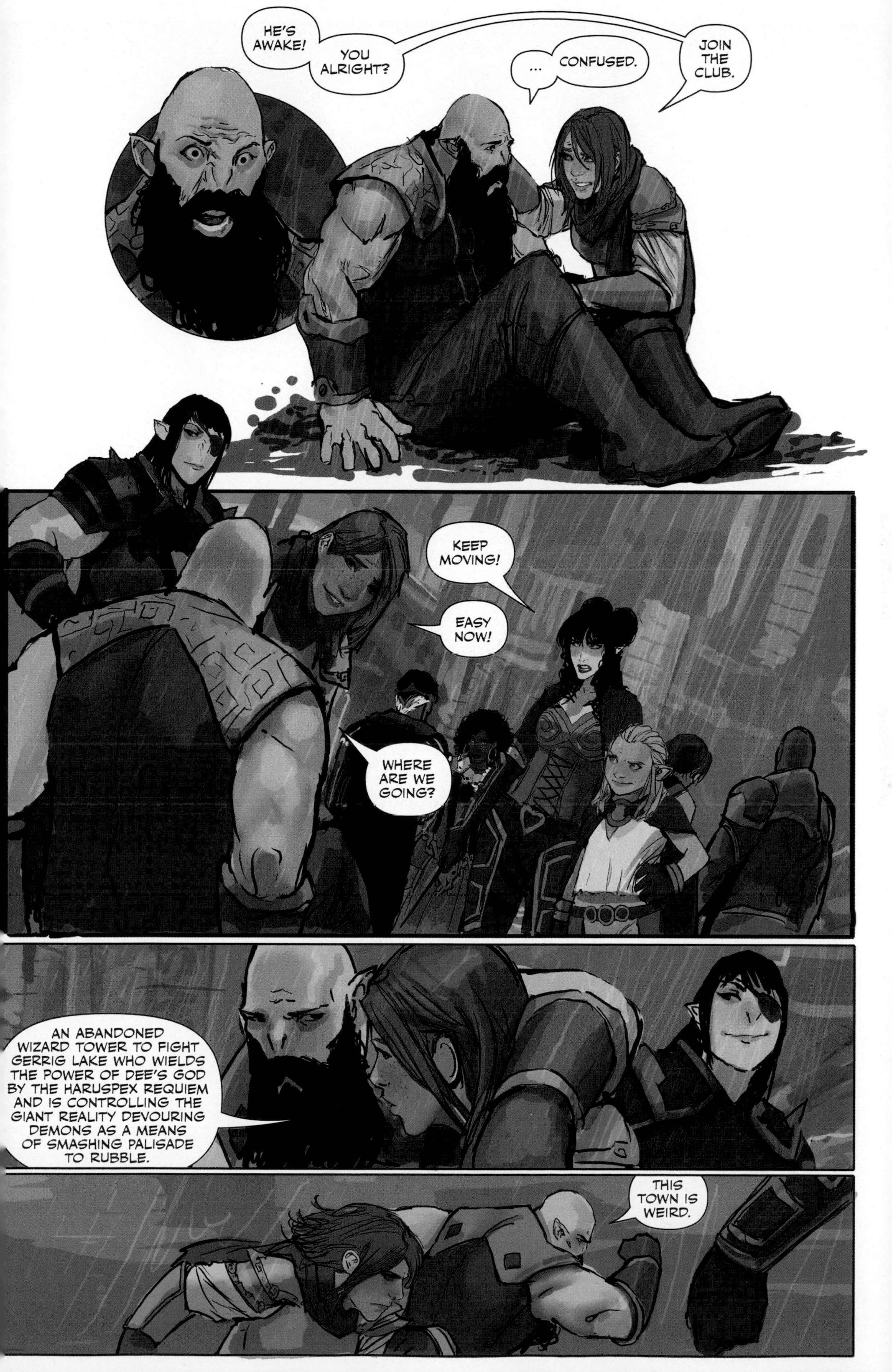
HE'S AWAKE!
YOU ALRIGHT?
... CONFUSED.
JOIN THE CLUB.
KEEP MOVING!
EASY NOW!
WHERE ARE WE GOING?
AN ABANDONED WIZARD TOWER TO FIGHT GERRIG LAKE WHO WIELDS THE POWER OF DEE'S GOD BY THE HARUSPEX REQUIEM AND IS CONTROLLING THE GIANT REALITY DEVOURING DEMONS AS A MEANS OF SMASHING PALISADE TO RUBBLE.
THIS TOWN IS WEIRD.

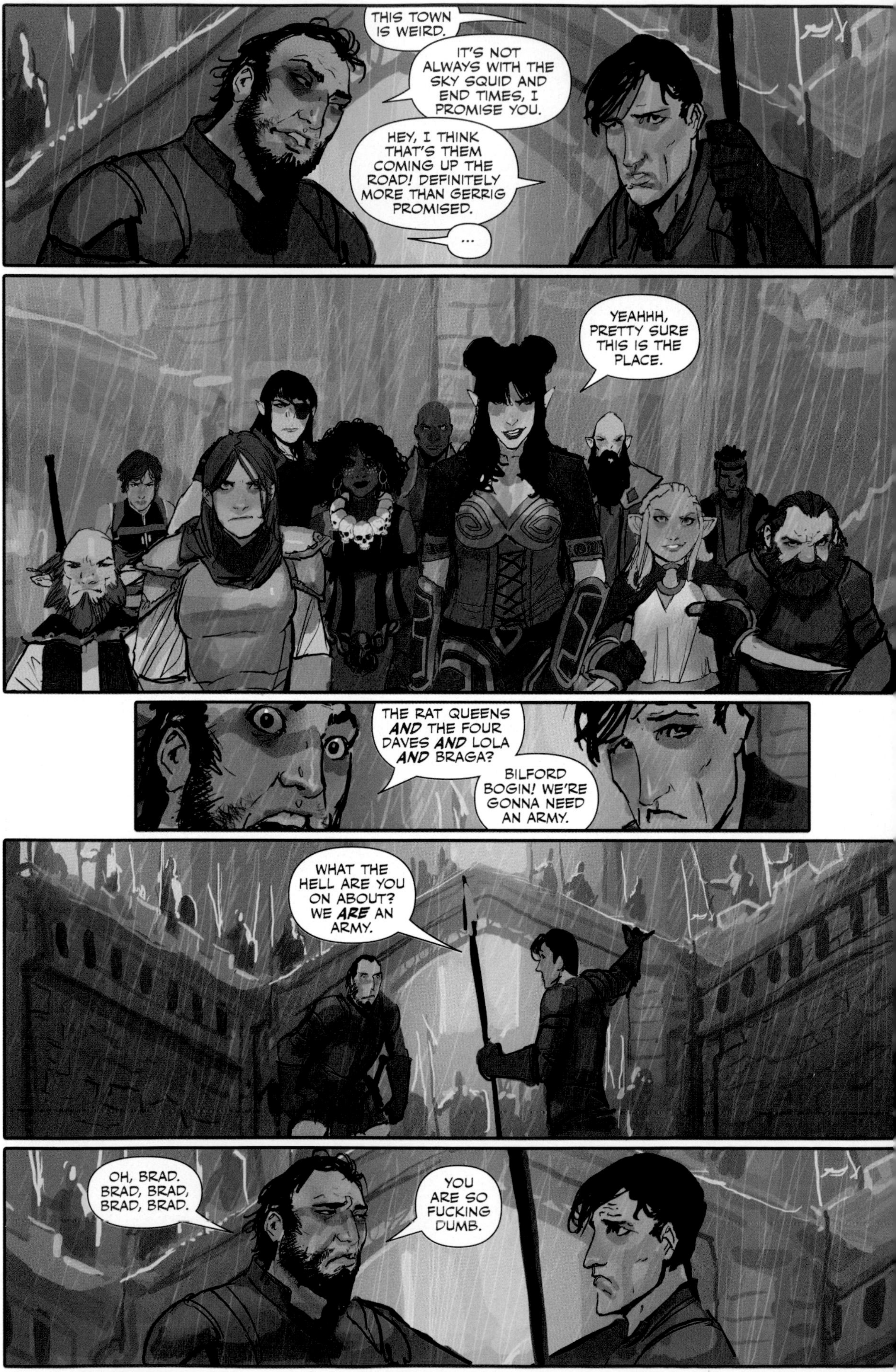
THIS TOWN IS WEIRD.
IT'S NOT ALWAYS WITH THE SKY SQUID AND END TIMES, I PROMISE YOU.
HEY, I THINK THAT'S THEM COMING UP THE ROAD! DEFINITELY MORE THAN GERRIG PROMISED.
...
YEAHHH, PRETTY SURE THIS IS THE PLACE.
THE RAT QUEENS *AND* THE FOUR DAVES *AND* LOLA *AND* BRAGA?
BILFORD BOGIN! WE'RE GONNA NEED AN ARMY.
WHAT THE HELL ARE YOU ON ABOUT? WE *ARE* AN ARMY.
OH, BRAD. BRAD, BRAD, BRAD, BRAD.
YOU ARE SO FUCKING DUMB.

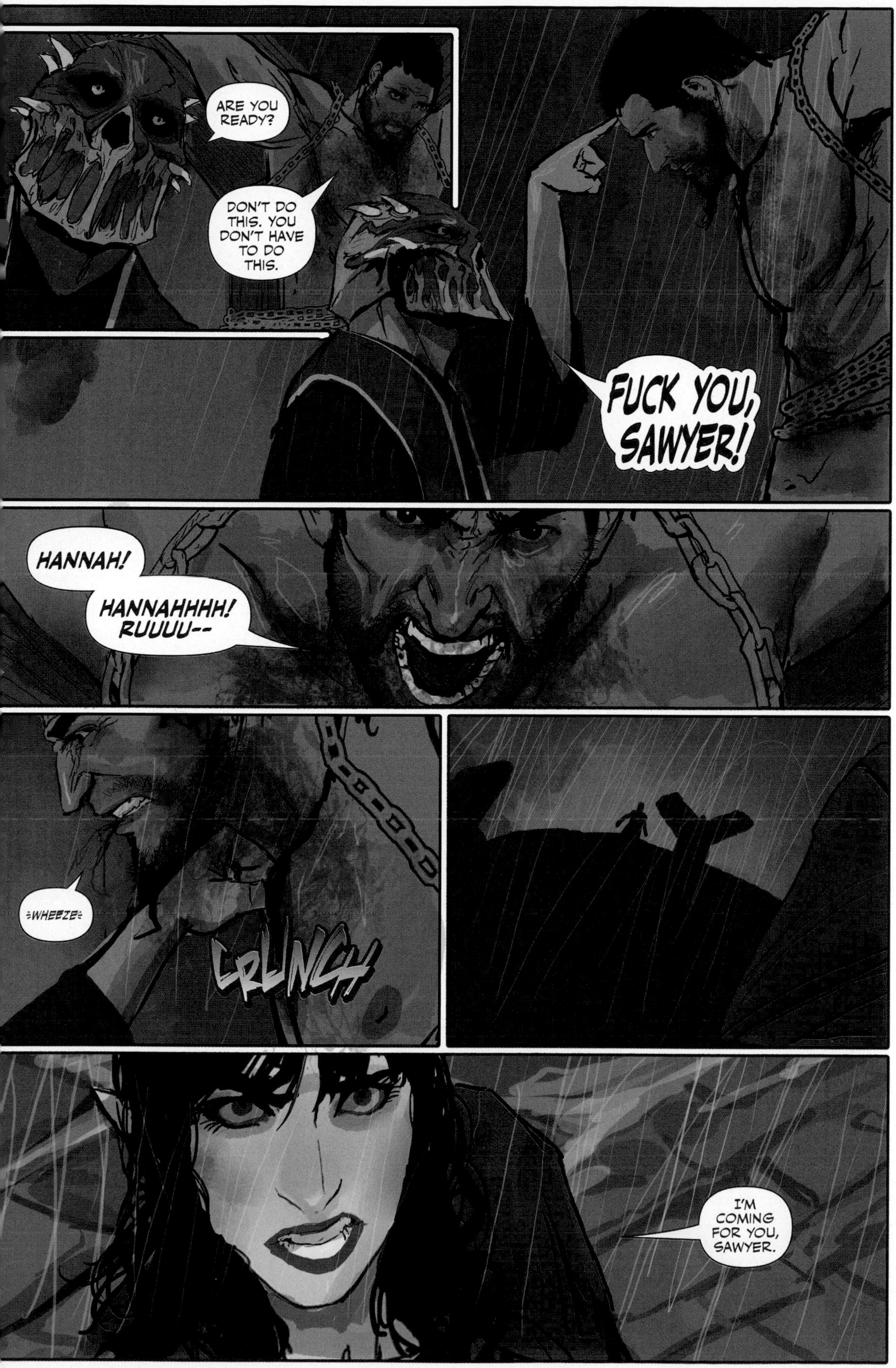
ARE YOU READY?
DON'T DO THIS. YOU DON'T HAVE TO DO THIS.
FUCK YOU, SAWYER!
HANNAH!
HANNAHHHH! RUUUU--
=WHEEZE=
CRUNCH
I'M COMING FOR YOU, SAWYER.

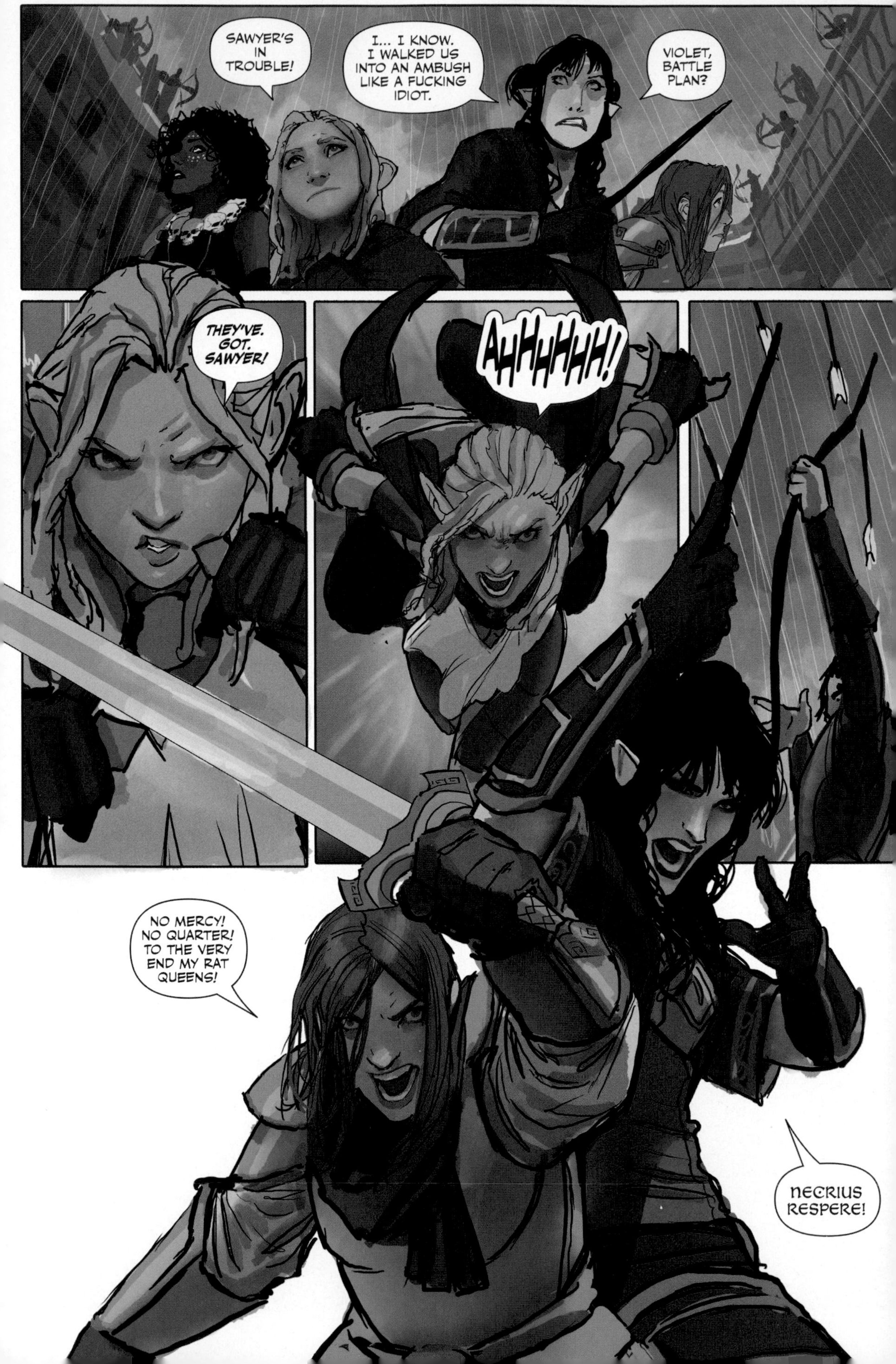
SAWYER'S IN TROUBLE!
I... I KNOW. I WALKED US INTO AN AMBUSH LIKE A FUCKING IDIOT.
VIOLET, BATTLE PLAN?
THEY'VE. GOT. SAWYER!
AHHHHHH!
NO MERCY! NO QUARTER! TO THE VERY END MY RAT QUEENS!
NECRIUS RESPERE!

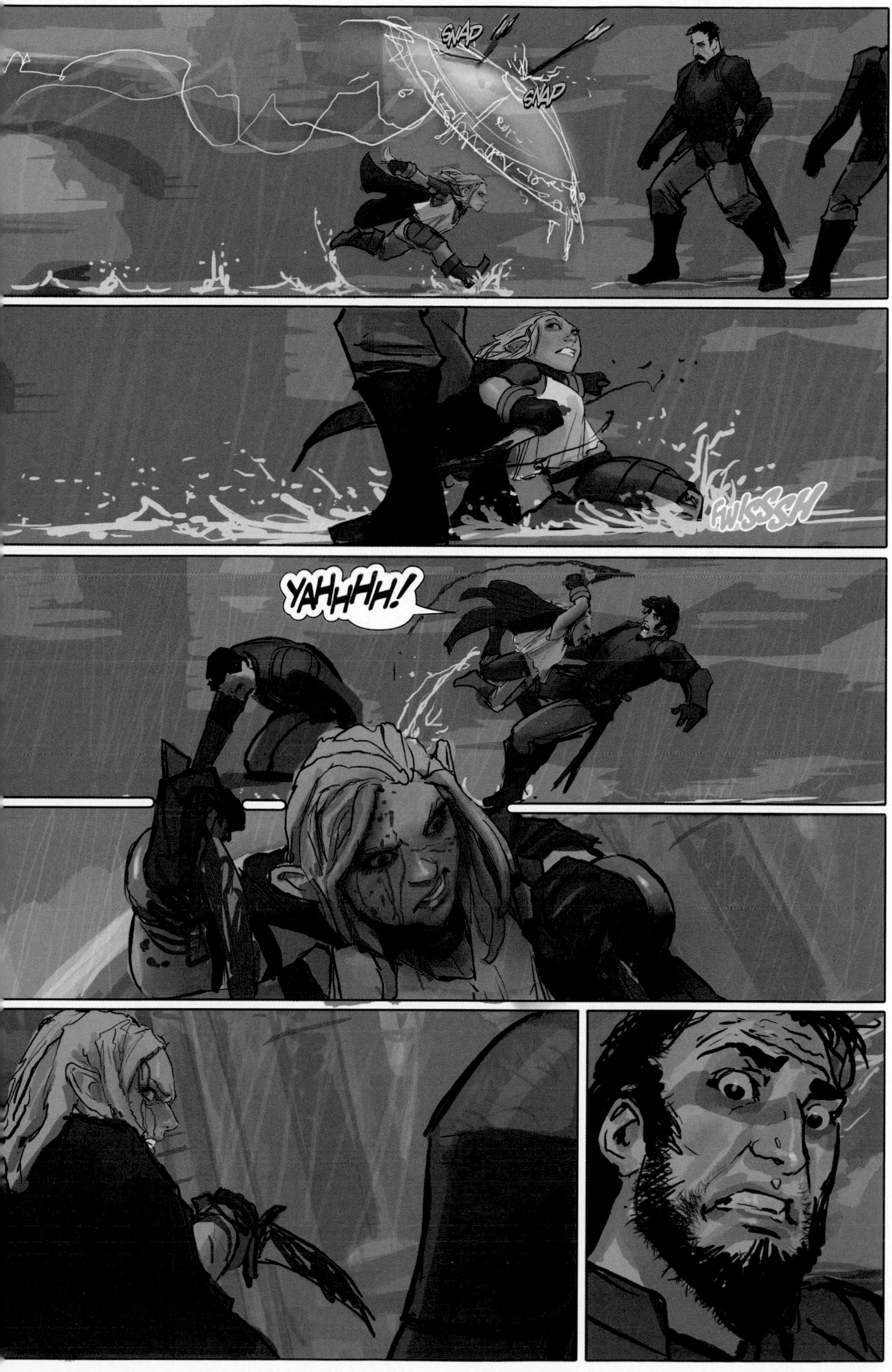
SNAP
SNAP
FWISSSH
YAHHHH!

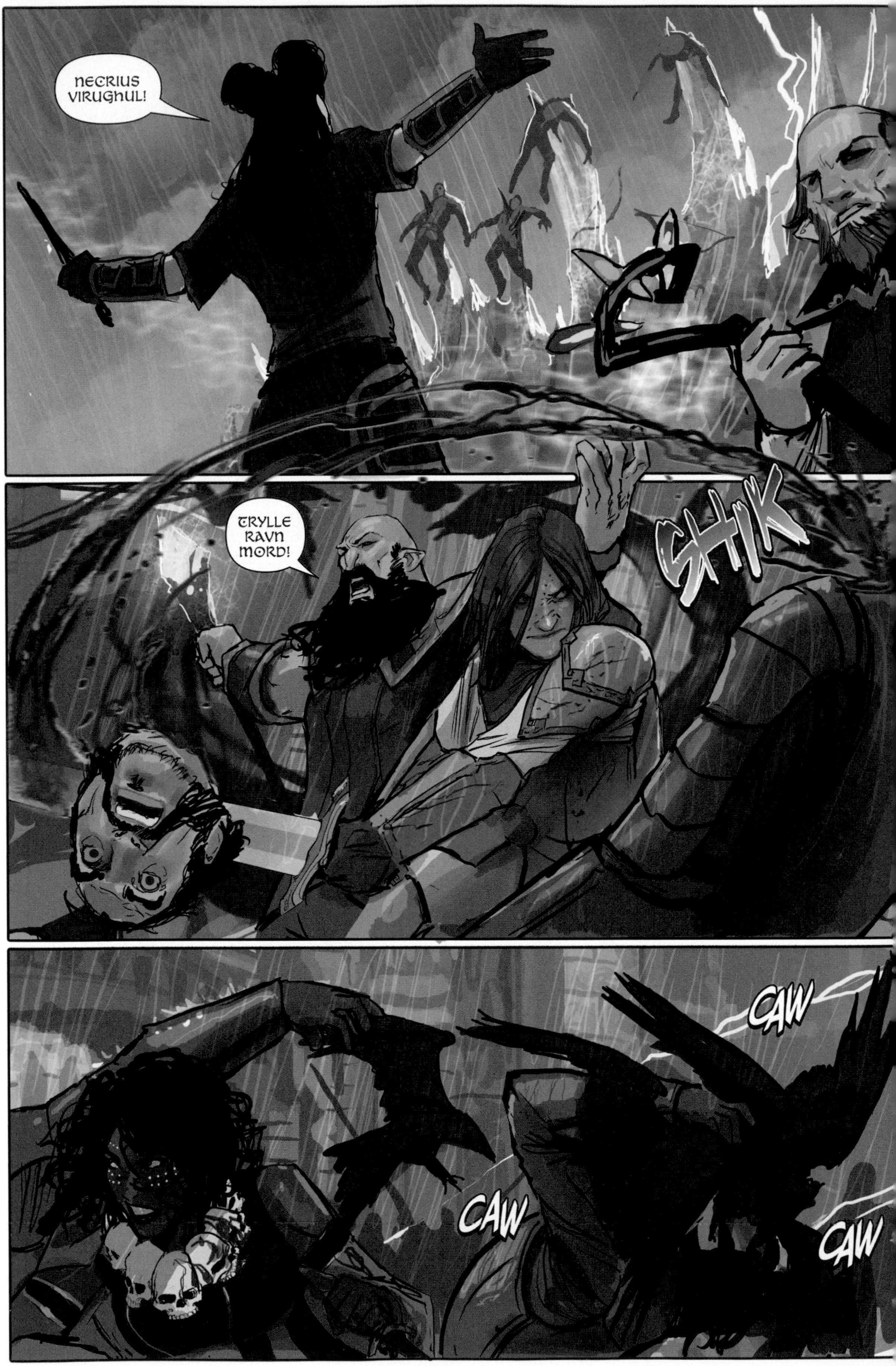
NECRIUS VIRUGHUL!
TRYLLE RAVN MORD!
SHIK
CAW
CAW
CAW

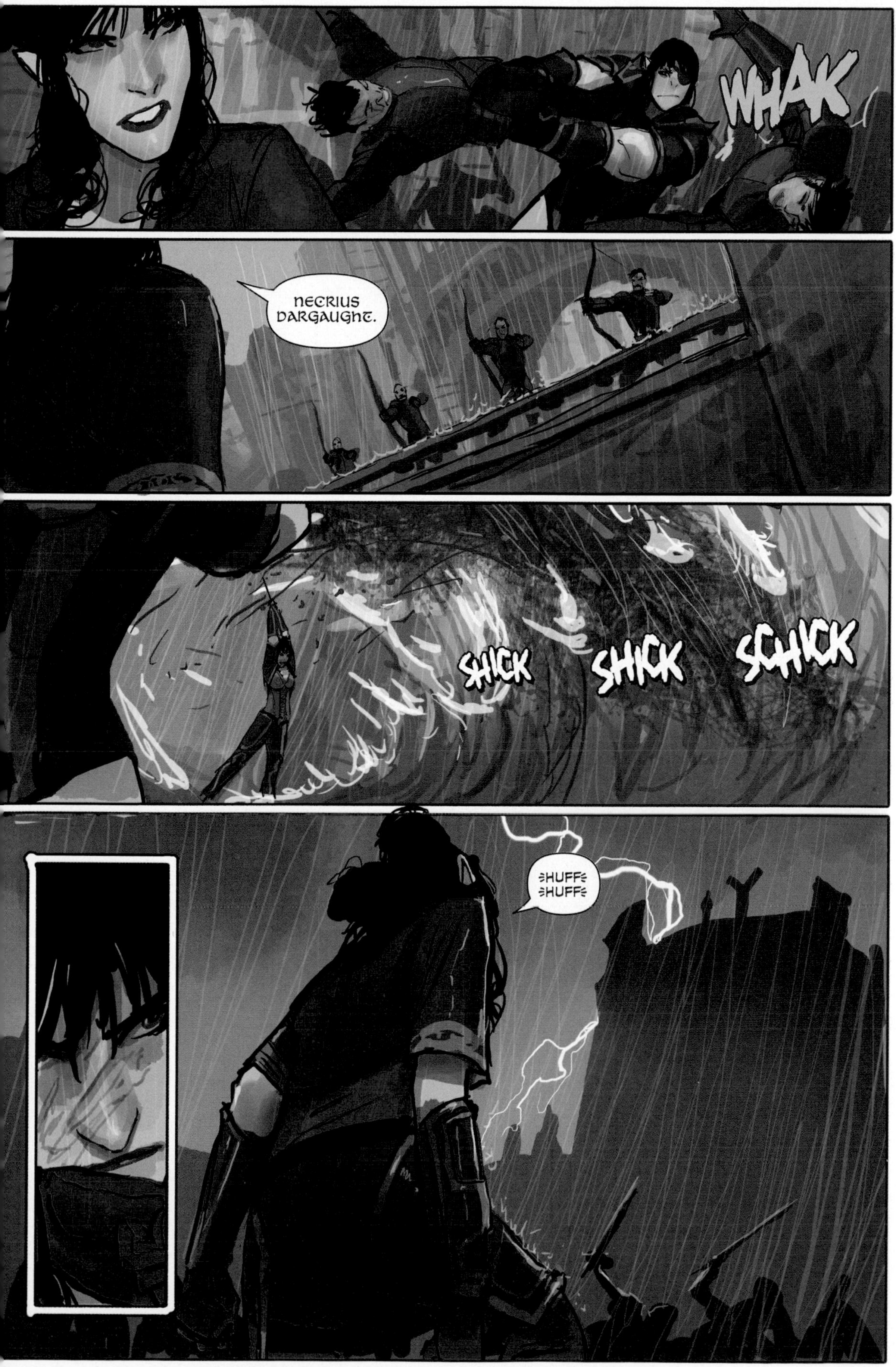
WHAK
NECRIUS DARGAUGHT.
SHICK
SHICK
SCHICK
HUFF HUFF

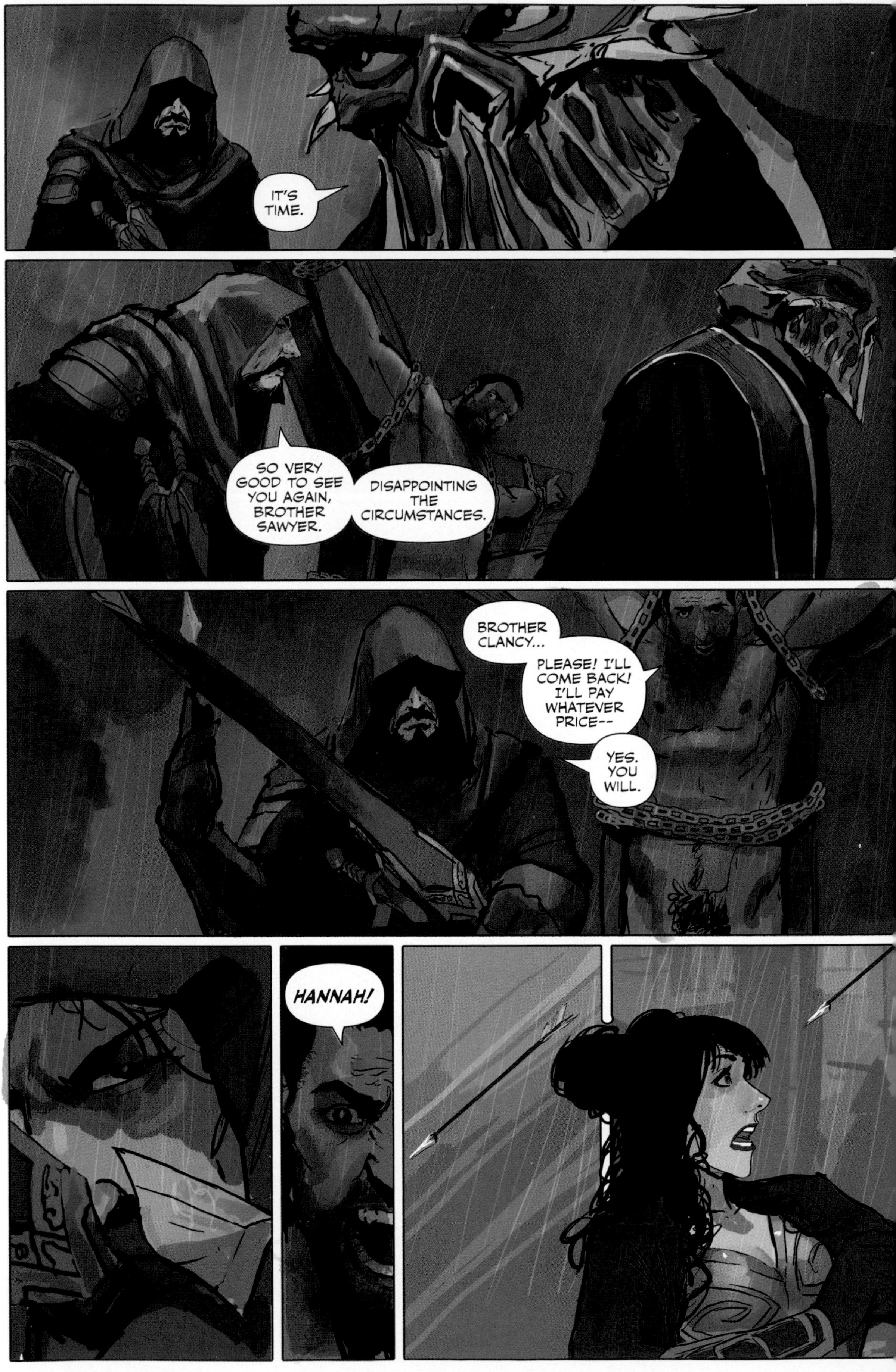
IT'S TIME.
SO VERY GOOD TO SEE YOU AGAIN, BROTHER SAWYER.
DISAPPOINTING THE CIRCUMSTANCES.
BROTHER CLANCY...
PLEASE! I'LL COME BACK! I'LL PAY WHATEVER PRICE--
YES. YOU WILL.
HANNAH!

CHAPTER TEN

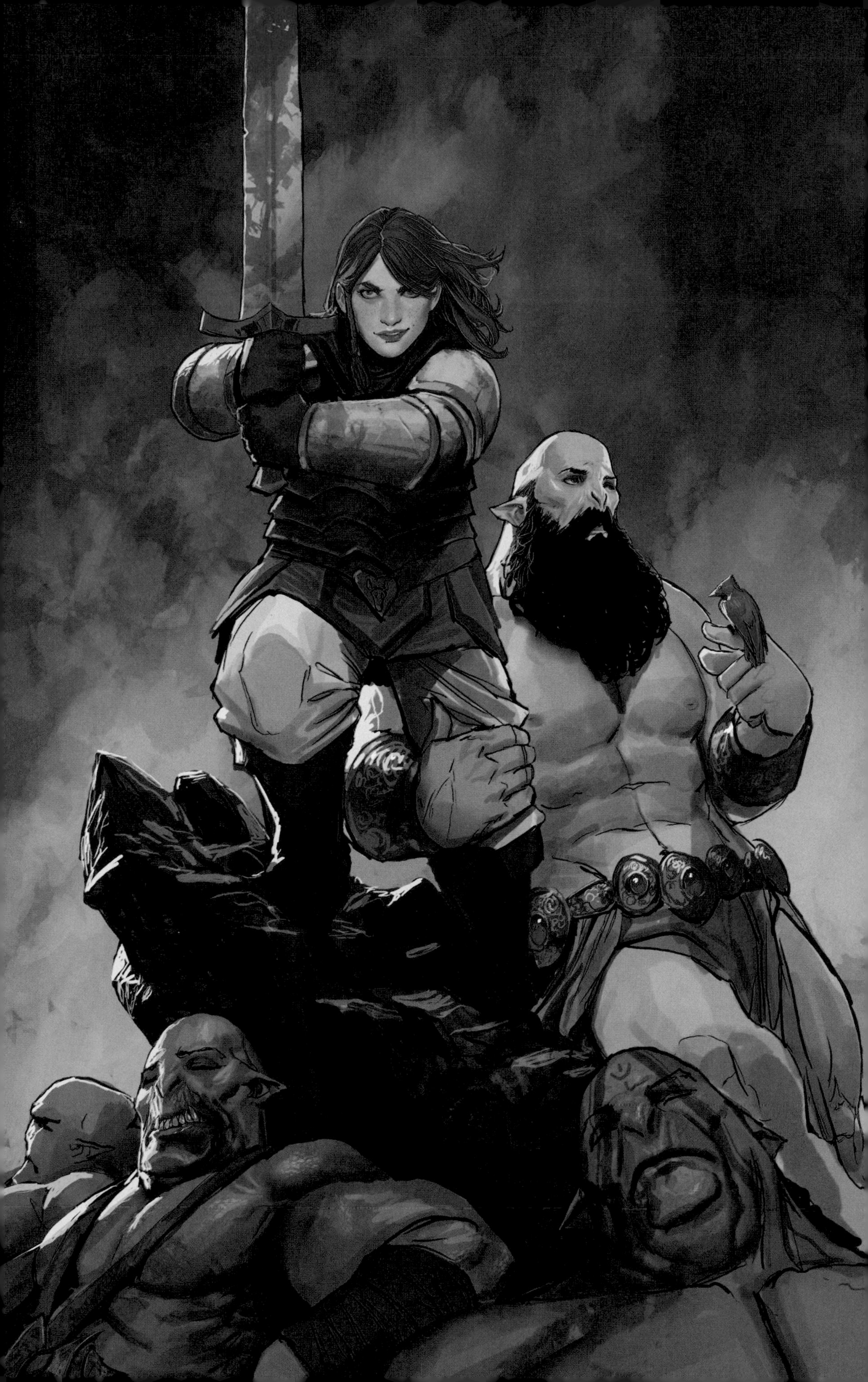

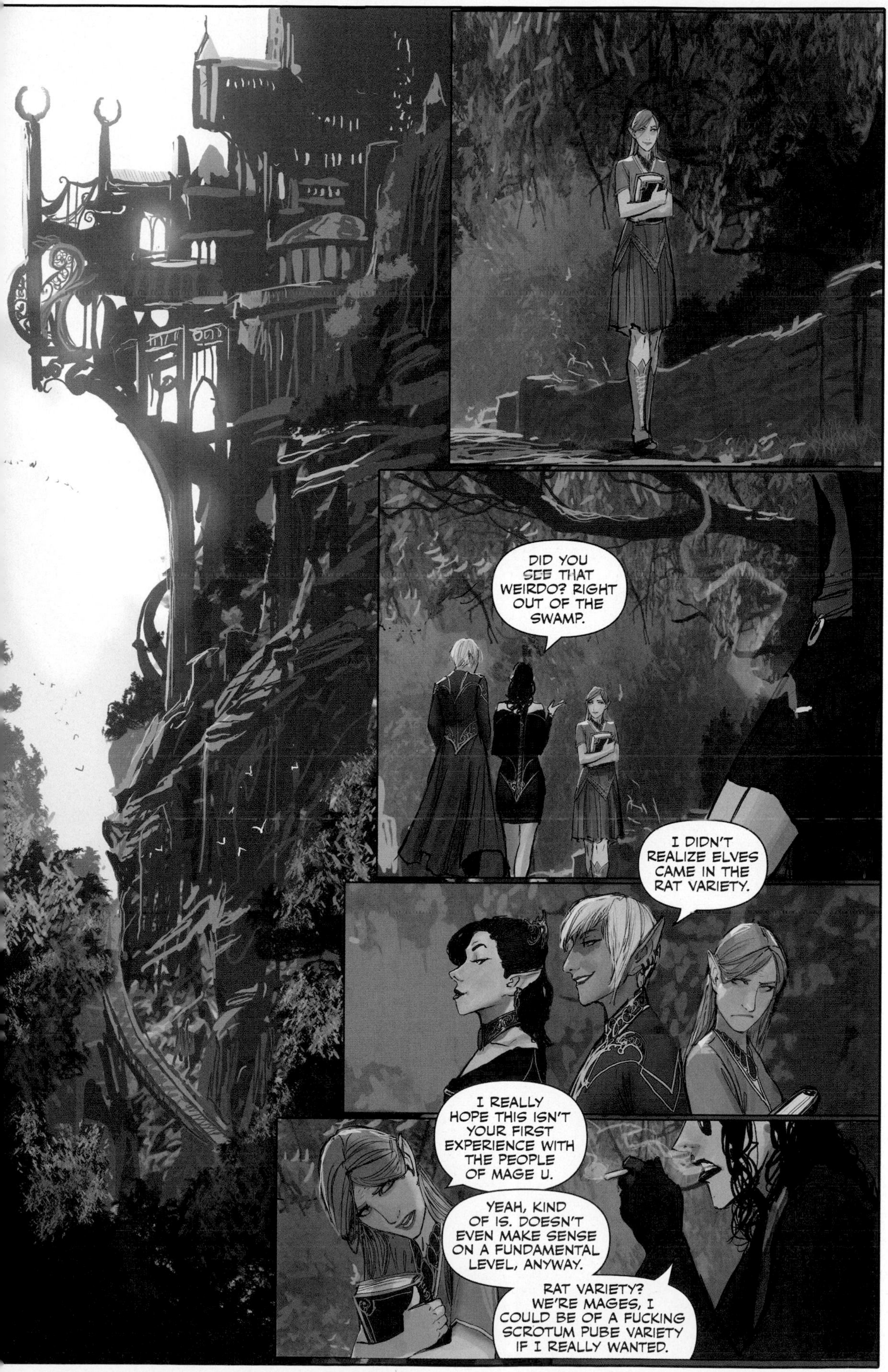
DID YOU SEE THAT WEIRDO? RIGHT OUT OF THE SWAMP.
I DIDN'T REALIZE ELVES CAME IN THE RAT VARIETY.
I REALLY HOPE THIS ISN'T YOUR FIRST EXPERIENCE WITH THE PEOPLE OF MAGE U.
YEAH, KIND OF IS. DOESN'T EVEN MAKE SENSE ON A FUNDAMENTAL LEVEL, ANYWAY.
RAT VARIETY? WE'RE MAGES, I COULD BE OF A FUCKING SCROTUM PUBE VARIETY IF I REALLY WANTED.

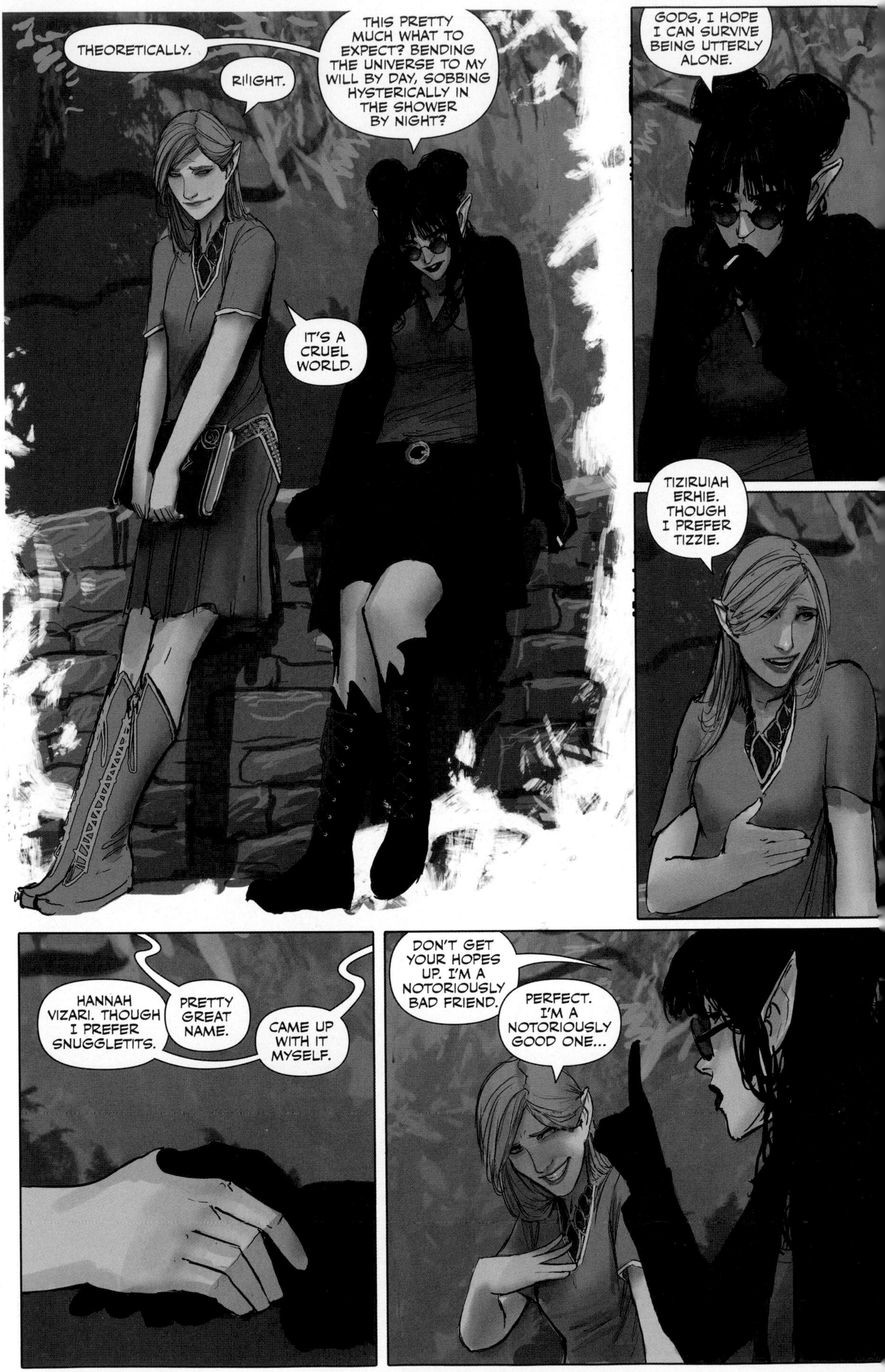
THEORETICALLY.
RIIIGHT.
THIS PRETTY MUCH WHAT TO EXPECT? BENDING THE UNIVERSE TO MY WILL BY DAY, SOBBING HYSTERICALLY IN THE SHOWER BY NIGHT?
IT'S A CRUEL WORLD.
GODS, I HOPE I CAN SURVIVE BEING UTTERLY ALONE.
TIZIRUIAH ERHIE. THOUGH I PREFER TIZZIE.
HANNAH VIZARI. THOUGH I PREFER SNUGGLETITS.
PRETTY GREAT NAME.
CAME UP WITH IT MYSELF.
DON'T GET YOUR HOPES UP. I'M A NOTORIOUSLY BAD FRIEND.
PERFECT. I'M A NOTORIOUSLY GOOD ONE...

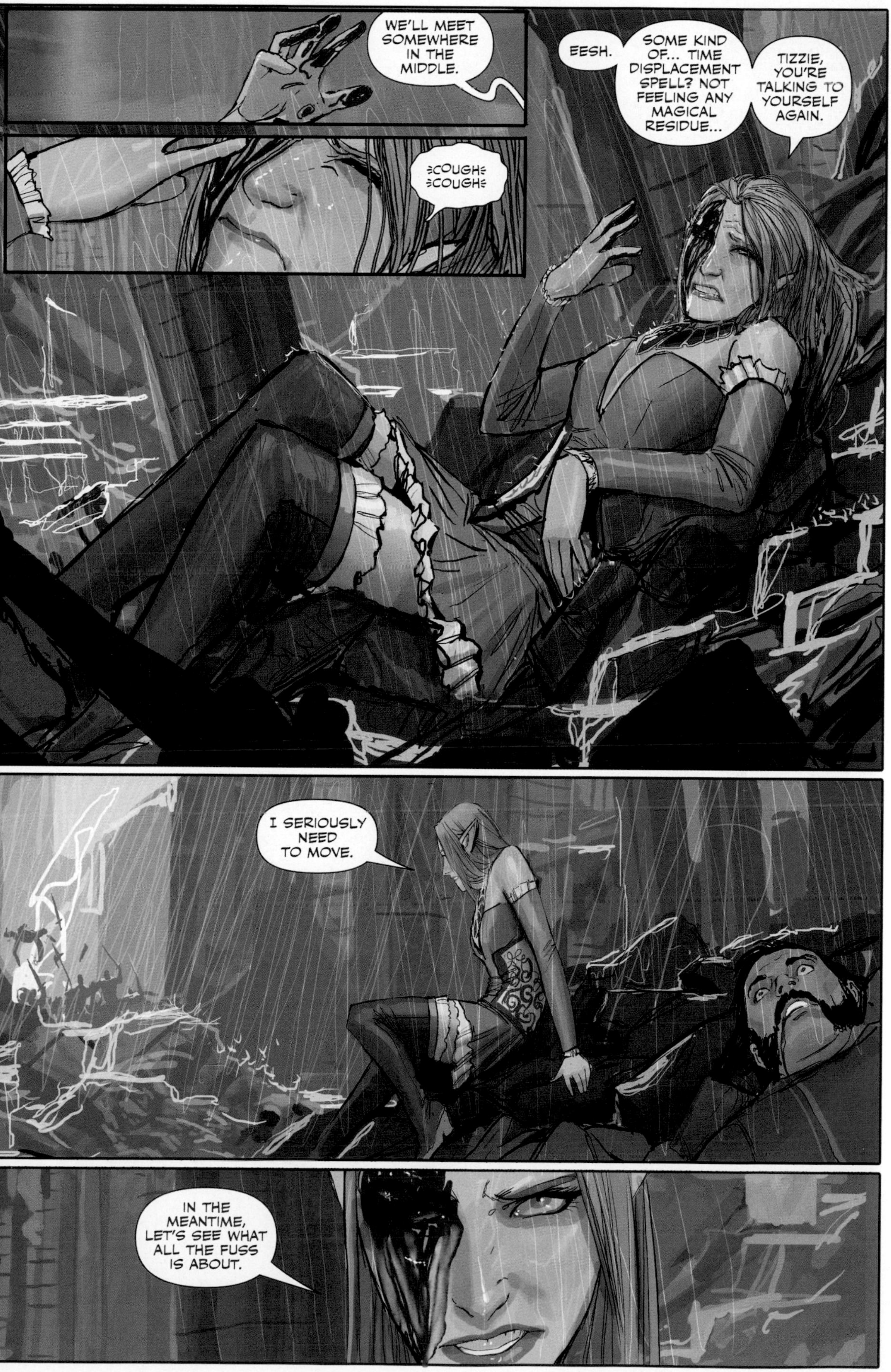
WE'LL MEET SOMEWHERE IN THE MIDDLE.
≈COUGH≈ ≈COUGH≈
EESH.
SOME KIND OF... TIME DISPLACEMENT SPELL? NOT FEELING ANY MAGICAL RESIDUE...
TIZZIE, YOU'RE TALKING TO YOURSELF AGAIN.
I SERIOUSLY NEED TO MOVE.
IN THE MEANTIME, LET'S SEE WHAT ALL THE FUSS IS ABOUT.

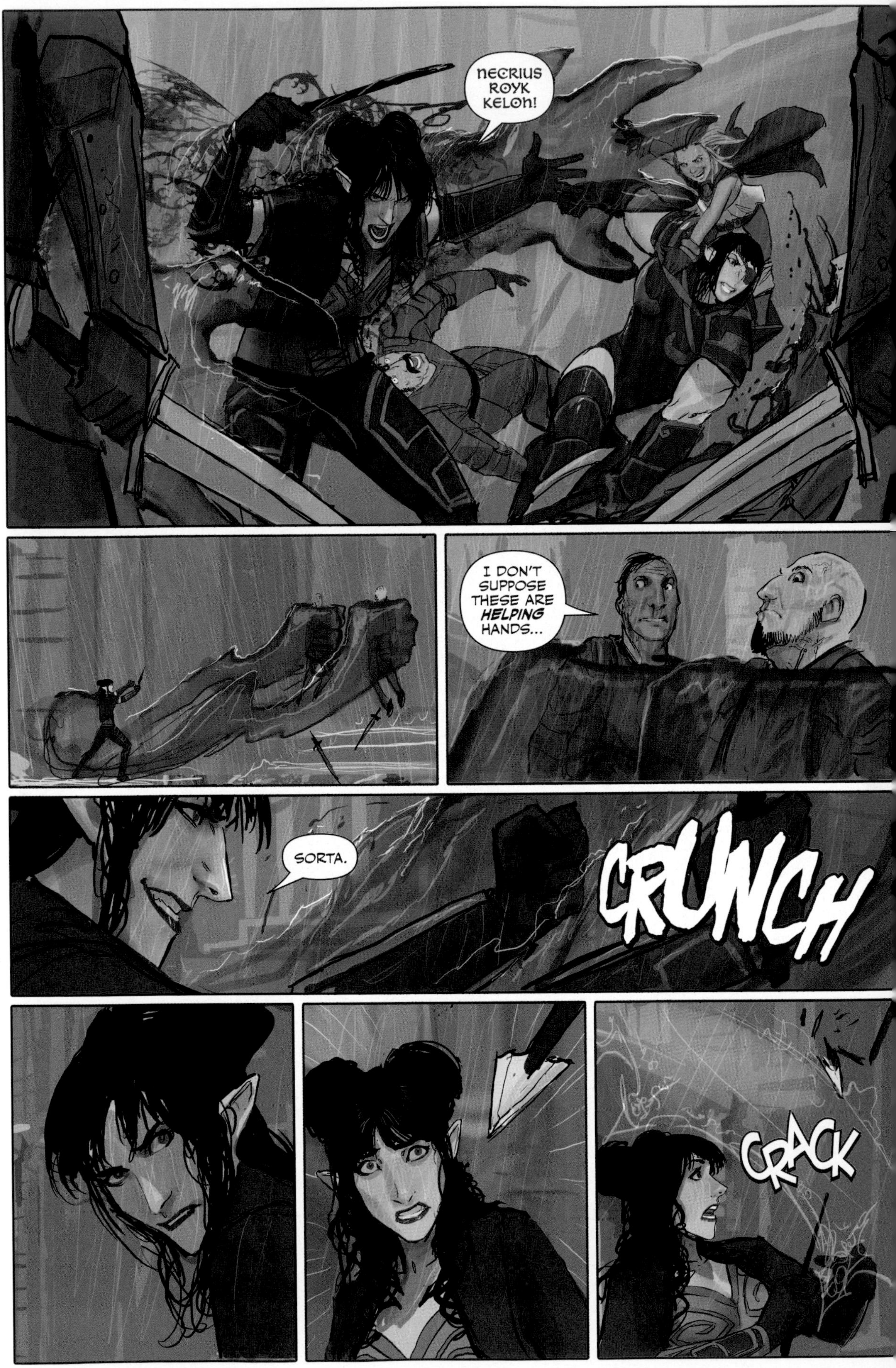
NECRIUS ROYK KELOH!
I DON'T SUPPOSE THESE ARE *HELPING* HANDS...
SORTA.
CRUNCH
CRACK

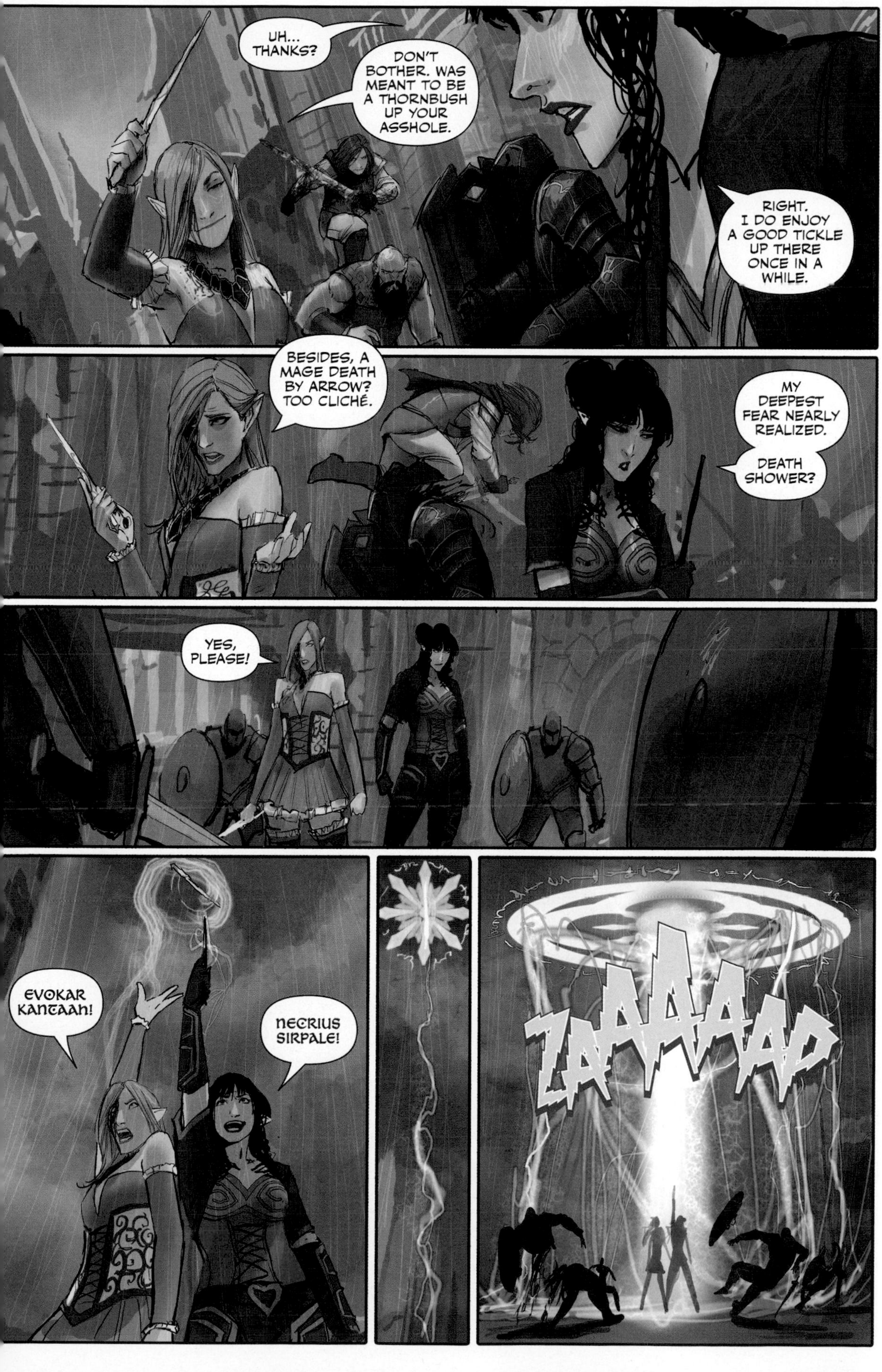

UH... THANKS?
DON'T BOTHER. WAS MEANT TO BE A THORNBUSH UP YOUR ASSHOLE.
RIGHT. I DO ENJOY A GOOD TICKLE UP THERE ONCE IN A WHILE.
BESIDES, A MAGE DEATH BY ARROW? TOO CLICHÉ.
MY DEEPEST FEAR NEARLY REALIZED.
DEATH SHOWER?
YES, PLEASE!
EVOKAR KANTAAH!
NECRIUS SIRPALE!
ZAAAAAD

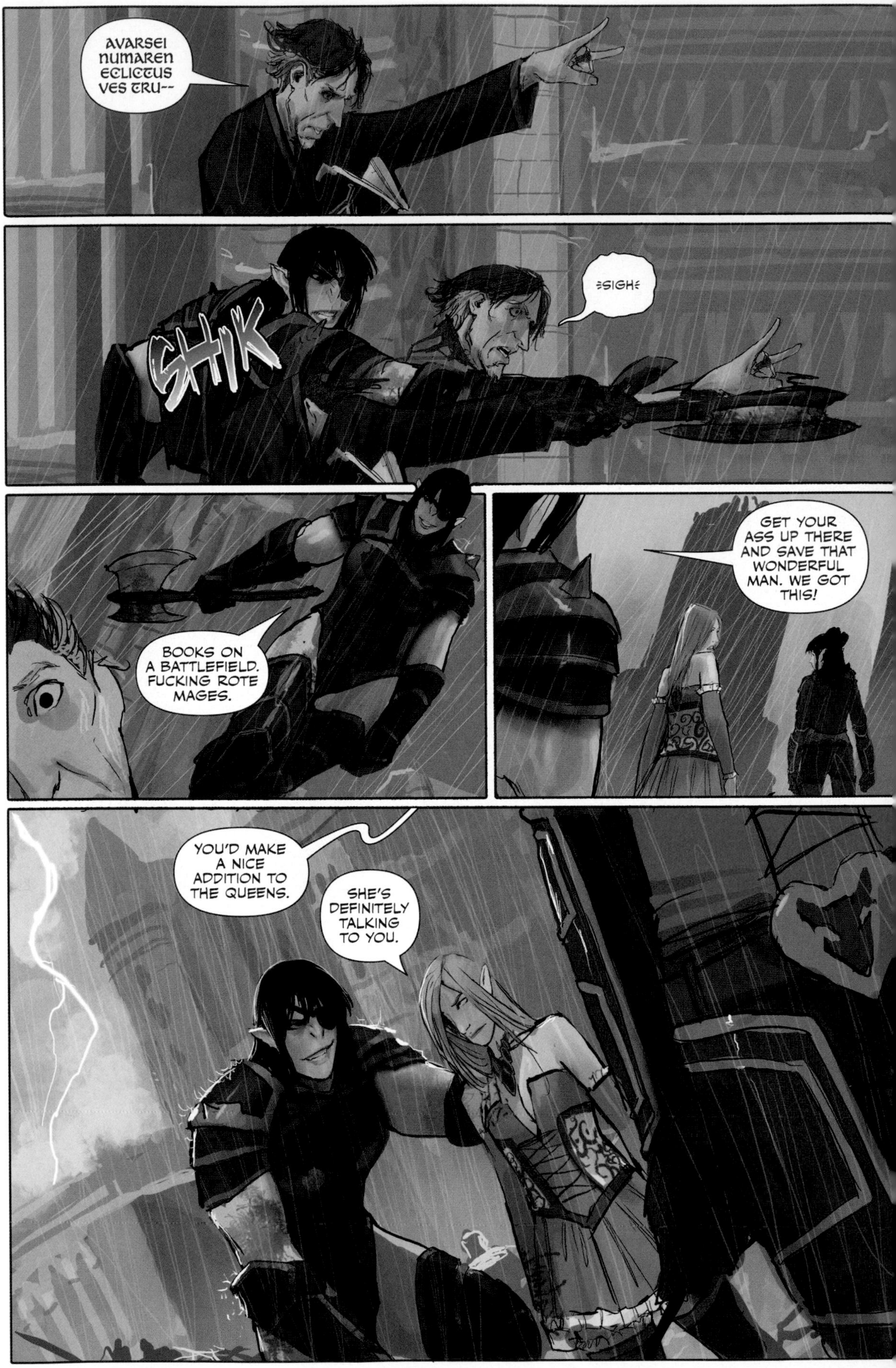
AVARSEI NUMAREN ECLICTUS VES TRU--
SHIK
SIGH
BOOKS ON A BATTLEFIELD. FUCKING ROTE MAGES.
GET YOUR ASS UP THERE AND SAVE THAT WONDERFUL MAN. WE GOT THIS!
YOU'D MAKE A NICE ADDITION TO THE QUEENS.
SHE'S DEFINITELY TALKING TO YOU.

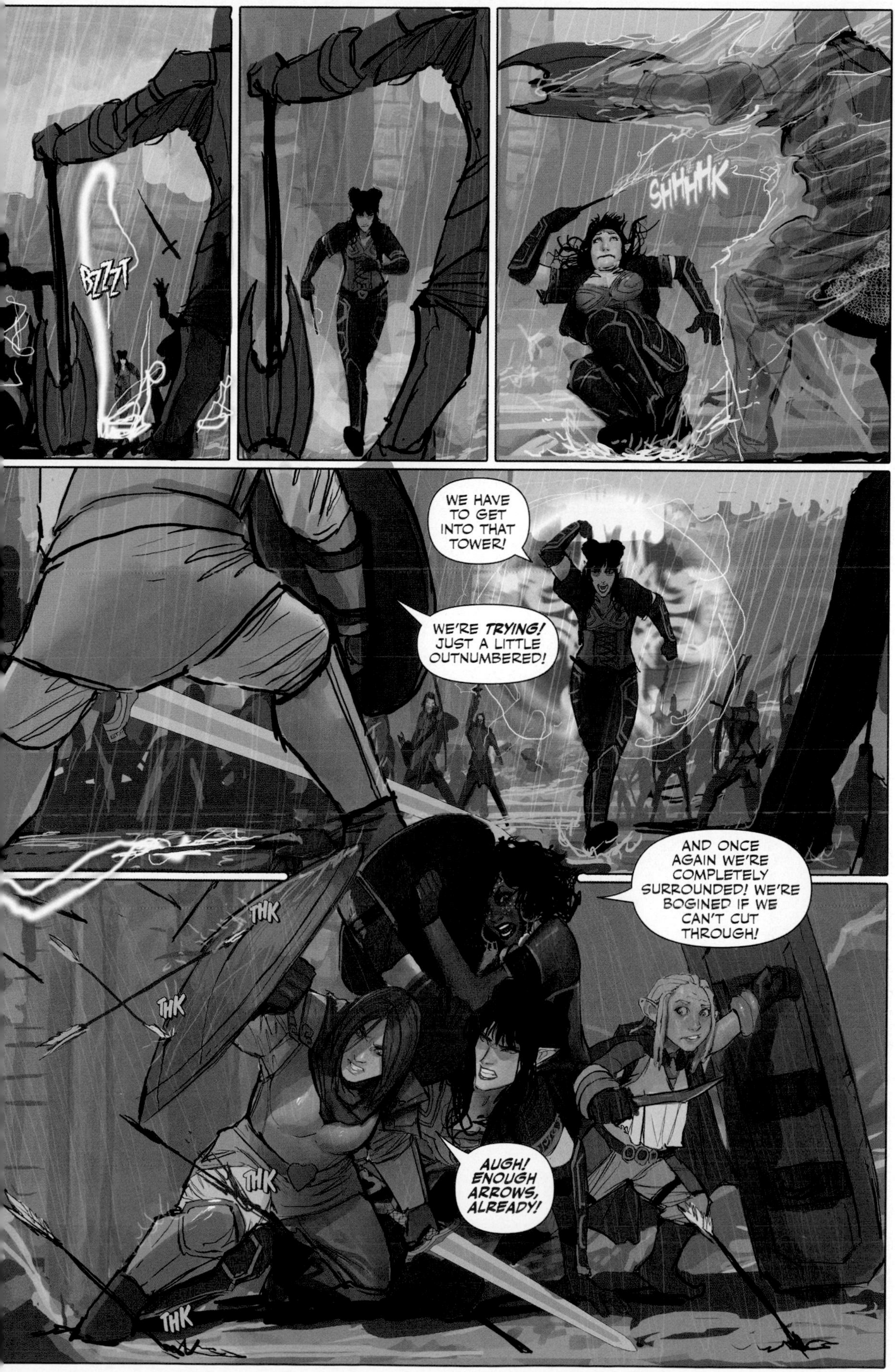
BZZZT
SHHHHK
WE HAVE TO GET INTO THAT TOWER!
WE'RE TRYING! JUST A LITTLE OUTNUMBERED!
AND ONCE AGAIN WE'RE COMPLETELY SURROUNDED! WE'RE BOGINED IF WE CAN'T CUT THROUGH!
THK
THK
AUGH! ENOUGH ARROWS, ALREADY!
THK
THK

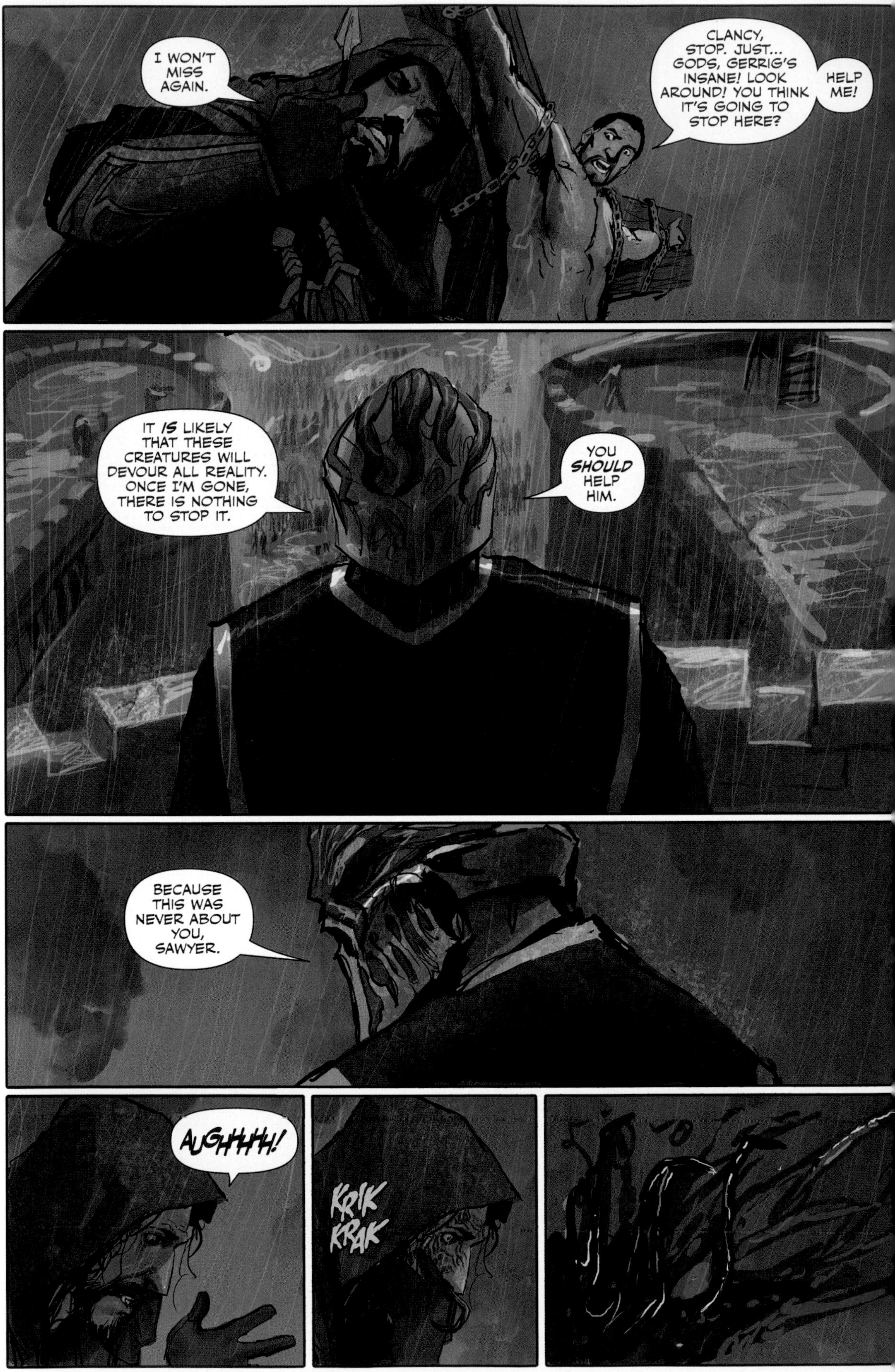
I WON'T MISS AGAIN.
CLANCY, STOP. JUST... GODS, GERRIG'S INSANE! LOOK AROUND! YOU THINK IT'S GOING TO STOP HERE?
HELP ME!
IT *IS* LIKELY THAT THESE CREATURES WILL DEVOUR ALL REALITY. ONCE I'M GONE, THERE IS NOTHING TO STOP IT.
YOU *SHOULD* HELP HIM.
BECAUSE THIS WAS NEVER ABOUT YOU, SAWYER.
AUGHHHH!
KRIK KRAK

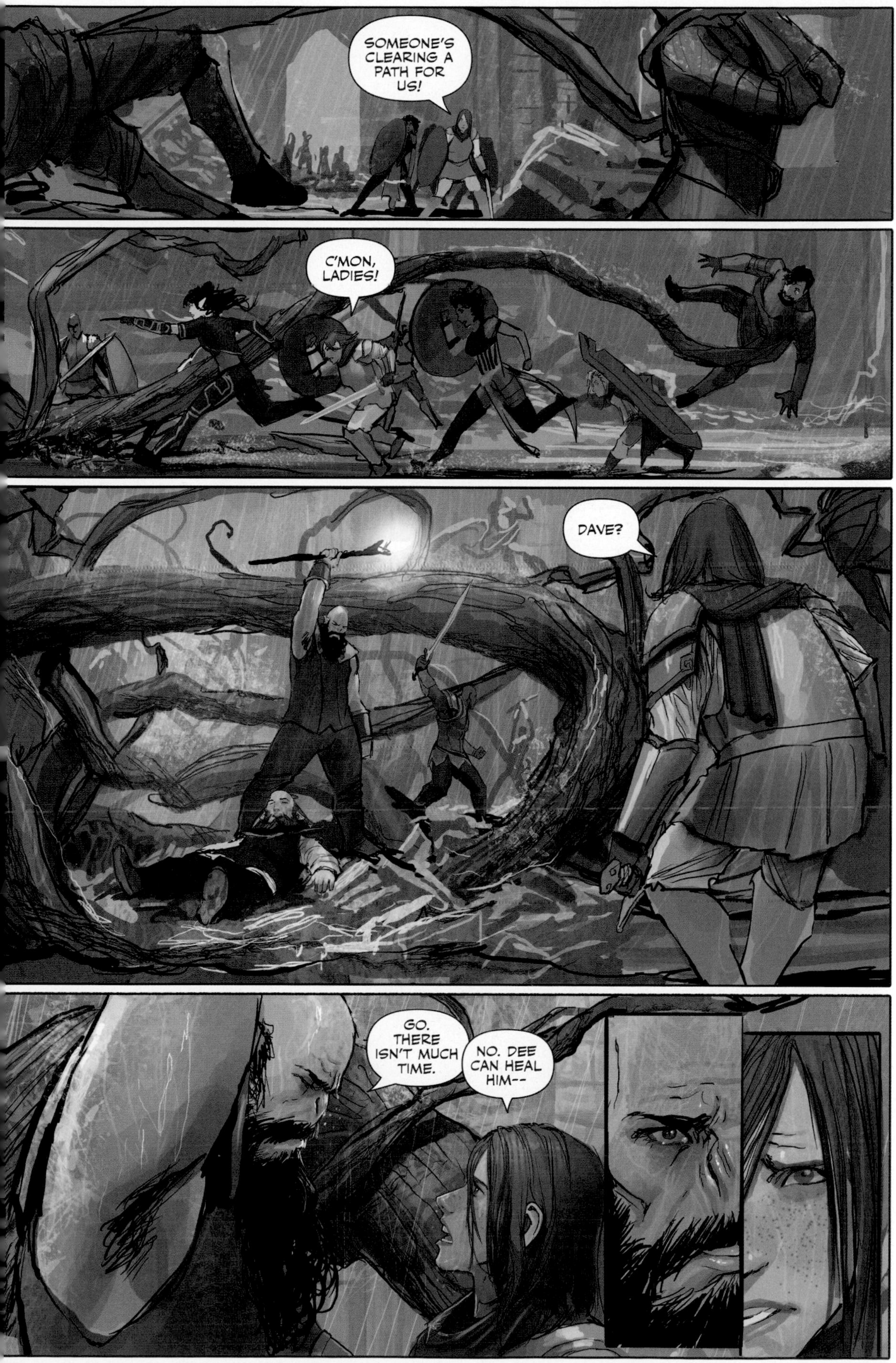
SOMEONE'S CLEARING A PATH FOR US!
C'MON, LADIES!
DAVE?
GO. THERE ISN'T MUCH TIME.
NO. DEE CAN HEAL HIM--

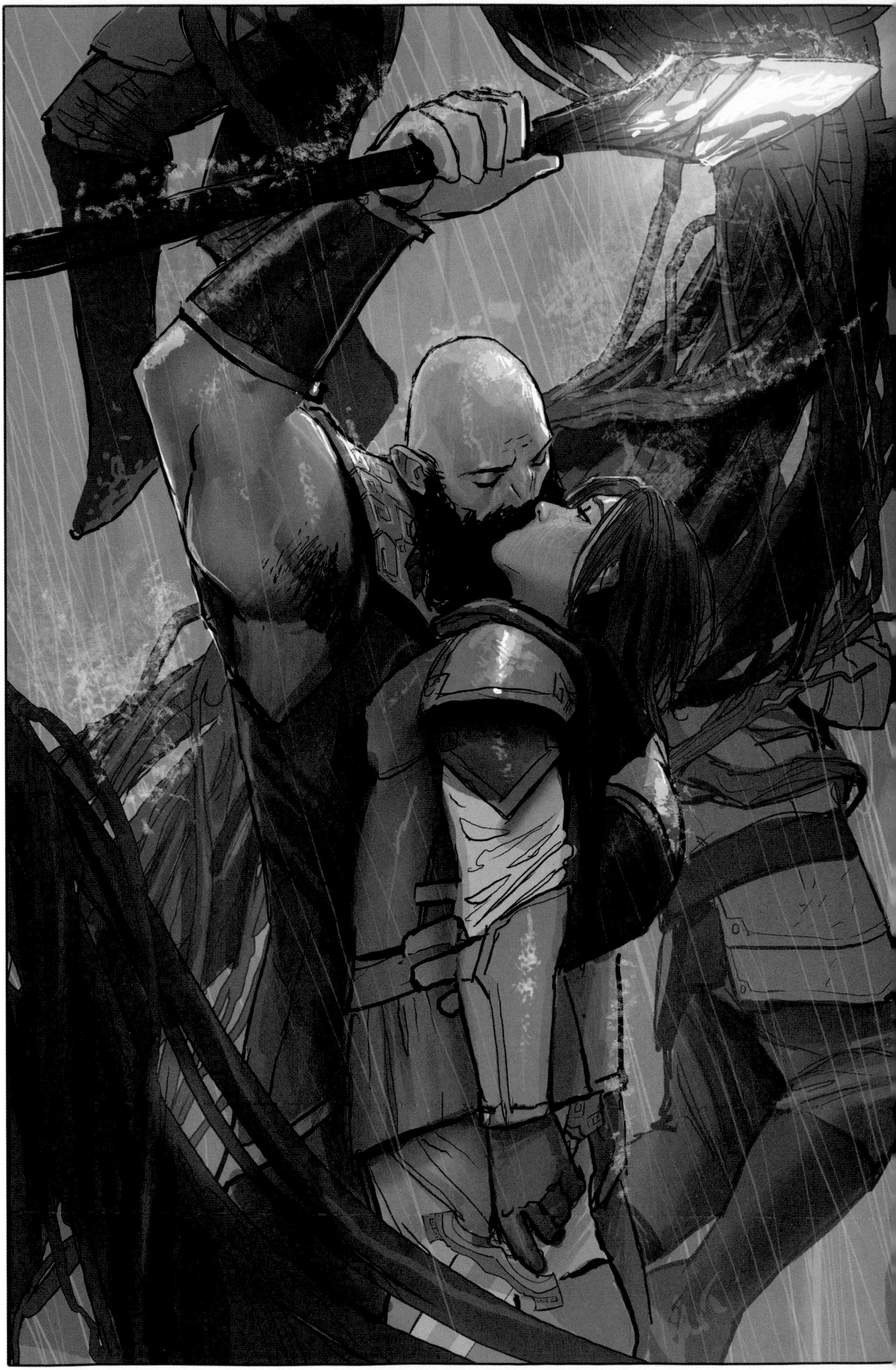

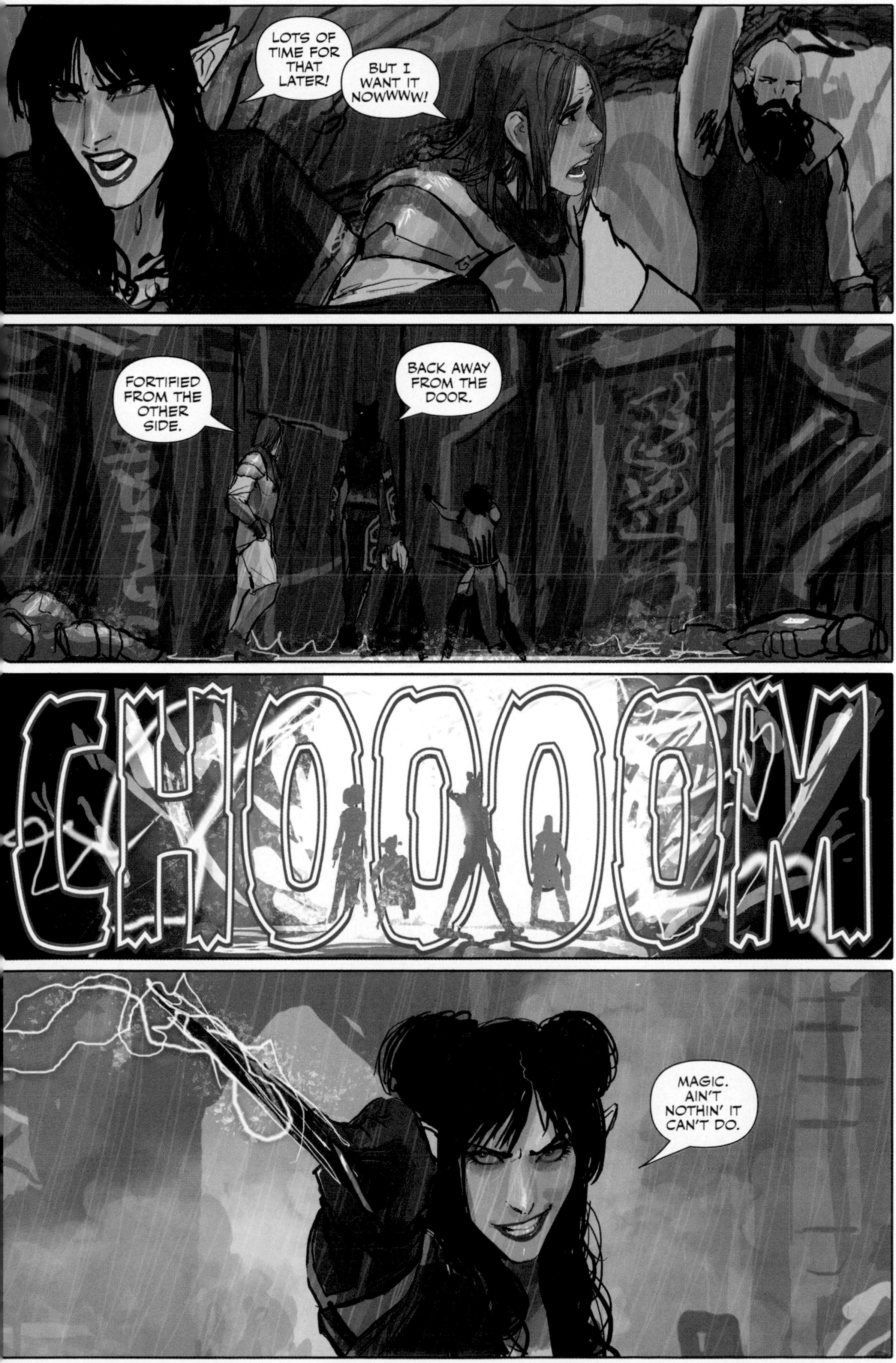
LOTS OF TIME FOR THAT LATER!
BUT I WANT IT NOWWWW!
FORTIFIED FROM THE OTHER SIDE.
BACK AWAY FROM THE DOOR.
CHOOOOM
MAGIC. AIN'T NOTHIN' IT CAN'T DO.

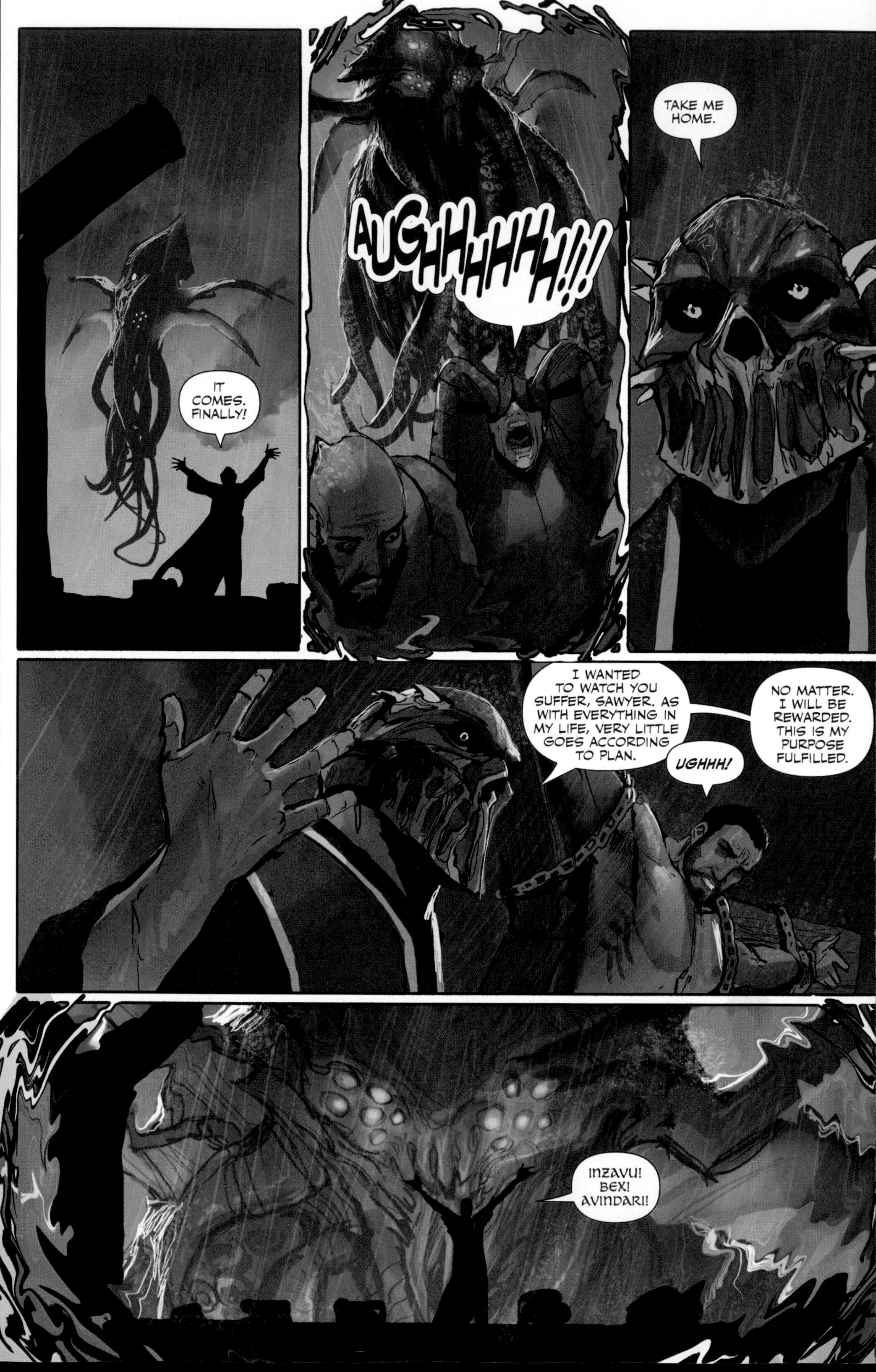
IT COMES. FINALLY!
AUGHHHHHH!!!
TAKE ME HOME.
I WANTED TO WATCH YOU SUFFER, SAWYER. AS WITH EVERYTHING IN MY LIFE, VERY LITTLE GOES ACCORDING TO PLAN.
UGHHH!
NO MATTER. I WILL BE REWARDED. THIS IS MY PURPOSE FULFILLED.
INZAVU! BEX! AVINDARI!

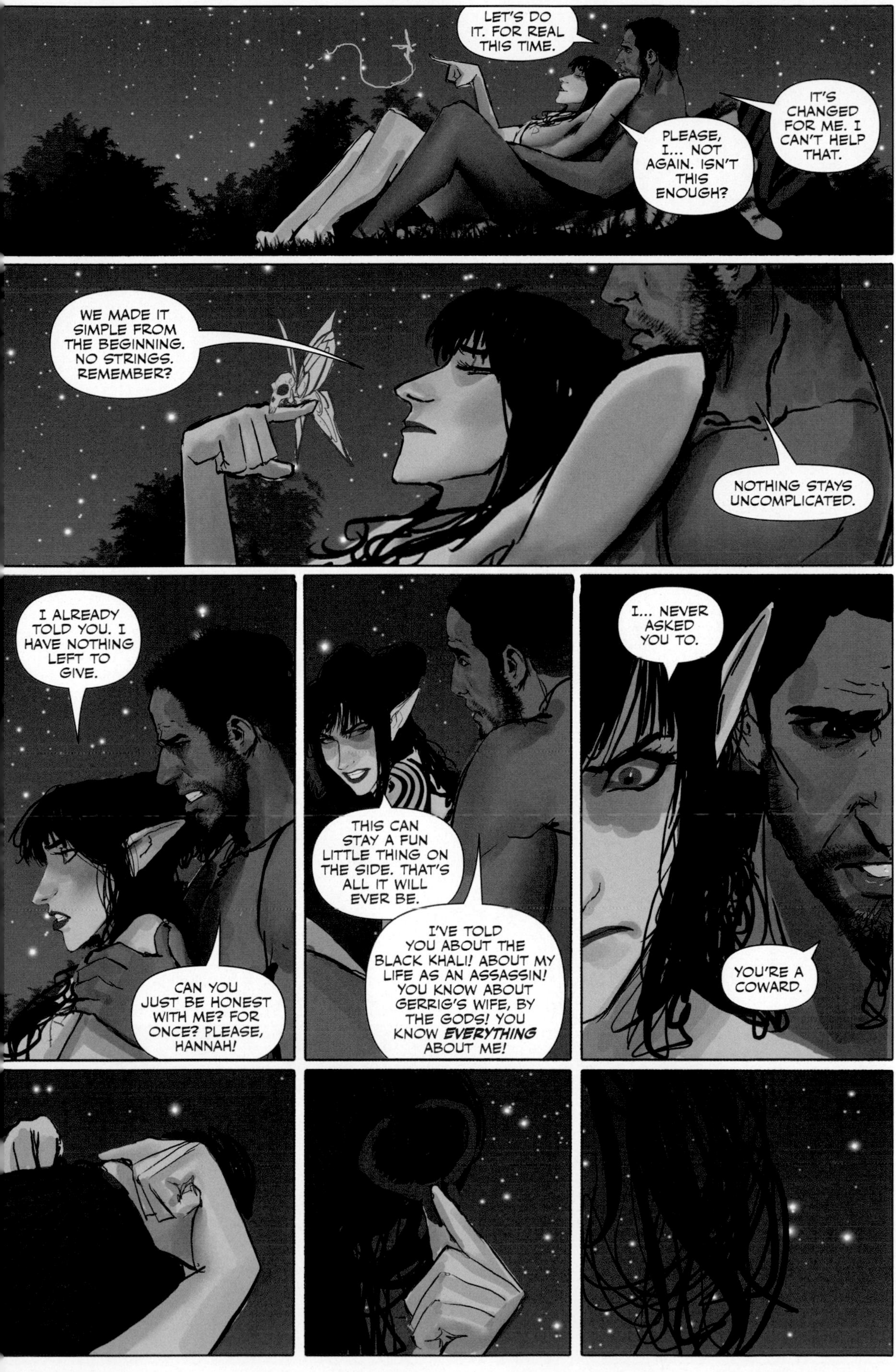
LET'S DO IT. FOR REAL THIS TIME.
PLEASE, I... NOT AGAIN. ISN'T THIS ENOUGH?
IT'S CHANGED FOR ME. I CAN'T HELP THAT.
WE MADE IT SIMPLE FROM THE BEGINNING. NO STRINGS. REMEMBER?
NOTHING STAYS UNCOMPLICATED.
I ALREADY TOLD YOU. I HAVE NOTHING LEFT TO GIVE.
CAN YOU JUST BE HONEST WITH ME? FOR ONCE? PLEASE, HANNAH!
THIS CAN STAY A FUN LITTLE THING ON THE SIDE. THAT'S ALL IT WILL EVER BE.
I'VE TOLD YOU ABOUT THE BLACK KHALI! ABOUT MY LIFE AS AN ASSASSIN! YOU KNOW ABOUT GERRIG'S WIFE, BY THE GODS! YOU KNOW *EVERYTHING* ABOUT ME!
I... NEVER ASKED YOU TO.
YOU'RE A COWARD.

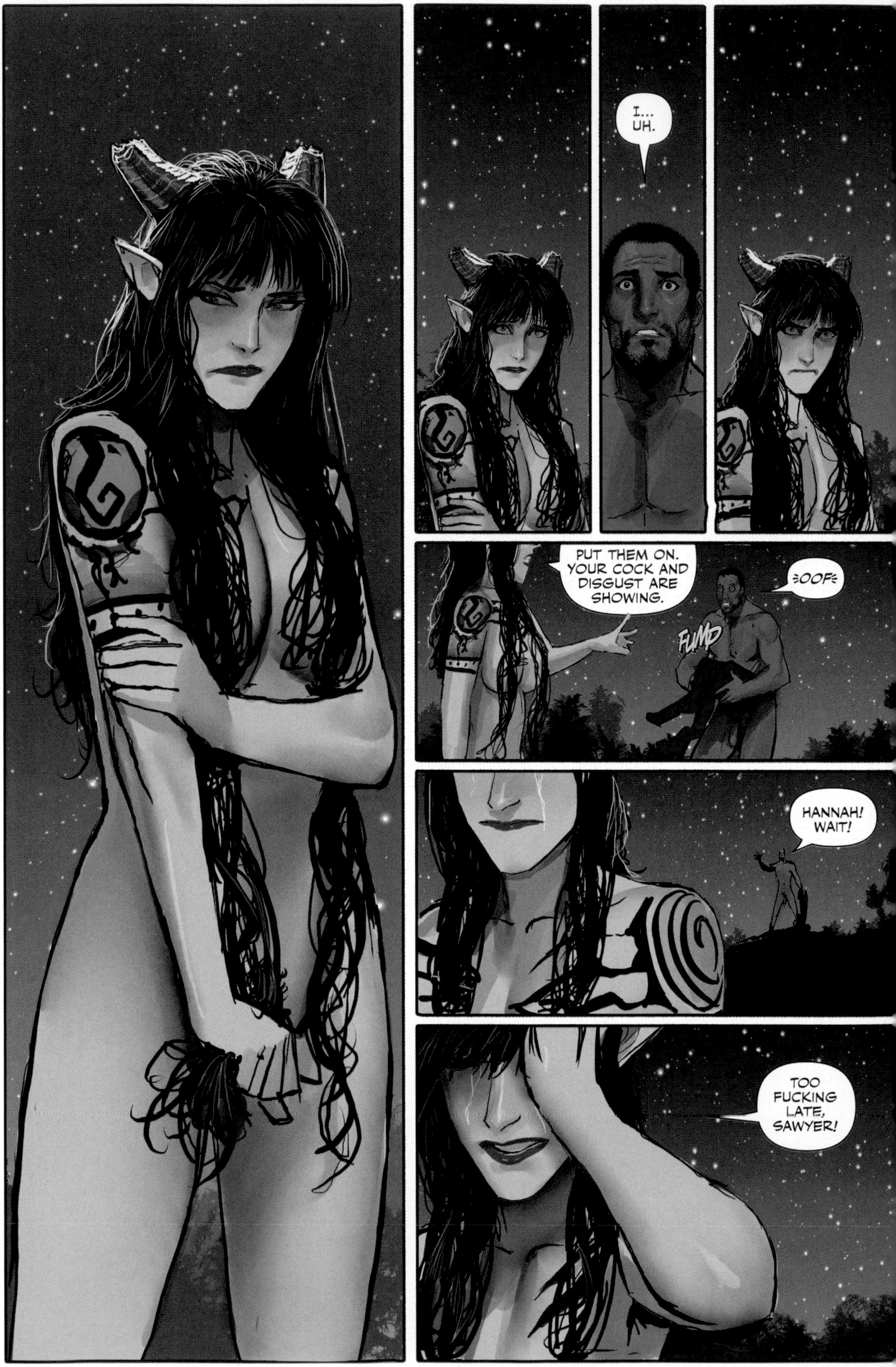

I... UH.
PUT THEM ON. YOUR COCK AND DISGUST ARE SHOWING.
FUMP
OOF
HANNAH! WAIT!
TOO FUCKING LATE, SAWYER!

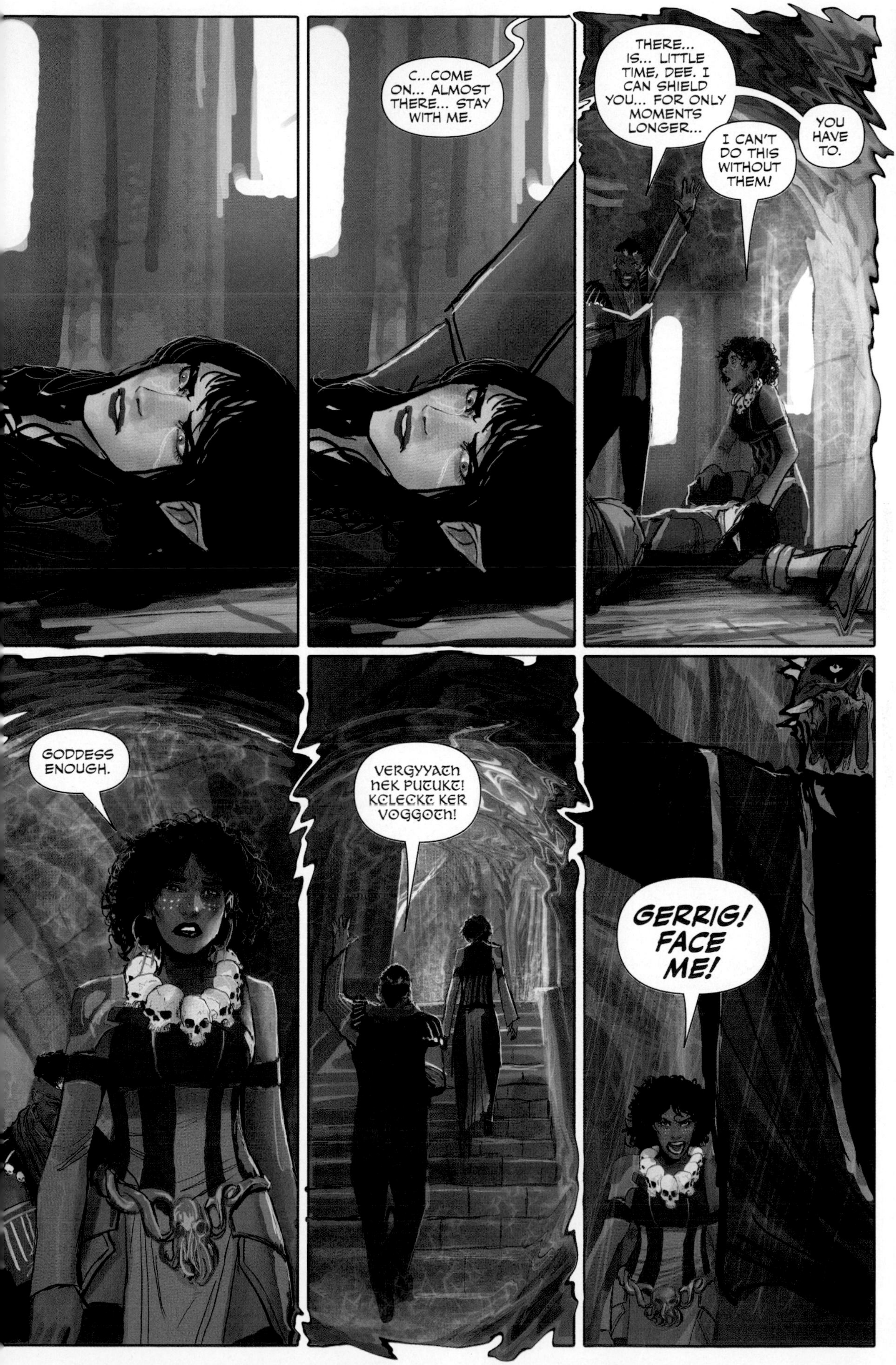
C...COME ON... ALMOST THERE... STAY WITH ME.
THERE... IS... LITTLE TIME, DEE. I CAN SHIELD YOU... FOR ONLY MOMENTS LONGER...
I CAN'T DO THIS WITHOUT THEM!
YOU HAVE TO.
GODDESS ENOUGH.
VERGYYATH HEK PUTUKT! KCLECKT KER VOGGOTH!
GERRIG! FACE ME!

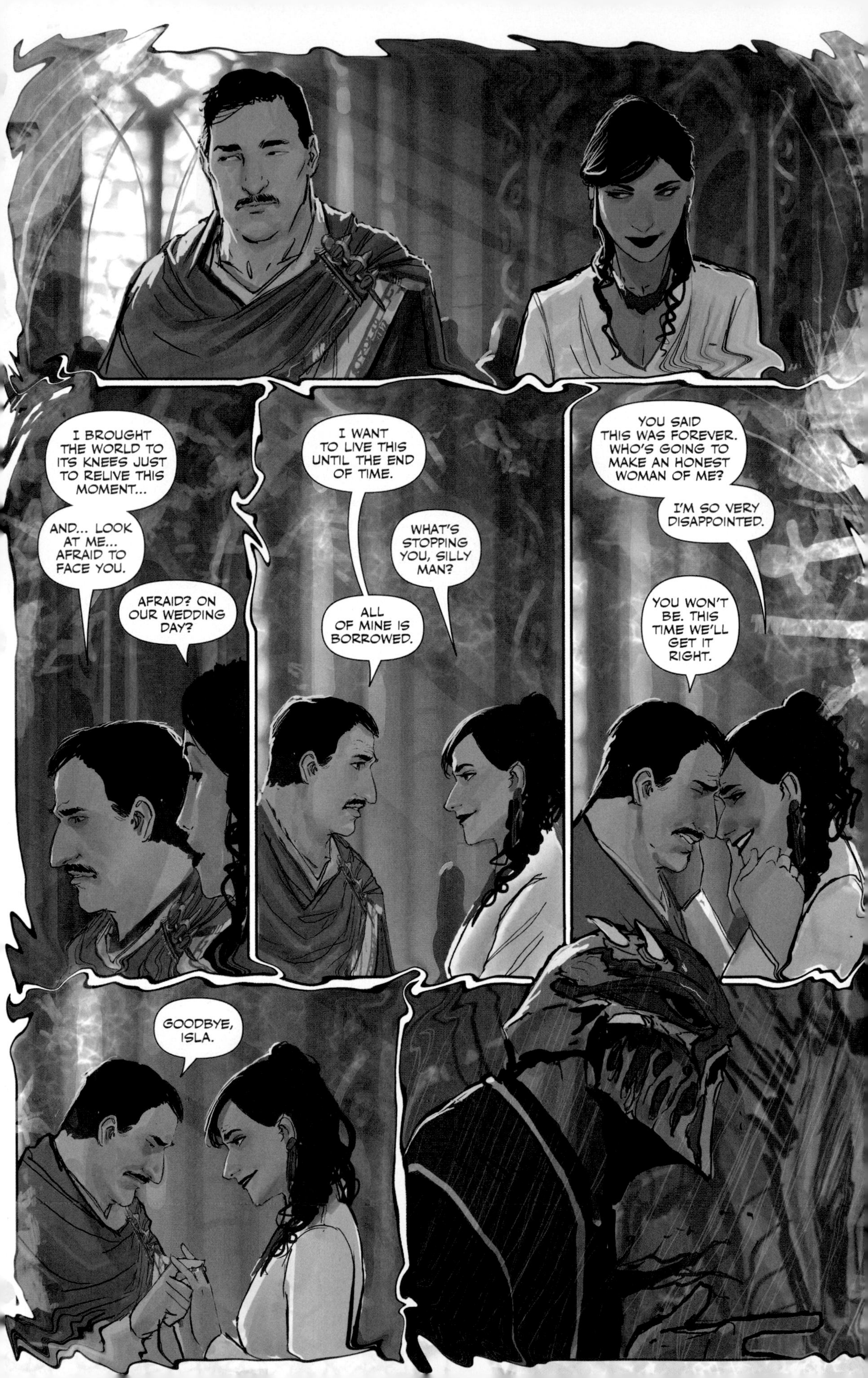
I BROUGHT THE WORLD TO ITS KNEES JUST TO RELIVE THIS MOMENT...
AND... LOOK AT ME... AFRAID TO FACE YOU.
AFRAID? ON OUR WEDDING DAY?
I WANT TO LIVE THIS UNTIL THE END OF TIME.
WHAT'S STOPPING YOU, SILLY MAN?
ALL OF MINE IS BORROWED.
YOU SAID THIS WAS FOREVER. WHO'S GOING TO MAKE AN HONEST WOMAN OF ME?
I'M SO VERY DISAPPOINTED.
YOU WON'T BE. THIS TIME WE'LL GET IT RIGHT.
GOODBYE, ISLA.

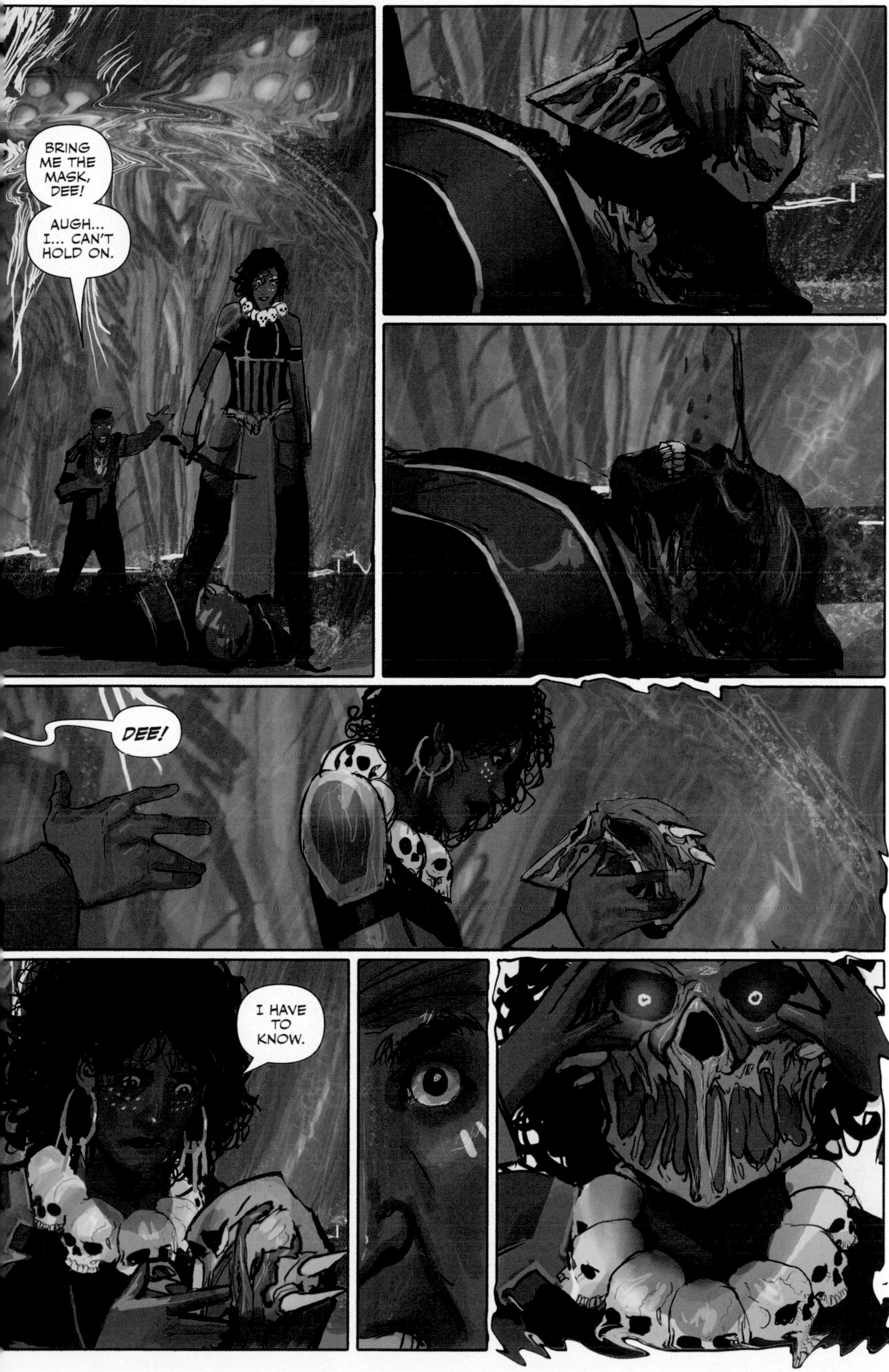
BRING ME THE MASK, DEE!
AUGH... I... CAN'T HOLD ON.
DEE!
I HAVE TO KNOW.

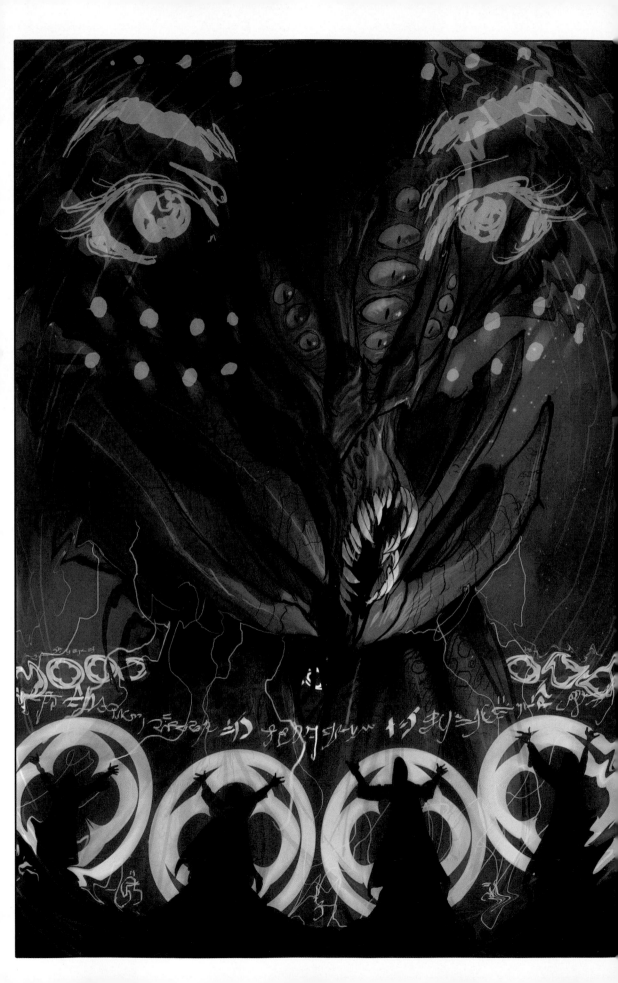

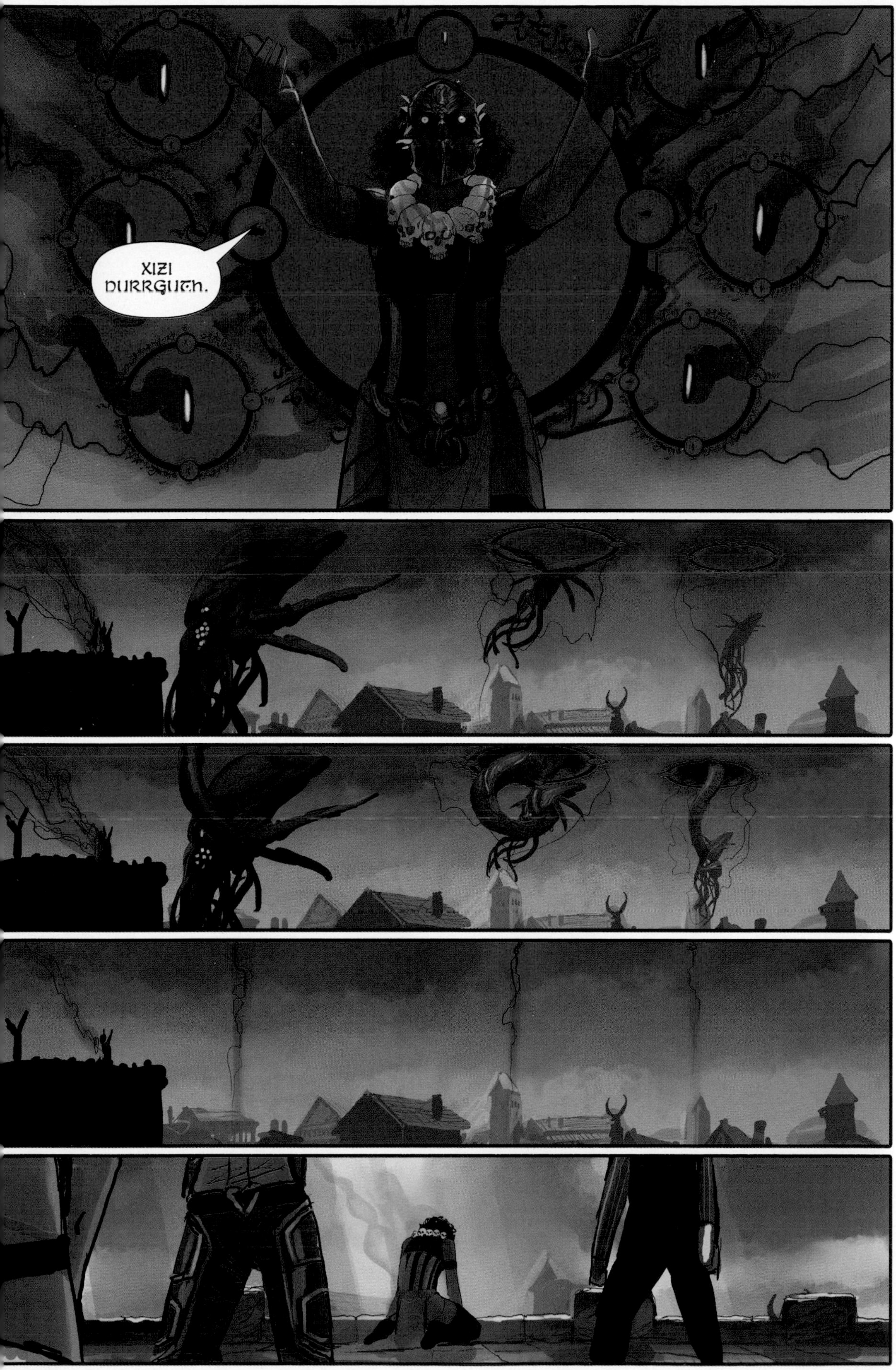
XIZI DURRGUTH.

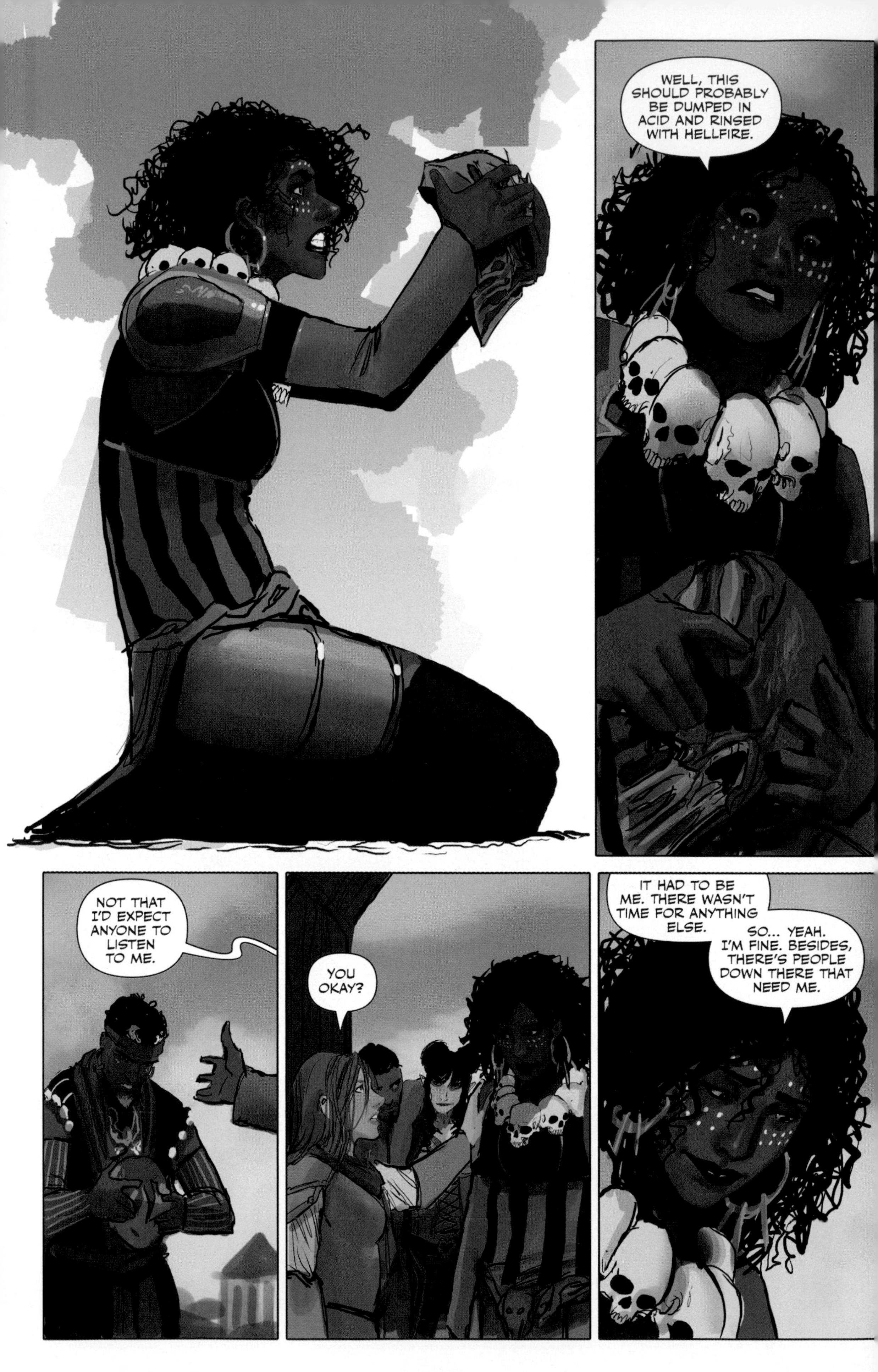
WELL, THIS SHOULD PROBABLY BE DUMPED IN ACID AND RINSED WITH HELLFIRE.
NOT THAT I'D EXPECT ANYONE TO LISTEN TO ME.
YOU OKAY?
IT HAD TO BE ME. THERE WASN'T TIME FOR ANYTHING ELSE.
SO... YEAH. I'M FINE. BESIDES, THERE'S PEOPLE DOWN THERE THAT NEED ME.

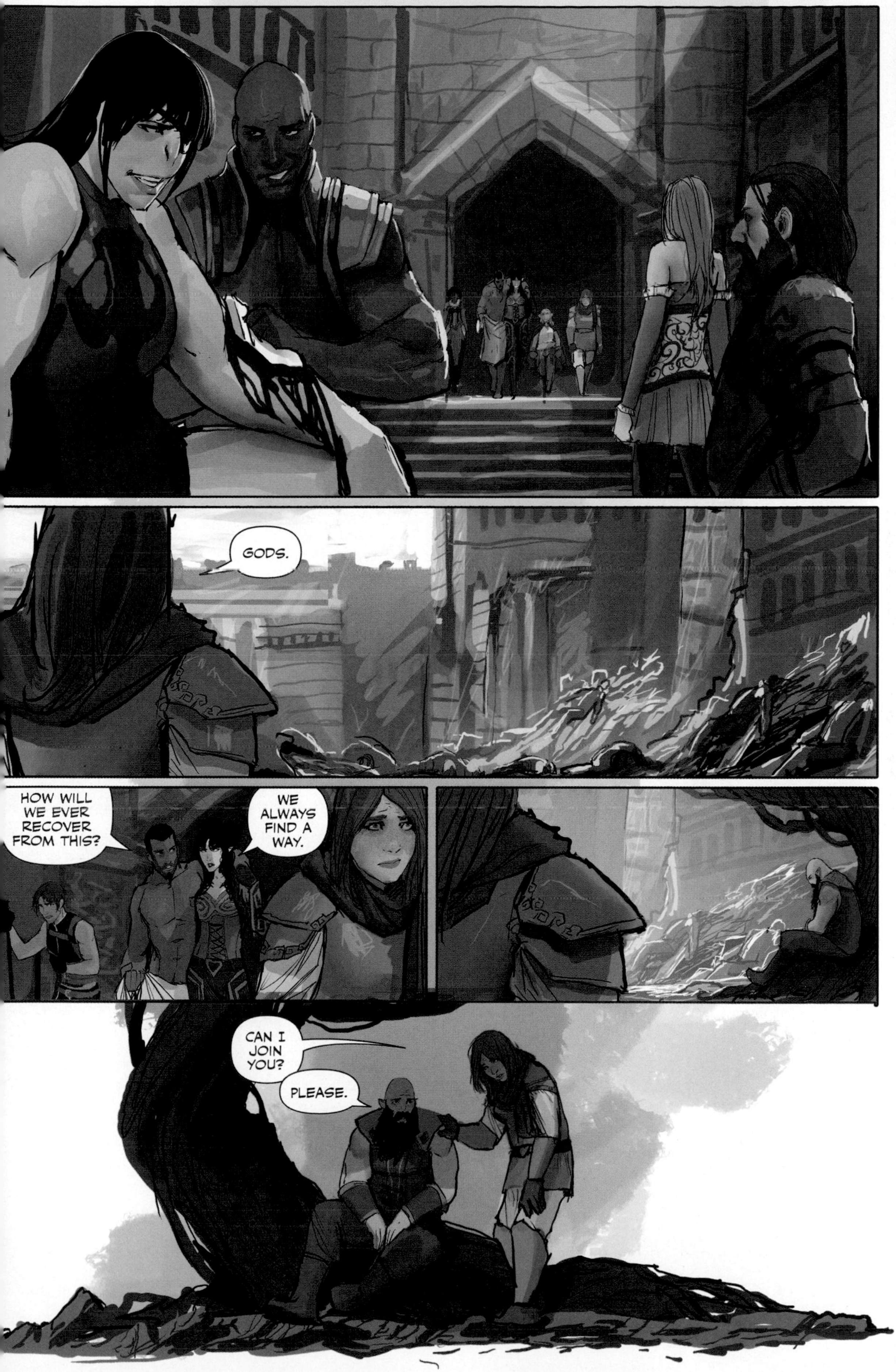
GODS.
HOW WILL WE EVER RECOVER FROM THIS?
WE ALWAYS FIND A WAY.
CAN I JOIN YOU?
PLEASE.

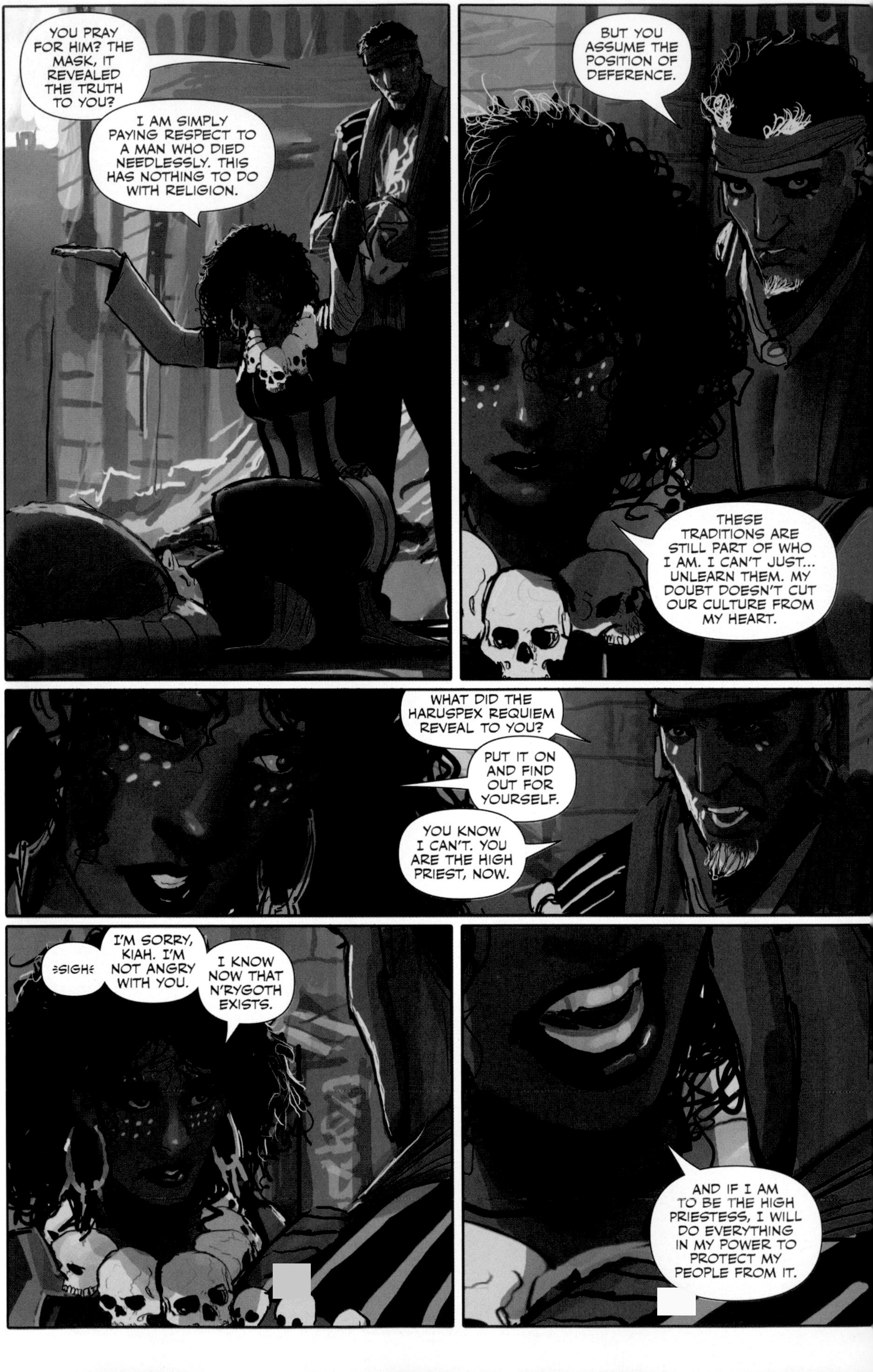
YOU PRAY FOR HIM? THE MASK, IT REVEALED THE TRUTH TO YOU?
I AM SIMPLY PAYING RESPECT TO A MAN WHO DIED NEEDLESSLY. THIS HAS NOTHING TO DO WITH RELIGION.
BUT YOU ASSUME THE POSITION OF DEFERENCE.
THESE TRADITIONS ARE STILL PART OF WHO I AM. I CAN'T JUST... UNLEARN THEM. MY DOUBT DOESN'T CUT OUR CULTURE FROM MY HEART.
WHAT DID THE HARUSPEX REQUIEM REVEAL TO YOU?
PUT IT ON AND FIND OUT FOR YOURSELF.
YOU KNOW I CAN'T. YOU ARE THE HIGH PRIEST, NOW.
SIGH
I'M SORRY, KIAH. I'M NOT ANGRY WITH YOU.
I KNOW NOW THAT N'RYGOTH EXISTS.
AND IF I AM TO BE THE HIGH PRIESTESS, I WILL DO EVERYTHING IN MY POWER TO PROTECT MY PEOPLE FROM IT.

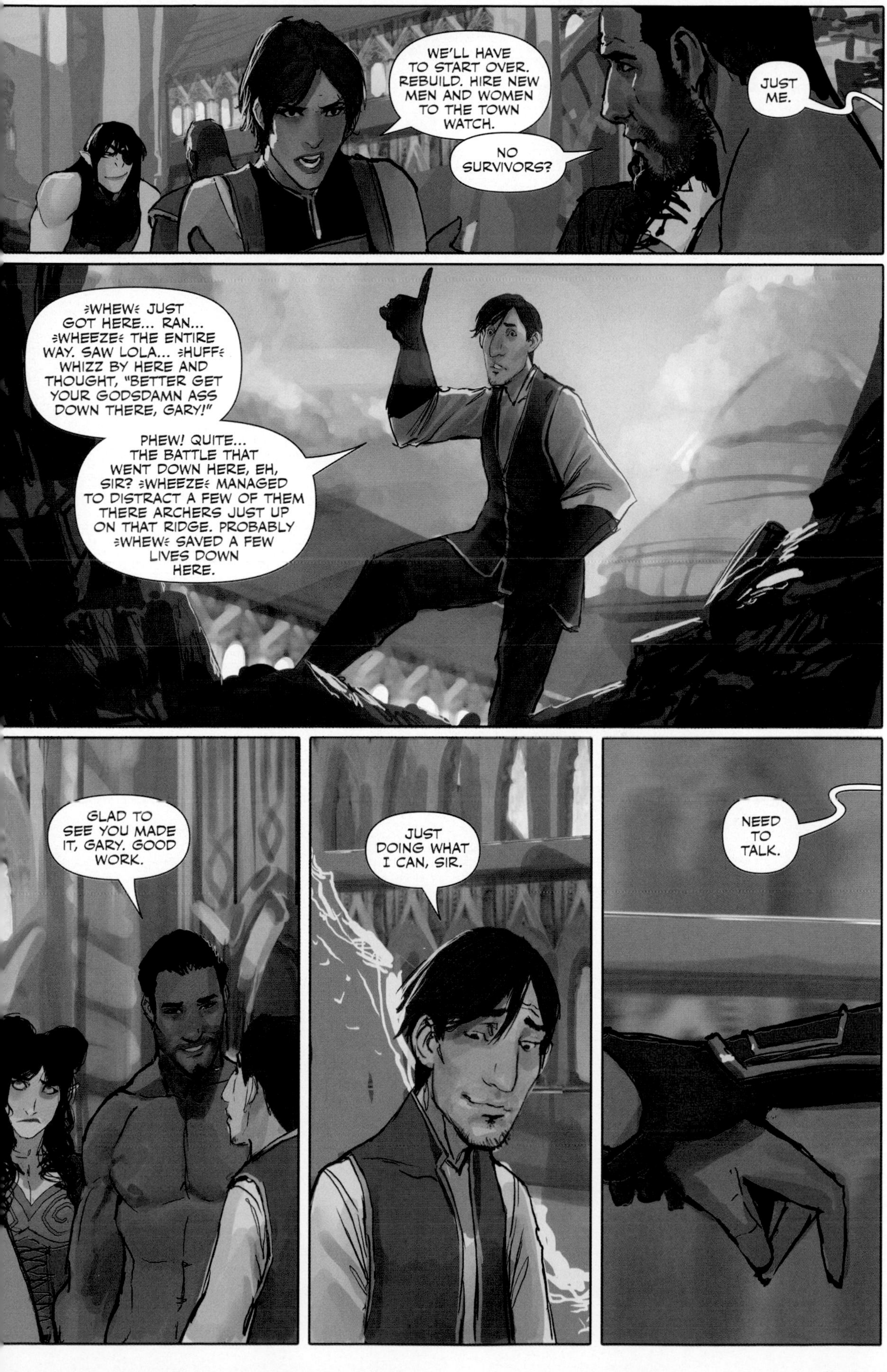
WE'LL HAVE TO START OVER. REBUILD. HIRE NEW MEN AND WOMEN TO THE TOWN WATCH.
NO SURVIVORS?
JUST ME.
≑WHEW≑ JUST GOT HERE... RAN... ≑WHEEZE≑ THE ENTIRE WAY. SAW LOLA... ≑HUFF≑ WHIZZ BY HERE AND THOUGHT, "BETTER GET YOUR GODSDAMN ASS DOWN THERE, GARY!"
PHEW! QUITE... THE BATTLE THAT WENT DOWN HERE, EH, SIR? ≑WHEEZE≑ MANAGED TO DISTRACT A FEW OF THEM THERE ARCHERS JUST UP ON THAT RIDGE. PROBABLY ≑WHEW≑ SAVED A FEW LIVES DOWN HERE.
GLAD TO SEE YOU MADE IT, GARY. GOOD WORK.
JUST DOING WHAT I CAN, SIR.
NEED TO TALK.

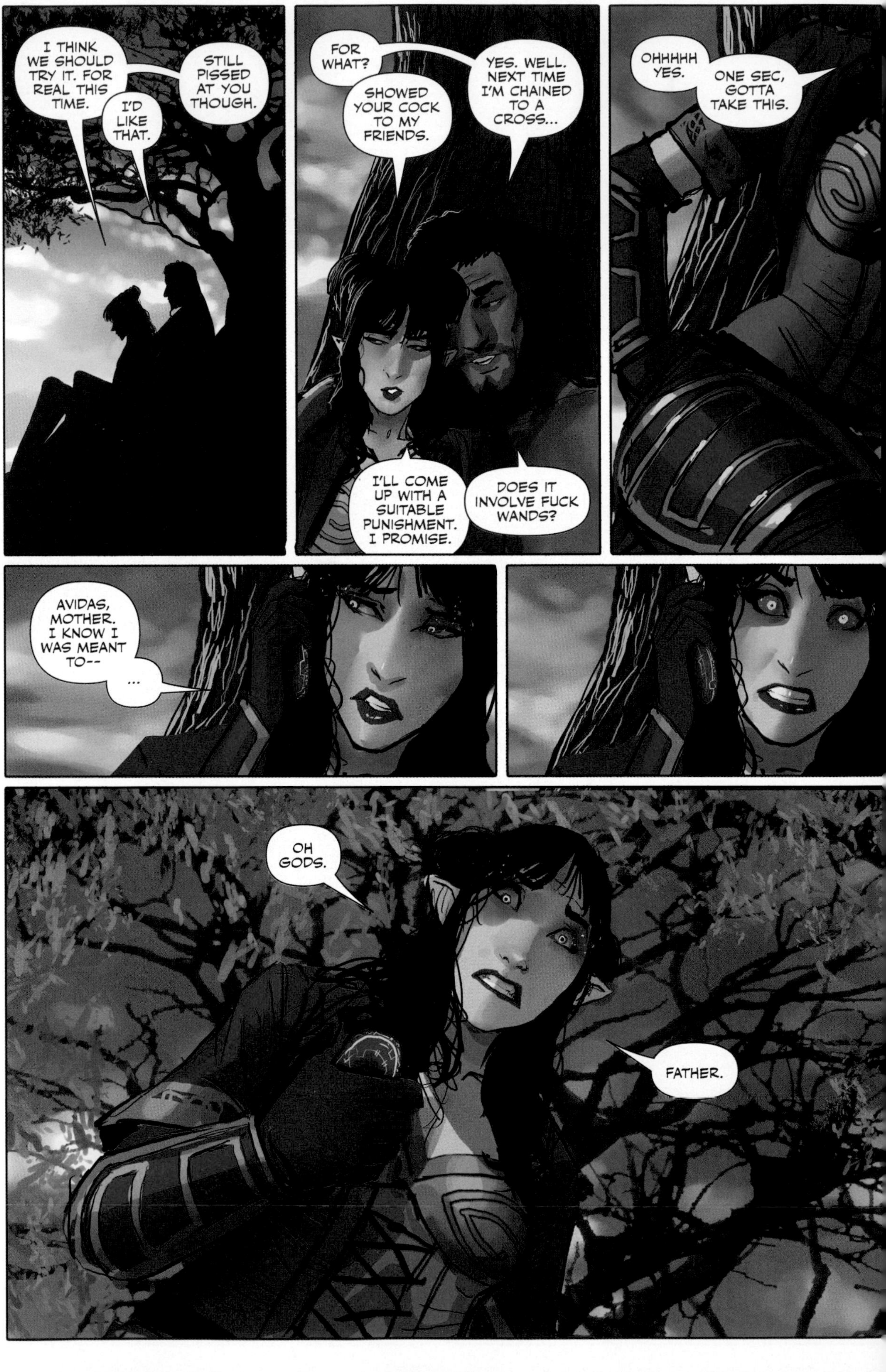
I THINK WE SHOULD TRY IT. FOR REAL THIS TIME.
STILL PISSED AT YOU THOUGH.
I'D LIKE THAT.
FOR WHAT?
YES. WELL. NEXT TIME I'M CHAINED TO A CROSS...
SHOWED YOUR COCK TO MY FRIENDS.
I'LL COME UP WITH A SUITABLE PUNISHMENT. I PROMISE.
DOES IT INVOLVE FUCK WANDS?
OHHHHH YES.
ONE SEC, GOTTA TAKE THIS.
AVIDAS, MOTHER. I KNOW I WAS MEANT TO--
...
OH GODS.
FATHER.

EXTRAS

Illustration by STJEPAN SEJIC

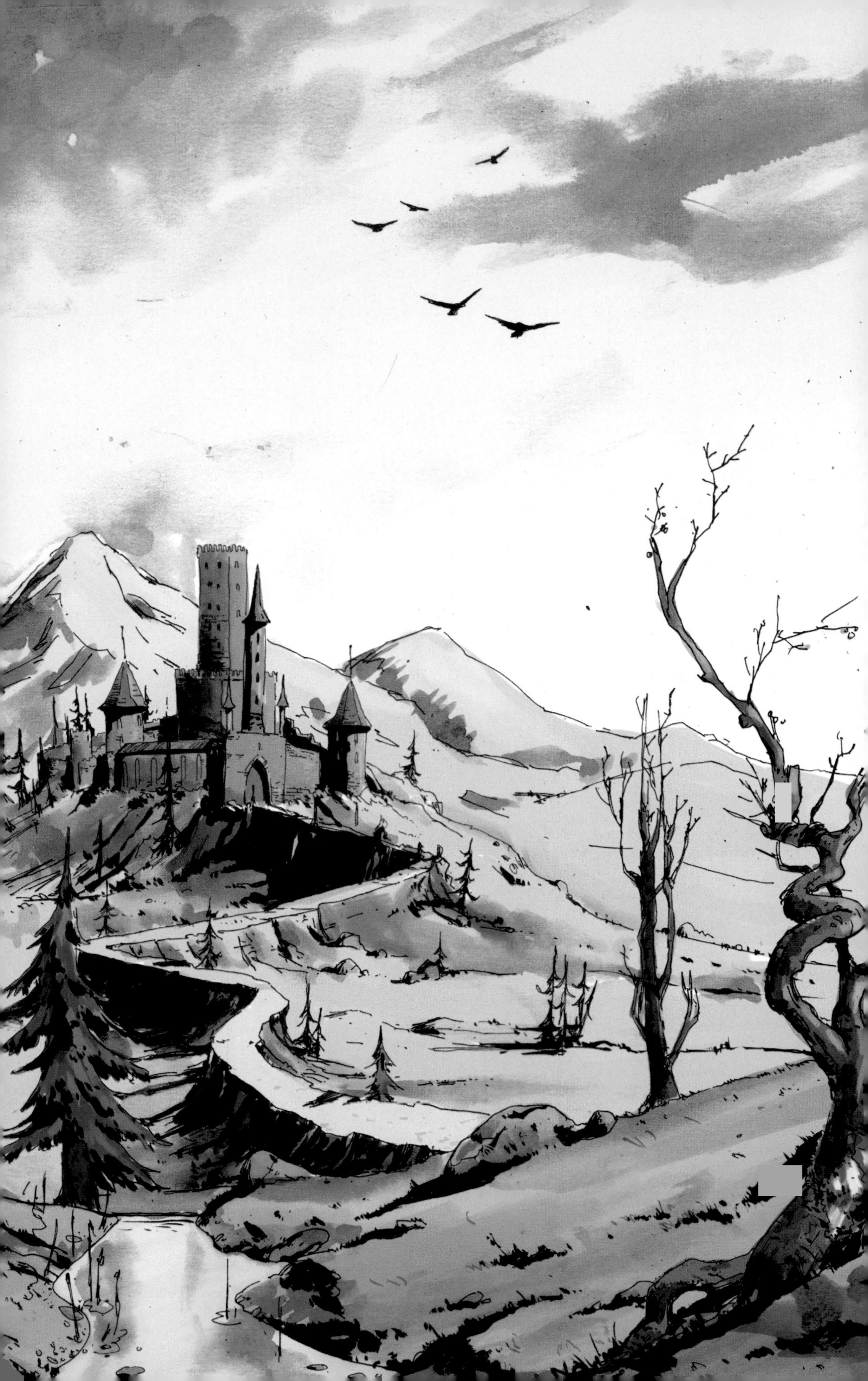

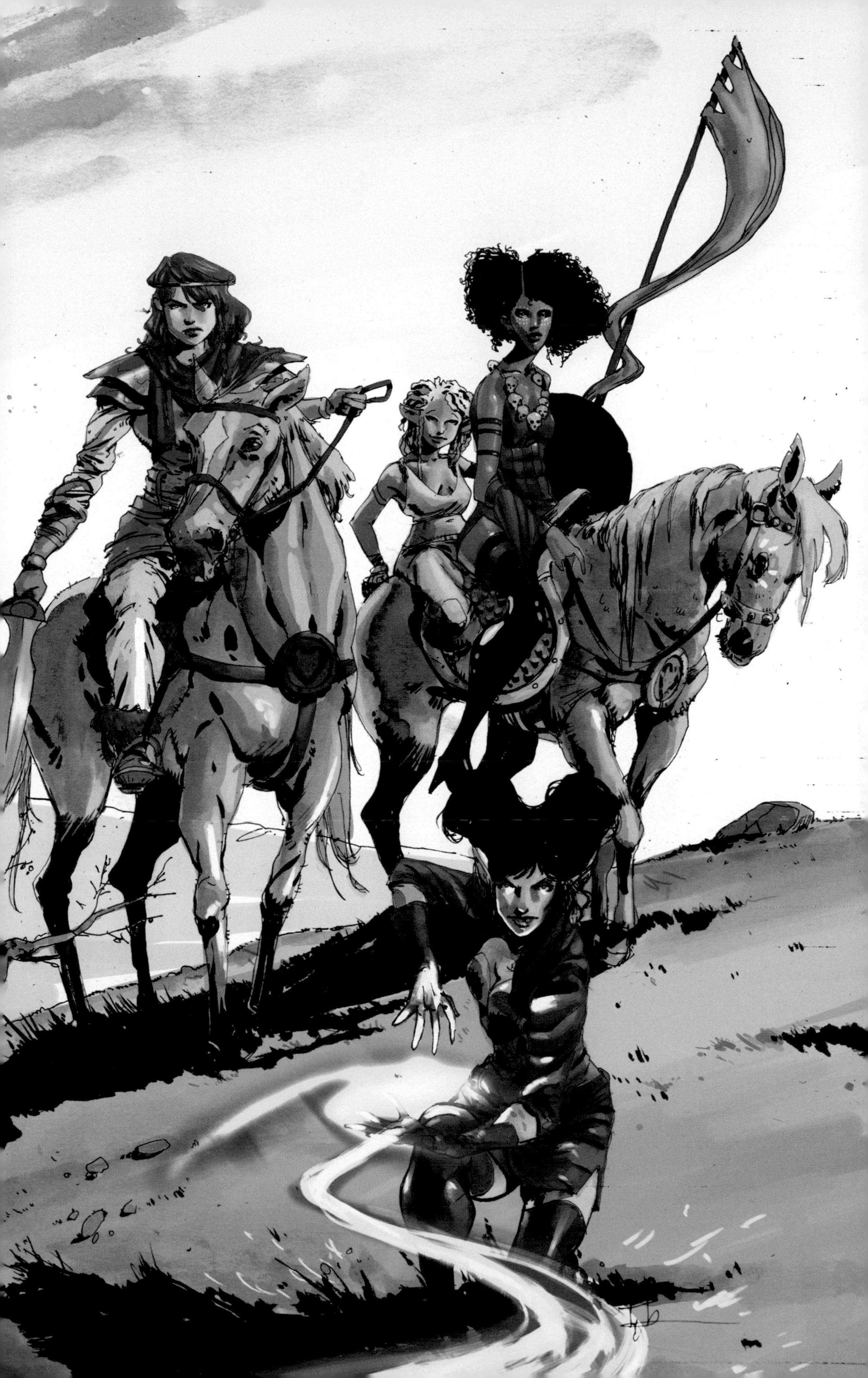

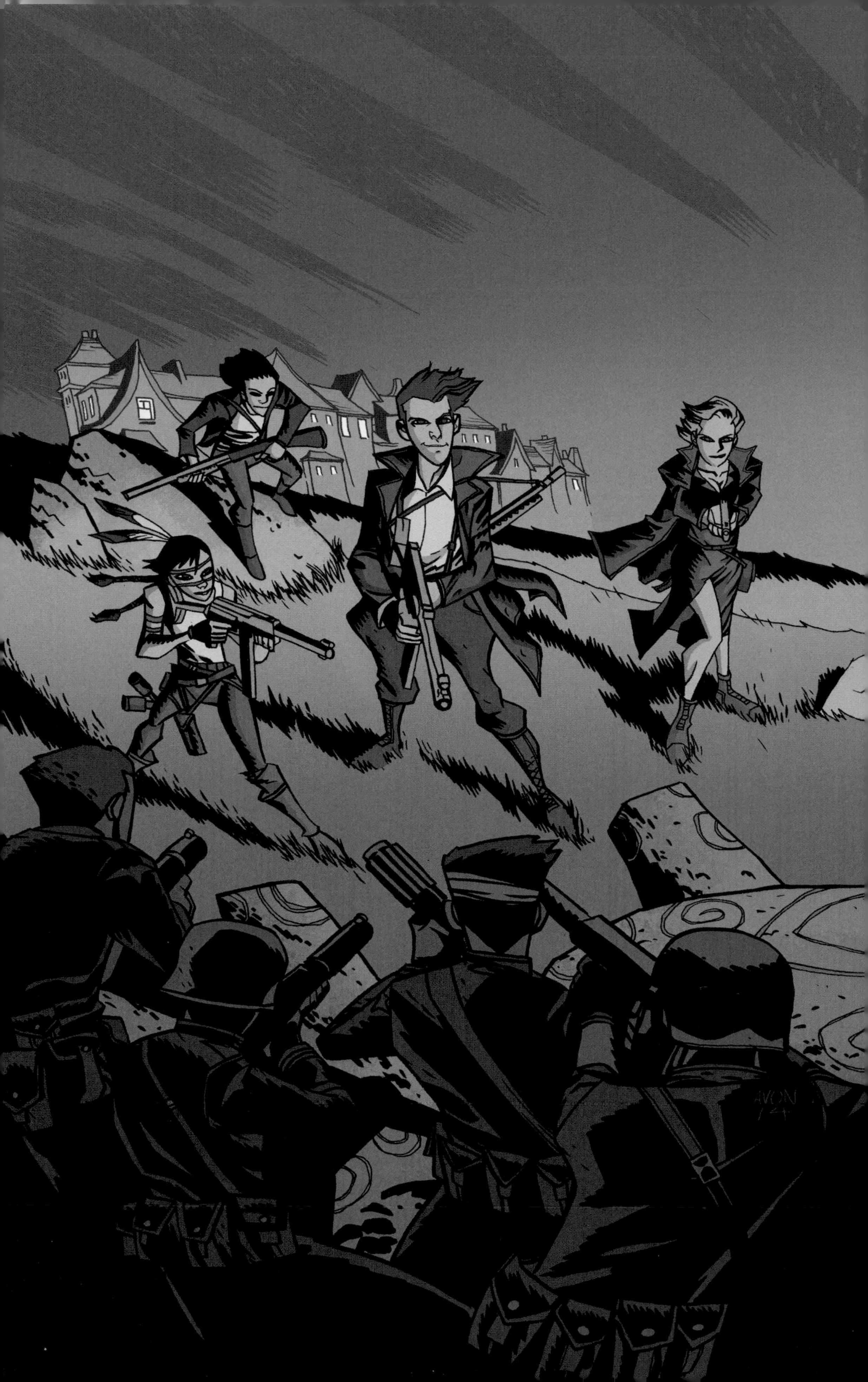

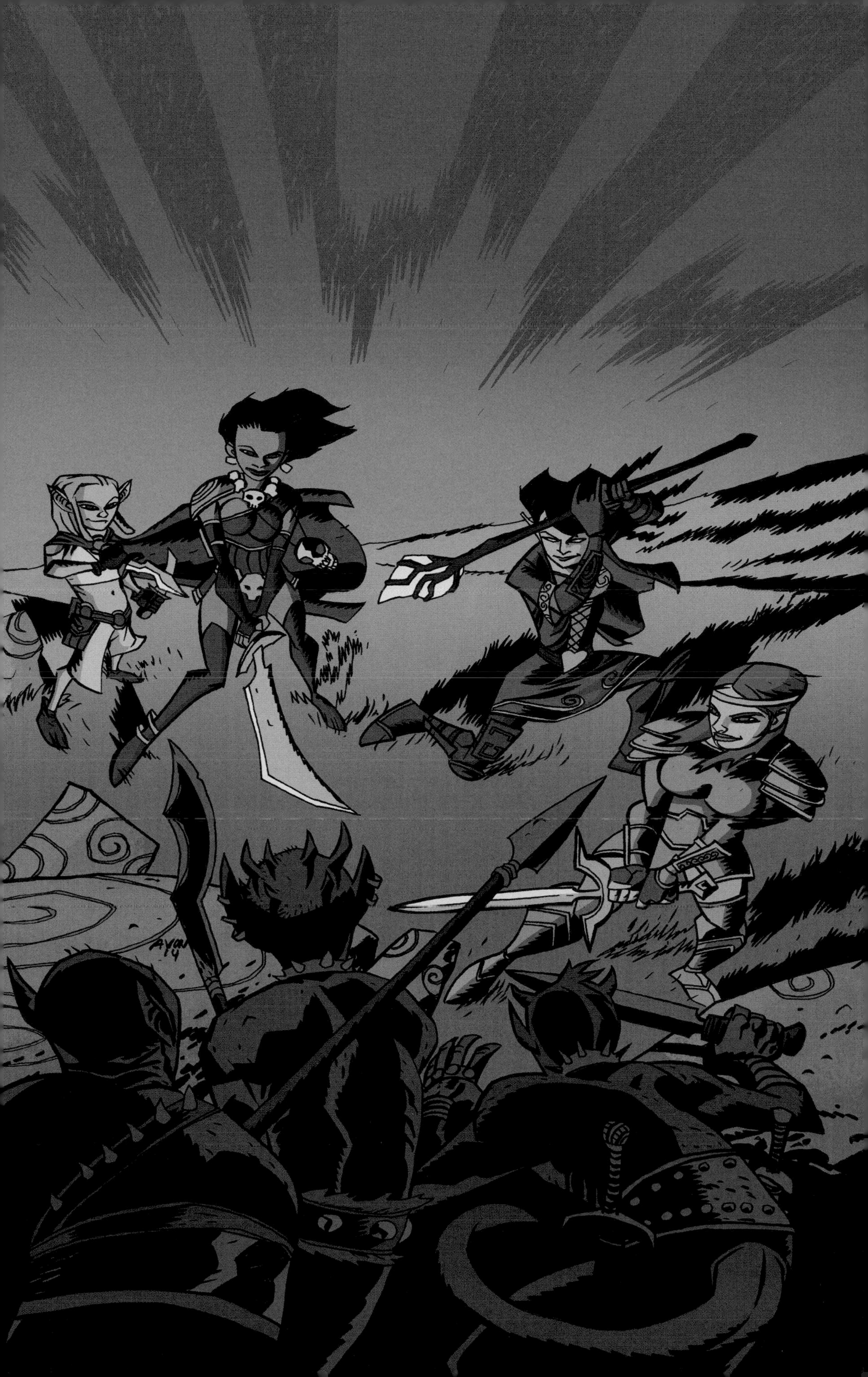

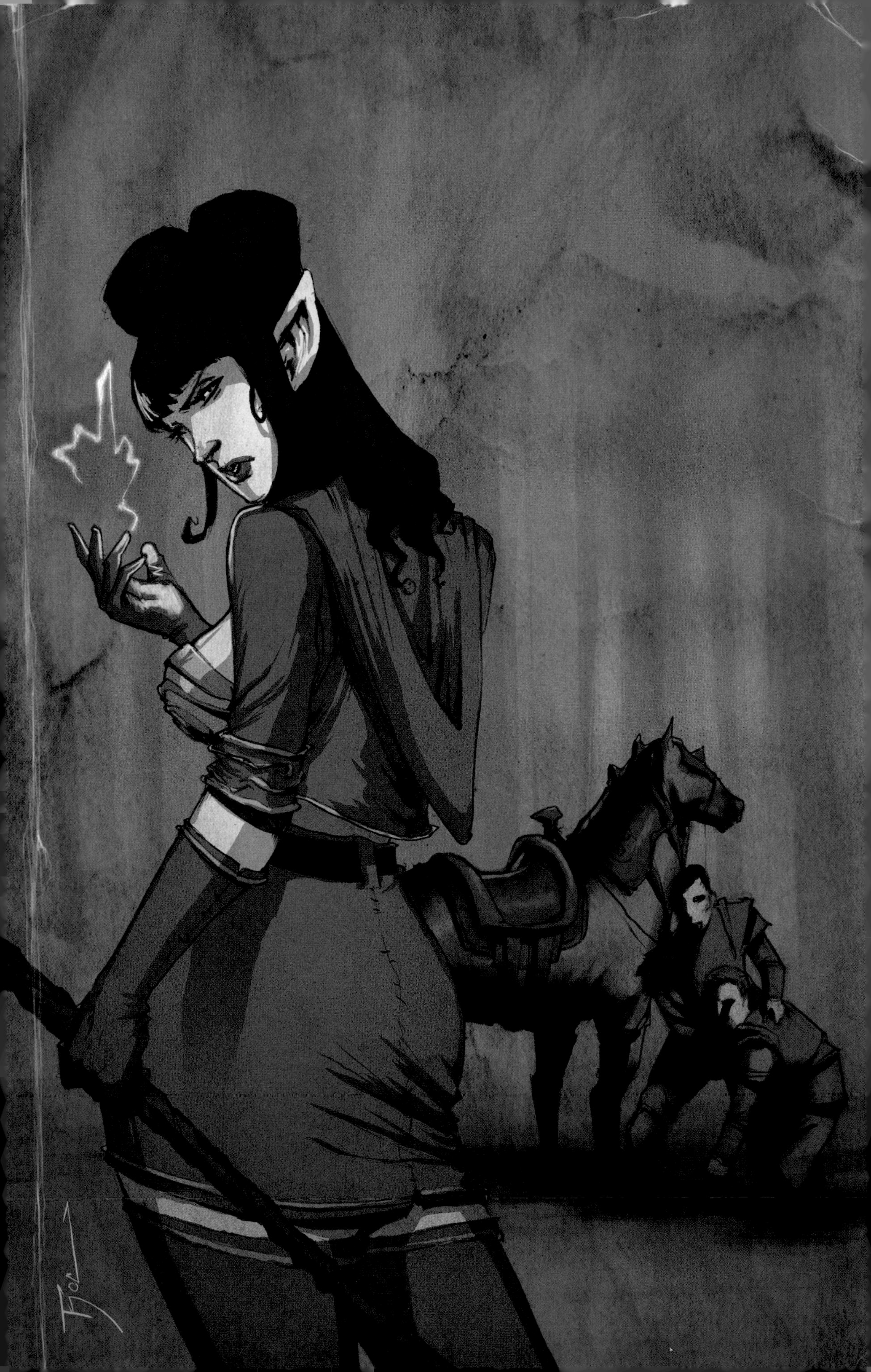

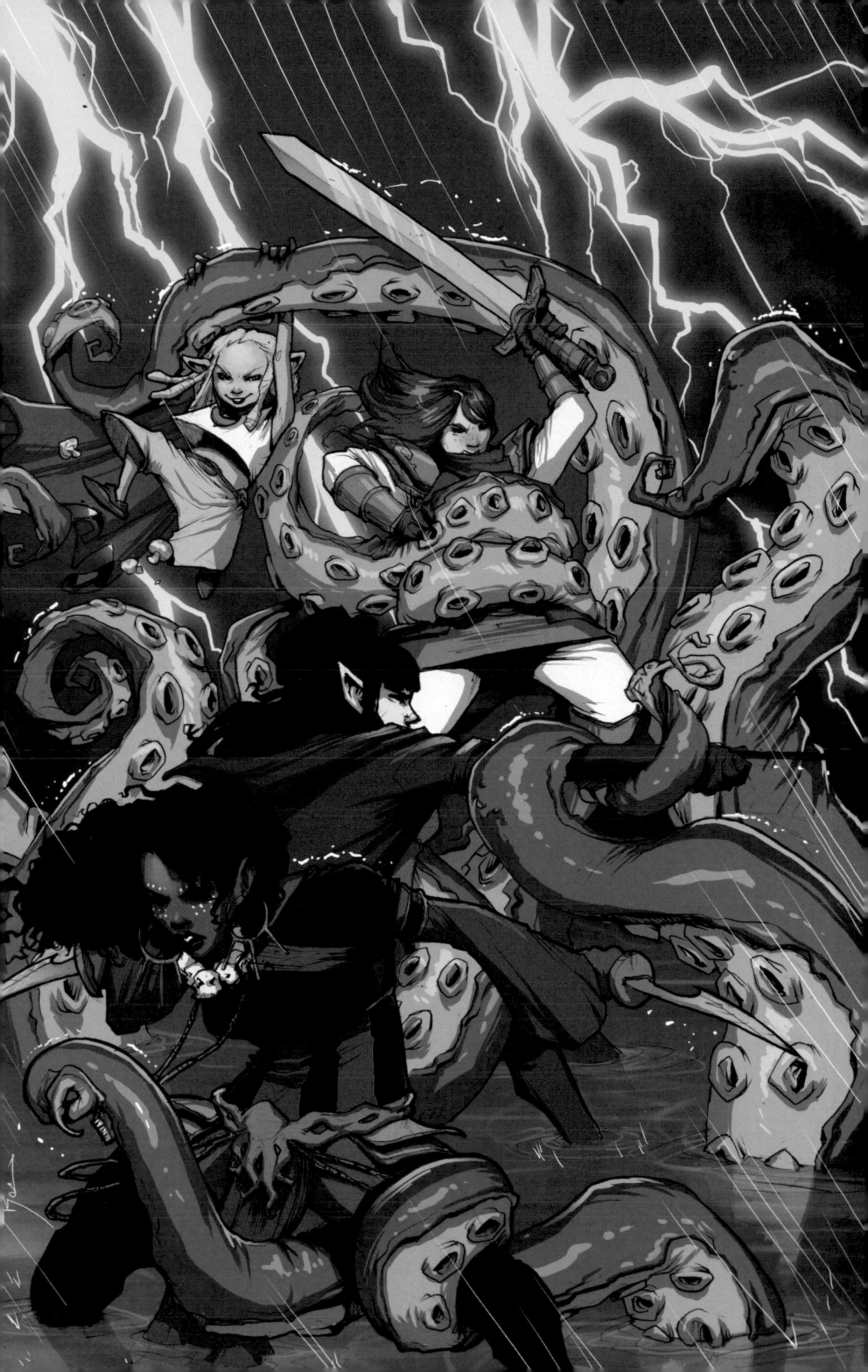

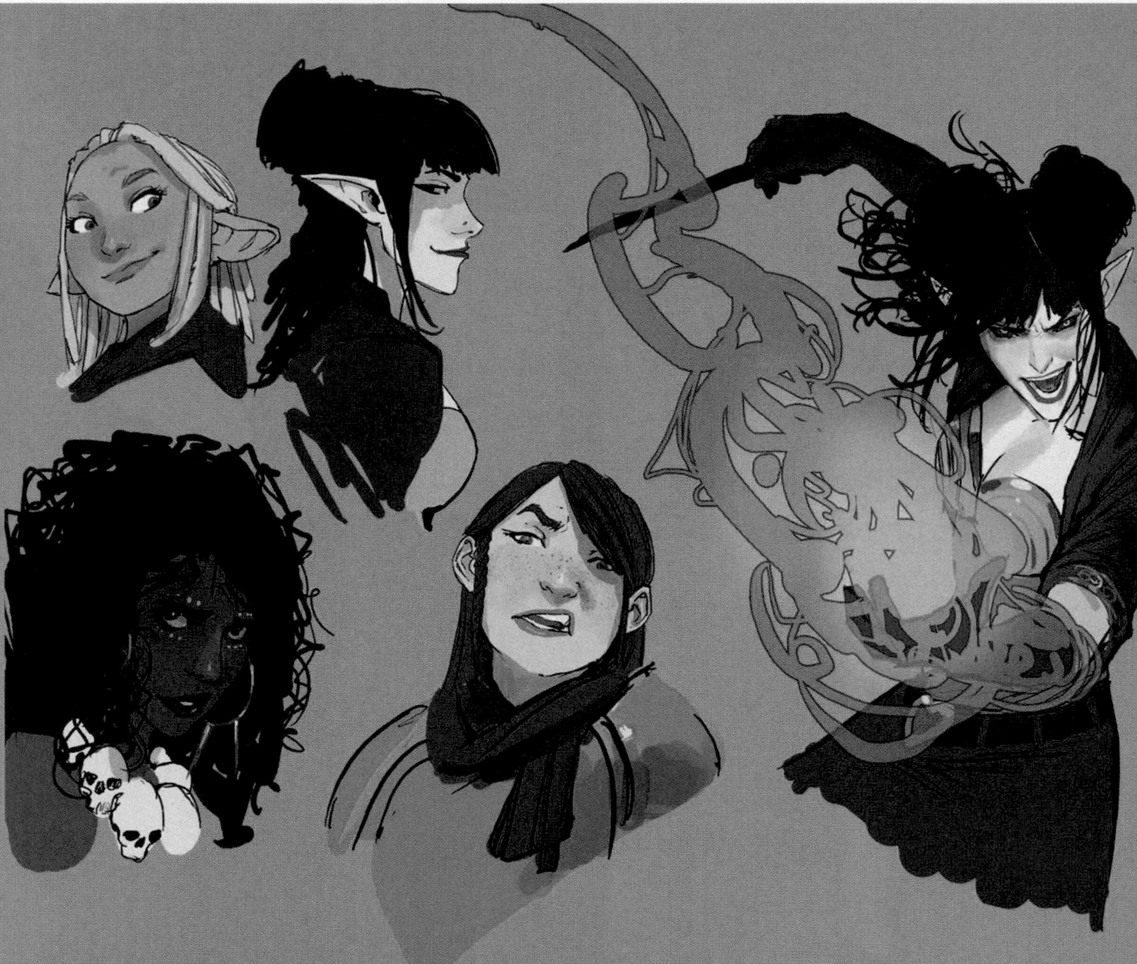

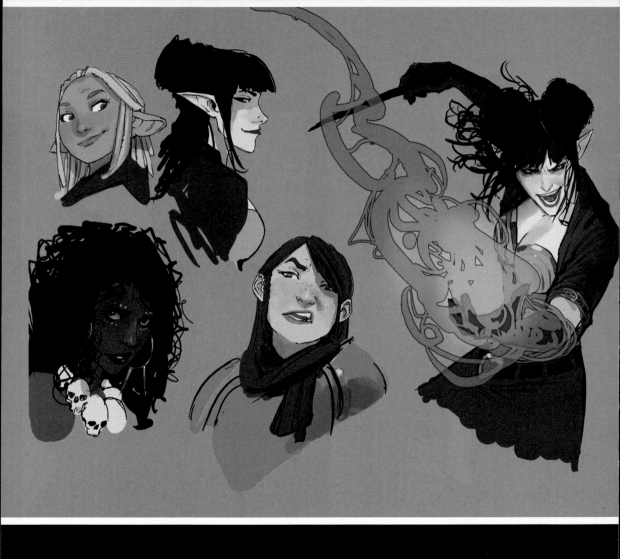

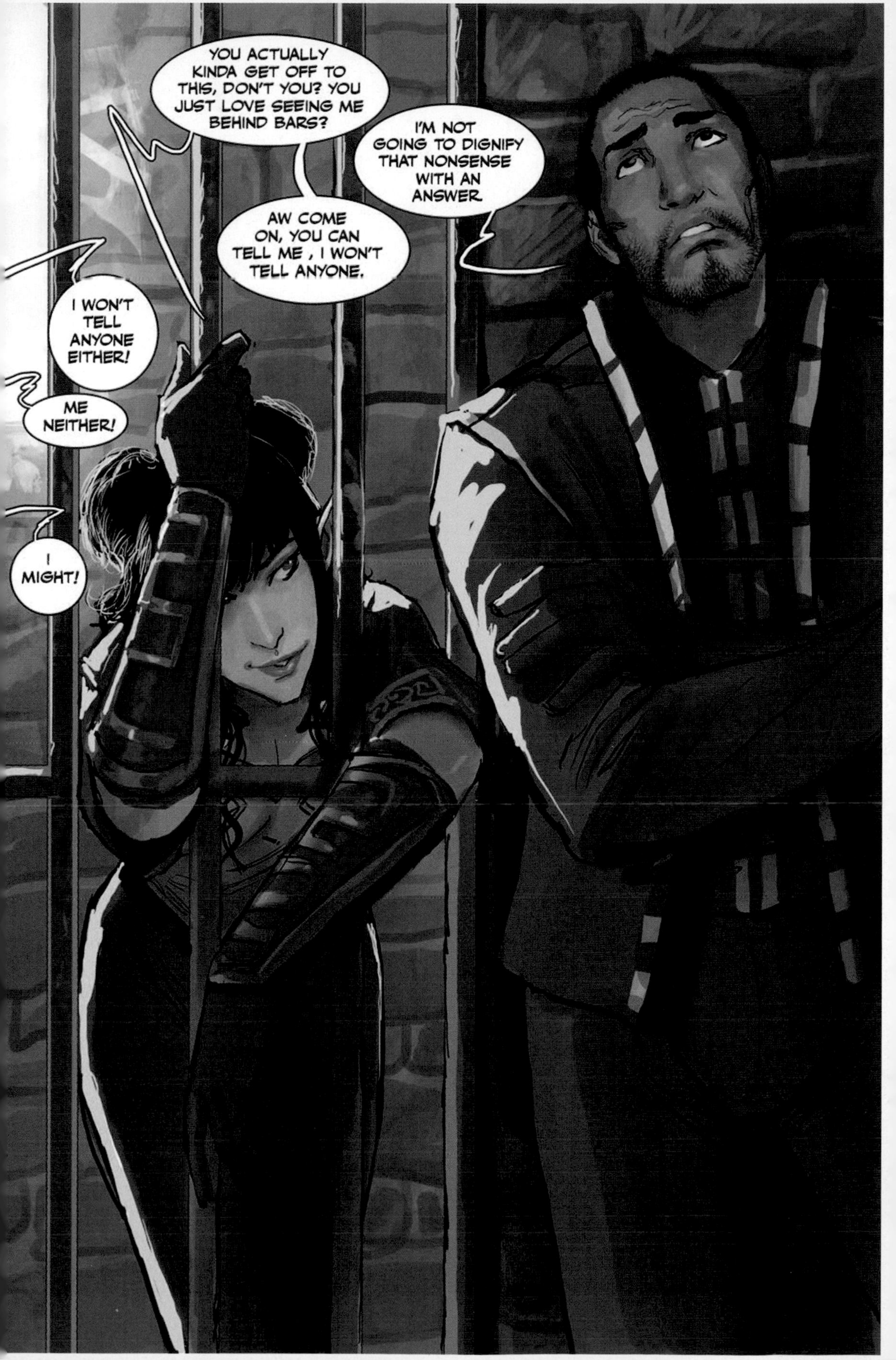

YOU ACTUALLY KINDA GET OFF TO THIS, DON'T YOU? YOU JUST LOVE SEEING ME BEHIND BARS?
I'M NOT GOING TO DIGNIFY THAT NONSENSE WITH AN ANSWER.
AW COME ON, YOU CAN TELL ME , I WON'T TELL ANYONE.
I WON'T TELL ANYONE EITHER!
ME NEITHER!
I MIGHT!

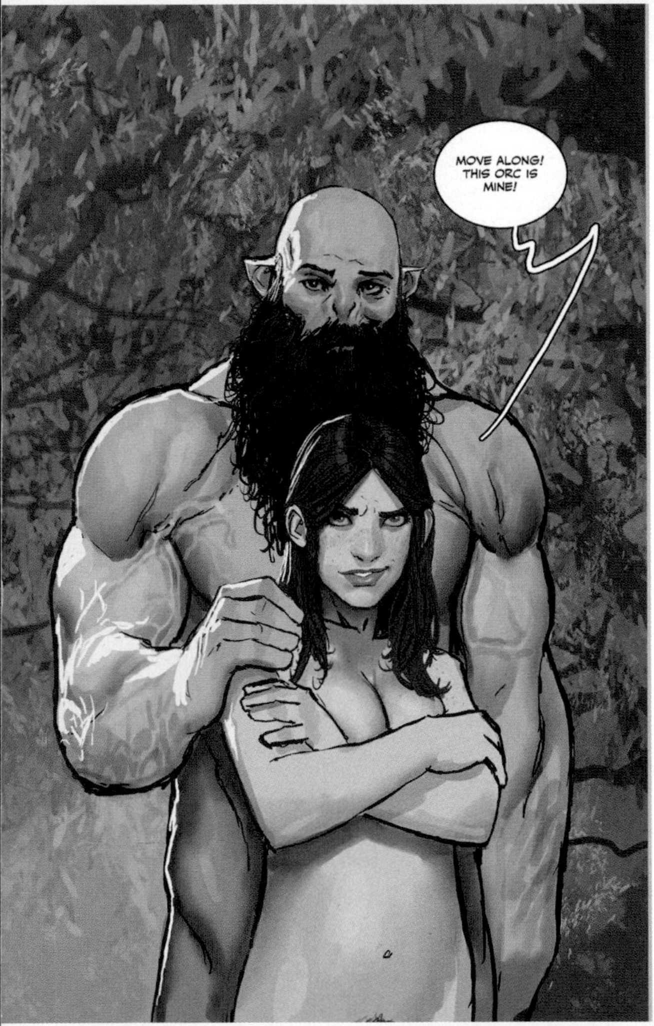
MOVE ALONG! THIS ORC IS MINE!

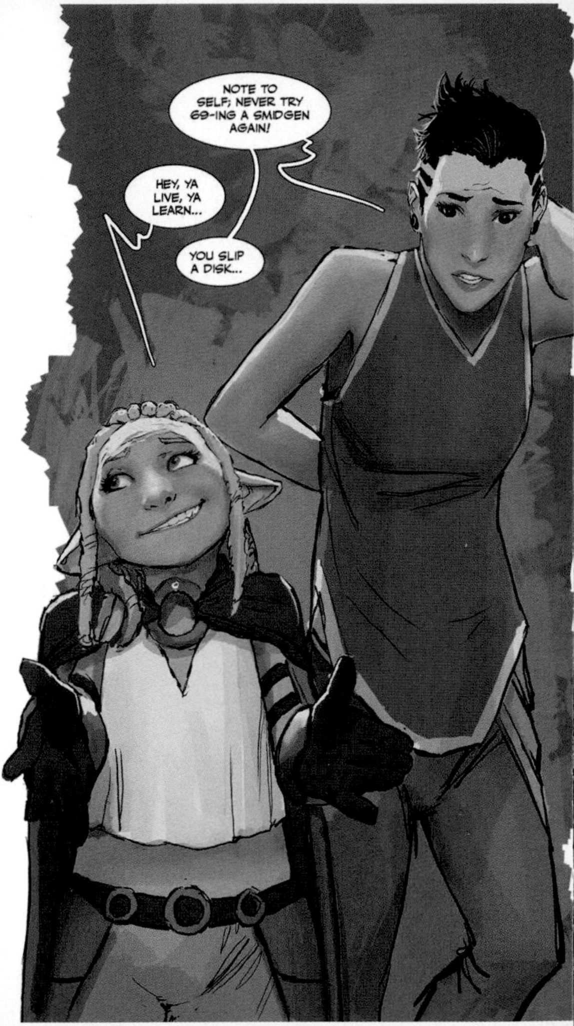
NOTE TO SELF; NEVER TRY 69-ING A SMIDGEN AGAIN!
HEY, YA LIVE, YA LEARN...
YOU SLIP A DISK...